普通高等院校"十三五"规划教材
普通高等院校"十一五"规划教材
普通高等院校机械类精品教材

# 编审委员会

**顾 问：** 杨叔子　华中科技大学
　　　　　李培根　华中科技大学
**总主编：** 吴昌林　华中科技大学
**委 员：** （按姓氏拼音顺序排列）

| | |
|---|---|
| 崔洪斌　河北科技大学 | 孟　逵　河南工业大学 |
| 冯　浩　景德镇陶瓷学院 | 芮执元　兰州理工大学 |
| 高为国　湖南工程学院 | 汪建新　内蒙古科技大学 |
| 郭钟宁　广东工业大学 | 王生泽　东华大学 |
| 韩建海　河南科技大学 | 闫占辉　长春工程学院 |
| 孔建益　武汉科技大学 | 杨振中　华北水利水电学院 |
| 李光布　上海师范大学 | 尹明富　天津工业大学 |
| 李　军　重庆交通大学 | 张　华　南昌大学 |
| 黎秋萍　华中科技大学出版社 | 张建钢　武汉科技学院 |
| 刘成俊　重庆科技学院 | 赵大兴　湖北工业大学 |
| 柳舟通　黄石理工学院 | 赵天婵　江汉大学 |
| 卢道华　江苏科技大学 | 赵雪松　安徽工程科技学院 |
| 鲁屏宇　江南大学 | 郑清春　天津理工大学 |
| 梅顺齐　武汉科技学院 | 周广林　黑龙江科技学院 |

普通高等院校"十三五"规划教材
普通高等院校"十一五"规划教材
普通高等院校机械类精品教材

顾　问　杨叔子　李培根

# 机械工程专业英语

主　编　李光布　饶锡新
编　委　郭冰菁　安爱琴　张春红
　　　　何凤琴　俞芙芳

华中科技大学出版社
http://www.hustp.com

中国·武汉

# 内 容 简 介

本教材是根据 21 世纪对机械工程人才培养的新要求,并结合机械工程领域所取得的最新研究成果进行编写的。

本教材的特点是:取材广泛、内容新颖、注重实践、突出练习。全书内容包括六大部分 39 课,第一部分机械设计共分 9 课,包括机械设计过程、金属和非金属材料、机械零部件、CAD 等,第二部分机械制造共分 8 课,包括机床、数控车床、快速成型、CAM、CIMS、先进制造过程、材料搬运等,第三部分机电一体化共分 8 课,包括机电一体化、自动化技术、工业机器人、开闭环控制、传感器技术、液压技术、交流电动机、直流电动机等,第四部分汽车共分 8 课,包括汽车构造、分类、发动机特性、电喷技术、发动机维修、悬挂系统、转向和制动系统等,第五部分企业管理共分 4 课,包括制造企业生产率、产品质量及其保障体系、ISO9000 国际标准及电子商务等,第六部分实用英语共分 2 课,包括书信、履历表、科技报告的格式、写作以及专业英语的特点、词汇和句子翻译技巧等。

本教材既可作为高等学校机械类各专业的教材,也可供大专、职业大学、成人高校等相关专业选用,还可供企业中的工程技术人员自学和参考。

```
图书在版编目(CIP)数据

机械工程专业英语/李光布,饶锡新主编. —武汉:华中科技大学出版社,2008.5(2024.7重印)
ISBN 978-7-5609-4253-7

Ⅰ.①机… Ⅱ.①李… ②饶… Ⅲ.①机械工程-英语-高等学校-教材 Ⅳ.①H31

中国版本图书馆 CIP 数据核字(2008)第 055653 号
```

**机械工程专业英语**　　　　　　　　　　　　　　　　　　李光布　饶锡新　主编

责任编辑:张　欣　　　　　　　　　　　　　　　　　　封面设计:潘　群
责任校对:李　琴　　　　　　　　　　　　　　　　　　责任监印:周治超

出版发行:华中科技大学出版社(中国·武汉)　　　电话:(027)81321913
　　　　　武汉市东湖新技术开发区华工科技园　　　邮编:430223

录　排:华中科技大学惠友文印中心
印　刷:武汉邮科印务有限公司

开本:787mm×1092mm　1/16　　　印张:19　插页:2　　　字数:472 0100
版次:2008 年 5 月第 1 版　　　　　印次:2024 年 7 月第 13 次印刷　　　定价:38.00 元
ISBN 978-7-5609-4253-7/H·623

(本书若有印装质量问题,请向出版社发行部调换)

"爆竹一声除旧,桃符万户更新。"在新年伊始,春节伊始,"十一五规划"伊始,来为"普通高等院校机械类精品教材"这套丛书写这个"序",我感到很有意义。

近十年来,我国高等教育取得了历史性的突破,实现了跨越式的发展,毛入学率由低于10%达到了高于20%,高等教育由精英教育而跨入了大众化教育。显然,教育观念必须与时俱进而更新,教育质量观也必须与时俱进而改变,从而教育模式也必须与时俱进而多样化。

以国家需求与社会发展为导向,走多样化人才培养之路是今后高等教育教学改革的一项重要任务。在前几年,教育部高等学校机械学科教学指导委员会对全国高校机械专业提出了机械专业人才培养模式的多样化原则,各有关高校的机械专业都在积极探索适应国家需求与社会发展的办学途径,有的已制定了新的人才培养计划,有的正在考虑深刻变革的培养方案,人才培养模式已呈现百花齐放、各得其所的繁荣局面。精英教育时代规划教材、一致模式、雷同要求的一统天下的局面,显然无法适应大众化教育形势的发展。事实上,多年来许多普通院校采用规划教材就十分勉强,而又苦于无合适教材可用。

"百年大计,教育为本;教育大计,教师为本;教师大计,教学为本;教学大计,教材为本。"有好的教材,就有章可循,有规可依,有鉴可借,有道可走。师资、设备、资料(首先是教材)是高校的三大教学基本建设。

"山不在高,有仙则名。水不在深,有龙则灵。"教材不在厚薄,内容不在深浅,能切合学生培养目标,能抓住学生应掌握的要言,能做到彼此呼应、相互配套,就行,此即教材要精、课程要精,能精则名、能精则灵、能精则行。

华中科技大学出版社主动邀请了一大批专家,联合了全国几十个应用型机械专业,在全国高校机械学科教学指导委员会的指导下,保证了当前形势下机械学科教学改革的发展方向,交流了各校的教改经验与教材建设计划,确定了一批面向普通高等院校机械学科精品课程的教材编写计划。特别要提出的,教育质量观、教材质量观必须随高等教育大众化而更新。大众化、多样化决不是降低质量，而是要面向、适应与满足人才市场的多样化需求，面向、符合、激活学生个性与能力的多样化特点。"和而不同"，才能生动活泼地繁荣与发展。脱离市场实际的、脱离学生实际的一刀切的质量不仅不是"万应灵丹"，而是"千篇一律"的桎梏。正因为如此，为了真正确保高等教育大众化时代的教学质量，教育主管部门正在对高校进行教学质量评估，各高校正在积极进行教材建设、特别是精品课程、精品教材建设。也因为如此，华中科技大学出版社组织出版普通高等院校应用型机械学科的精品教材，可谓正得其时。

我感谢参与这批精品教材编写的专家们！我感谢出版这批精品教材的华中科技大学出版社的有关同志！我感谢关心、支持与帮助这批精品教材编写与出版的单位与同志们！我深信编写者与出版者一定会同使用者沟通，听取他们的意见与建议，不断提高教材的水平！

特为之序。

中国科学院院士<br>
教育部高等学校机械学科指导委员会主任<br>
杨叔子<br>
2006.1

# 前　言

本书是普通高等院校"十一五"规划教材,是在总结机械工程专业英语教学改革和教材建设成果的基础上编写的。本书的目的,是使读者掌握机械工程专业英语术语及用法,培养和提高读者阅读、翻译专业英语文献资料的能力。

本书力求突出以下四个特点:①内容全面、结构合理,不仅有机械设计、机械制造及机电一体化,还有汽车、企业管理、实用英语等内容。②突出重点、强调难点,每篇课文后都有重点和难点解释和翻译。③内容新、取材广,大多数资料取材于最新出版的原版教材。④注重实践、突出练习。本书配阅读材料和练习题供自学。

本书由上海师范大学李光布教授、南昌大学饶锡新副教授任主编。参加编写工作的有:上海师范大学李光布教授(第一部分,第六部分第38课),张春红讲师(第一部分第1~8课),福建工程学院俞芙芳教授(第一部分第9课),河南科技大学郭冰菁副教授(第二部分第10~15课,第六部分第39课),南昌大学饶锡新副教授(第二部分第16、第17课,第三部分第24、第25课和第四部分),上海师范大学何凤琴讲师(第三部分第18~23课),河南科技学院安爱琴讲师(第五部分)。全书由李光布和饶锡新统稿。

林菁教授、上官芡倩副教授、董淑冷讲师、研究生曹椋焱等为本教材的编写提供了许多资料和帮助,在此谨表谢意。

由于作者水平有限,缺点和错误在所难免,敬请广大师生和读者多提宝贵意见。

编　者
2007年8月

# CONTENTS

## Part I  Mechanical Design

Lesson 1　The Mechanical Design Process ……………………………………… (3)
Lesson 2　Carbon and Alloy Steel ……………………………………………… (10)
Lesson 3　Plastics and Composite Materials …………………………………… (17)
Lesson 4　Gears …………………………………………………………………… (23)
Lesson 5　Keys, Couplings and Seals …………………………………………… (28)
Lesson 6　Rolling Contact Bearings ……………………………………………… (34)
Lesson 7　Belt and Chain Drives ………………………………………………… (40)
Lesson 8　CAD …………………………………………………………………… (47)
Lesson 9　Extruding ……………………………………………………………… (53)

## Part II  Manufacturing

Lesson 10　Lathe, Shaper, Grinding and Milling Machine …………………… (59)
Lesson 11　Numerical Control …………………………………………………… (68)
Lesson 12　Rapid-Prototyping Operations …………………………………… (76)
Lesson 13　Fabrication of Micro-electromechanical Devices and Systems (MEMS)
　　　　　 ……………………………………………………………………… (84)
Lesson 14　CAM ………………………………………………………………… (93)
Lesson 15　CIMS ………………………………………………………………… (101)
Lesson 16　Advanced Machining Processes …………………………………… (110)
Lesson 17　Material Handling and Movement ………………………………… (116)

## Part III  Mechatronics

Lesson 18　Mechatronics ………………………………………………………… (125)
Lesson 19　Automation ………………………………………………………… (132)
Lesson 20　Industrial Robots …………………………………………………… (139)
Lesson 21　Open-Loop Control and Closed-Loop Control …………………… (145)
Lesson 22　Sensor Technology ………………………………………………… (151)
Lesson 23　An Introduction to Hydraulics …………………………………… (157)
Lesson 24　AC Motors …………………………………………………………… (163)
Lesson 25　DC Motors …………………………………………………………… (170)

## Part IV  Automobile

Lesson 26　The Layout and Main Components of Automobile ……………… (181)
Lesson 27　Engine Classification and Overall Mechanics …………………… (187)
Lesson 28　Diesel Engine ………………………………………………………… (195)
Lesson 29　Electronic Fuel Injection System ………………………………… (201)

| Lesson 30 | Engine Service and Maintenance | (208) |
| Lesson 31 | Clutchs and Transmissions | (214) |
| Lesson 32 | Drive Axles and Suspension Systems | (222) |
| Lesson 33 | Brake System | (231) |

## Part Ⅴ  Management of Enterprise

| Lesson 34 | Productivity in Manufacturing | (241) |
| Lesson 35 | Product Quality Control and Quality Assurance | (246) |
| Lesson 36 | ISO 9000 | (252) |
| Lesson 37 | E-business | (258) |

## Part Ⅵ  Practical English

| Lesson 38 | Writing Skills in Application Articles | (267) |
| Lesson 39 | Translating Skills | (282) |

参考文献 ………………………………………………………………… (294)

# Part I

# Mechanical Design

# Lesson 1 The Mechanical Design Process

## TEXT

### 1. The Mechanical Design Process

The ultimate objective of mechanical design is to produce a useful product that satisfies the needs of a customer and that is safe, efficient, reliable, economical, and practical to manufacture. Think broadly when answering the question, "Who is the customer for the product or system I am about to design?"

It is essential that you know the desires and expectations of all customers before product design. Marketing professionals are often employed to manage the definition of customer expectations, but designers will likely work with them as a part of a product development team.

Many methods are used to determine what the customer wants. One popular method, called quality function deployment or QFD, seeks (1) to identify all of the features and performance factors that customers desire and (2) to assess the relative importance of these factors. The result of the QFD process is a detailed set of functions and design requirements for the product.

It is also important to consider how the design process fits with all functions that must happen to deliver a satisfactory product to the customer and to service the product throughout its life cycle. In fact, it is important to consider how the product will be disposed of after it has served its useful life. The total of all such functions that affect the product is sometimes called the product realization process or PRP. Some of the factors included in PRP are as follows:

- Marketing functions to assess customer requirements
- Research to determine the available technology that can reasonably be used in the product
  - Availability of materials and components that can be incorporated into the product
  - Product design and development
  - Performance testing
  - Documentation of the design
  - Vendor relationships and purchasing functions
  - Consideration of global sourcing of materials and global marketing
  - Work-force skills
  - Physical plant and facilities available
  - Capability of manufacturing systems
  - Production planning and control of production systems

- Production support systems and personnel
- Quality systems requirements
- Sales operations and time schedules
- Cost targets and other competitive issues
- Customer service requirements
- Environmental concerns during manufacture, operation and disposal of the product
- Legal requirements
- Availability of financial capital

Can you add to this list? You should be able to see that the design of a product is but one part of a comprehensive process. In this text, we will focus more carefully on the design process itself, but the producibility of designs must always be considered. This simultaneous consideration of product design and manufacturing process design is often called concurrent engineering.

## 2. Skills Needed in Mechanical Design

Product engineers and mechanical designers use a wide range of skills and knowledge in their daily work. These skills and knowledge are included in the following:
- Sketching, technical drawing, and computer-aided design
- Properties of materials, materials processing, and manufacturing processes
- Applications of chemistry, such as corrosion protection, plating, and painting
- Statics, dynamics, strength of materials, kinematics, and mechanisms
- Fluid mechanics, thermodynamics, and heat transfer
- Fluid power, the fundamentals of electrical phenomena, and industrial controls
- Experimental design and performance testing of materials and mechanical systems
- Stress analysis
- Specialized knowledge of the behavior of machine elements, such as gears, belt drives, chain drives, shafts, bearings, keys, splines, couplings, seals, springs, connections (bolted, riveted, welded, adhesive), electric motors, linear motion devices, clutches, and brakes
- Creativity, problem solving, and project management
- Oral communication, listening, technical writing, and teamwork skills

## 3. Functions, Design Requirements and Evaluation Criteria

Section 1 emphasized the importance of carefully identifying the needs and expectations of the customer prior to beginning the design of a mechanical device. You can formulate these by producing clear, complete statements of functions, design requirements, and evaluation criteria:
- Functions tell us what the device must do, using general, nonquantitative statements that employ action phrases such as "to support a load", "to lift a crate", "to transmit power", or "to hold two structural members together", etc.
- Design requirements are detailed, usually quantitative statements of expected

performance levels, environmental conditions in which the device must operate, limitations on space or weight, or available materials and components that may be used.

● Evaluation criteria are statements of desirable qualitative characteristics of a design that assist the designer in deciding which alternative design is optimum—that is, the design that maximizes benefits while minimizing disadvantages.

Together these elements can be called the specifications for the design.

Most designs progress through a cycle of activities are outlined in Figure1.1. You should typically propose more than one possible alternative design concept. This is where creativity is exercised to produce truly novel designs. Each design concept must satisfy the functions and design requirements. A critical evaluation of the desirable features, advantages, and disadvantages of each design concept should be completed. Then a rational decision analysis technique should use the evaluation criteria to decide which design concept is the optimum and, therefore, should be produced.

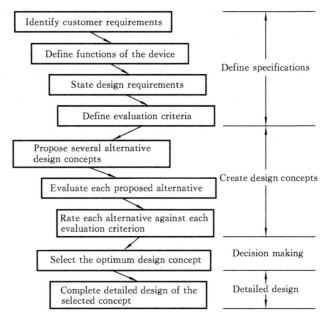

Figure 1.1　Steps in the design process

## NEW WORDS AND EXPRESSIONS

scenario [si'nɑːriəu] *n.* 设想,情节
spline [splain] *n.* 花键
thermodynamics *n.* 热动力学
plating ['pleitiŋ] *n.* 电镀
painting ['peintiŋ] *n.* 油漆
clutch [klʌtʃ] *n.* 离合器

quality function deployment 质量功能展开
product realization process 产品实现过程
performance test 性能测试
stress analysis 应力分析
evaluation criteria 评定标准
concurrent engineering 并行工程,同步工程

# NOTES

1) Marketing professionals are often employed to manage the definition of customer expectations, but designers will likely work with them as a part of a product development team.

经常请市场专业人员来对顾客期望进行评定,但设计人员却很可能作为产品开发小组的一部分与市场专业人员一起合作。

2) One popular method, called quality function deployment or QFD, seeks (1) to identify all of the features and performance factors that customer desire and (2) to assess the relative importance of these factors.

一种通用的方法,称为质量功能展开(简称 QFD),寻求识别顾客期望的所有特征和性能因素,并用于评定这些因素之间的相对重要性。

质量功能展开就是将顾客的需求转换成明确的代用特性,确定产品的设计质量,然后经过各功能、部件的质量,直至各部门的质量和工序要素,对其中的关系进行系统展开,包括质量展开、技术展开、成本展开和可靠性展开。

3) It is also important to consider how the design process fits with all functions that must happen to deliver a satisfactory product to the customer and to service the product throughout its life cycle.

考虑设计过程如何满足所有功能也是很重要的,这些功能必须恰好把满意的产品交给顾客,并在整个产品的生命周期内服务该产品。

4) Section 1 emphasized the importance of carefully identifying the needs and expectations of the customer prior to beginning the design of a mechanical device.

在第一部分强调了在开始设计机械装置之前仔细地了解顾客要求与期望的重要性。

# EXERCISES

1. After reading the text above, summarize the main ideas in oral.
2. Fill in the blanks with proper words or phrases according to the text (note the proper tense).

(1) In fact, it is important to consider how the product will be d_____ after it has served its useful life.

(2) This is where creativity is e_____ to produce truly novel designs.

(3) It is also important to consider how the design process f_____ all functions that must happen to deliver a satisfactory product to the customer and to service the product throughout its life cycle.

(4) One popular method, called quality function deployment or QFD, seeks ① to i_____ all of the features and performance factors that customers desire and ② to a_____ the relative importance of these factors.

(5) You should typically propose more than one possible a_____ design concept.

(6) This simultaneous consideration of product design and manufacturing process design is often called c_____.

3. Translate the following phrases into Chinese according to the text.
(1) quality function deployment  (2) product realization process
(3) materials processing  (4) concurrent engineering
(5) disposal of  (6) incorporate into
(7) life cycle

4. Translate the following phrases into English according to the text.
(1) 实验设计  (2) 性能测试
(3) 联轴器  (4) 质量体系要求
(5) 项目管理  (6) 带传动
(7) 链传动

5. Write a 100-word summary according to the text.

# READING MATERIAL

Mechanical design is the process of designing and/or selecting mechanical components and putting them together to accomplish a desired function. Of course, machine elements must be compatible, must fit well together, and must perform safely and efficiently. The designer must consider not only the performance of the element being designed at a given time, but also the elements with which it must interface.

To illustrate how the design of machine elements must be integrated with a larger mechanical design, let us consider the design of a speed reducer for the small tractor. Suppose that, to accomplish the speed reduction, you decide to design a double-reduction, spur gear speed reducer. You specify four gears, three shafts, six bearings, and a housing to hold the individual elements in proper relation to each other. The primary elements of the speed reducer are:

● The input shaft is to be connected to the power source, a gasoline engine whose output shaft rotates at 2 000 rpm. A flexible coupling is to be employed to minimize difficulties with alignment.

● The first pair of gears, A and B, causes a reduction in the speed of the intermediate shaft proportional to the ratio of the numbers of teeth in the gears. Gear B and C are both mounted to intermediate shaft and rotate at the same speed.

● A key is used at the interface between the hub of each gear and the shaft on which it is mounted to transmit torque between the gear and the shaft.

● The second pair of gears, C and D, further reduces the speed of gear D and the output shaft to the range of 290 rpm to 295 rpm.

● The output shaft is to carry a chain sprocket. The chain drive ultimately is to be connected to the drive wheel of the tractor.

● Each of the three shafts is supported by two ball bearings, making them statically determinate and allowing the analysis of forces and stresses using standard principles of mechanics.

● The bearings are held in a housing that is to be attached to the frame of the tractor. Note the manner of holding each bearing so that the inner race rotates with the shaft while the outer race is held stationary.

● Seals are on the input and output shafts to prohibit contaminants from entering the housing.

● Details of how the active elements are to be installed, lubricated, and aligned are only suggested at this stage of the design process to demonstrate feasibility. One possible assembly process could be as follows:

Start by placing the gears, keys, spacers, and bearings on their respective shafts.

Then insert input shaft into its bearing seat on the left side of the housing.

Insert the left end of intermediate shaft into its bearing seat while engaging the teeth of gears A and B.

Install the center bearing support to provide support for the bearing at the right side of input shaft.

Install output shaft by placing its left bearing into the seat on the center bearing support while engaging gears C and D.

Install the right side cover for the housing while placing the final two bearings in their seats.

Ensure careful alignment of the shafts.

Place gear lubricant in the lower part of the housing.

The arrangement of the gears, the placement of the bearings so that they straddle the gears, and the general configuration of the housing are also design decisions. The design process cannot rationally proceed until these kinds of decisions are made. When the overall design is conceptualized, the design of the individual machine elements in the speed reducer can proceed. You should recognize that you have already made many design decisions by rendering such a sketch. First, you choose spur gears rather than helical gears, a worm and worm gear, or bevel gears. In fact, other types of speed reduction devices—belt drives, chain drives, or many others—could be appreciate.

## 1. Gears

For the gear pairs, you must specify the number of teeth in each gear, the pitch (size) of the teeth, the pitch diameters, the face width, and the material and its heat treatment. These specifications depend on considerations of strength and wear of the gear teeth and the motion requirements (kinematics). You must also recognize that the gears must be mounted on shafts in a manner that ensures proper location of the gears, adequate torque transmitting capability from the gears to the shafts (as through keys) and safe shaft design.

## 2. Shafts

Having designed the gear pairs, next you will consider the shaft design. The shaft is loaded in bending and torsion because of the forces acting at the gear teeth. Thus, its design must consider strength and rigidity, and it must permit the mounting of the gears and bearings. Shafts of varying diameters may be used to provide shoulders against which to seat the gears and bearings. There may be keyseats cut into the shaft. The input and output shafts will extend beyond the housing to permit coupling with the engine and the drive axle. The type of coupling must be considered, as it can have a dramatic effect on the shaft stress analysis. Seals on the input and output shafts protect internal components.

### 3. Bearings

Design of the bearings is next. If rolling contact bearings are to be used, you will probably select commercially available bearings from a manufacturer's catalog, rather than design a unique one. You must first determine the magnitude of the loads on each bearing from the shaft analysis and the gear designs. The rotational speed and reasonable design life of the bearings and their compatibility with the shaft on which they are to be mounted must also be considered. For example, on the basis of the shaft analysis, you could specify the minimum allowable diameter at each bearing seat location to ensure safe stress levels. The bearing selected to support a particular part of the shaft, then, must have a bore (inside diameter) no smaller than the safe diameter of the shaft. Of course, the bearing should not be grossly larger than necessary. When a specific bearing is selected, the diameter or the shaft at the bearing seat location and allowable tolerances must be specified, according to the bearing manufacturer's recommendations, to achieve proper operation and life expectancy of the bearing.

# Lesson 2  Carbon and Alloy Steel

## TEXT

Steel is probably the most widely used material for machine elements because of its properties of high strength, high stiffness, durability and relative ease of fabrication. The term *steel* refers to an alloy of iron, carbon, manganese and one or more other significant elements. Carbon has a very strong effect on the strength, hardness and ductility of any steel alloy. The other elements affect hardenability, toughness, corrosion resistance, machinability and strength retention at high temperatures. The primary alloying elements present in the various alloy steels are sulfur, phosphorus, silicon, nickel, chromium, molybdenum and vanadium.

### 1. Importance of Carbon

Although most steel alloys contain less than 1.0% carbon, it is included in the designation because of its effect on the properties of steel. As Figure 1.2 illustrates, the last two digits indicate carbon content in hundredths of a percent. As carbon content increases, strength and hardness also increase under the same conditions of processing and heat treatment. Since ductility decreases with increasing carbon content, selecting a suitable steel involves some compromise between strength and ductility.

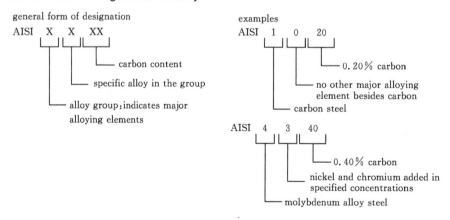

Figure 1.2  Steel designation system

As a rough classification scheme, a low-carbon steel is one having fewer than 30 points of carbon (0.30%). These steels have relatively low strength but good formability. In machine element applications where high strength is not required, low-carbon steels are frequently specified. If wear is a potential problem, low-carbon steels can be carburized to increase the carbon content in the very outer surface of the part and to improve the combination of properties.

Medium-carbon steels contain 30 to 50 points of carbon (0.30%—0.50%). Most machine elements having moderate to high strength requirements with fairly good ductility and moderate hardness requirements come from this group.

High-carbon steels have 50 to 95 points of carbon (0.50%—0.95%). The high carbon content provides better wear properties suitable for applications requiring durable cutting edges and for applications where surfaces are subjected to constant abrasion. Tools, knives, chisels, and many agricultural implement components are among these uses.

## 2. Stainless Steels

The term *stainless steel* characterizes the high level of corrosion resistance. To be classified as a stainless steel, the alloy must have a chromium content of at least 10%. Most have 12% to 18% chromium.

The three main groups of stainless steels are austenitic, ferritic, and martensitic. Austenitic stainless steels fall into the AISI 200 and 300 series. They are general-purpose grades with moderate strength. Most are not heat-treatable, and their final properties are determined by the amount of working. These alloys are nonmagnetic and are typically used in food processing equipment.

Ferritic stainless steels belong to the AISI 400 series, designated as 405, 409, 430, 446, and so on. They are magnetic and perform well at elevated temperatures, from 1 300 °F to 1 900 °F (700°C—1 040°C). They are not heat-treatable, but they can be cold-worked to improve properties. Typical applications include heat exchanger tubing, petroleum refining equipment, automotive trim, furnace parts, and chemical equipment.

Martensitic stainless steels are also members of the AISI 400 series, including 403, 410, 414, 416, 420, 431 and 440 types. They are magnetic, can be heat-treated, and have higher strength than the AISI 200 and 300 series, while retaining good toughness. Typical uses include turbine engine parts, cutlery, scissors, pump parts, valve parts, surgical instruments, aircraft fittings, and marine hardware.

## 3. Structural Steels

Most structural steels are designated by ASTM numbers established by American Society for Testing and Materials. The most common grade is ASTM A36, which has a minimum yield point of 36 000 psi (248 MPa) and is very ductile. It is basically a low-carbon, hot-rolled steel available in sheet, plate, bar, and structural shapes, such as wide-flange beams, American standard beams, channels and angles.

Most wide-flange beams are currently made using ASTM A992 structural steel, which has a yield point of 50 ksi to 65 ksi and a minimum tensile strength of 65 ksi. An additional requirement is that the maximum ratio of the yield point to the tensile strength is 0.85. This is a highly ductile steel, having a minimum of 21% elongation in a 2.00-inch gage length. Using this steel instead of the lower strength ASTM A36 steel typically allows smaller, lighter structural members at little or no additional cost.

Hollow structural sections (HSS) are typically made from ASTM A500 steel that is cold-formed and either welded or made seamless. Included are round tubes and square rectangular shapes. There are different strength grades can be specified. Some of these HSS products are made from ASTM A501 hot-formed steel having properties similar to the ASTM A36 hot-rolled steel.

Many higher-strength grades of structural steel are available for use in construction, vehicular, and machine applications. They provide yield points in the range from 42 000 psi to 100 000 psi (290 MPa—700 MPa).

### 4. Tool Steels

Tool steels refers to a group of steels typically used for cutting tools, punches, dies, shearing blades, chisels and similar uses. The numerous varieties of tool steel materials have been classified into seven general types. Whereas most uses of tool steels are related to the field of manufacturing engineering, they are also pertinent to machine design where the ability to maintain a keen edge under abrasive conditions is required. Also, some tool steels have rather high shock resistance which may be desirable in machine components such as parts for mechanical clutches, pawls, blades, guides for moving materials and clamps.

## NEW WORDS

durability [ˌdjuərəˈbiliti] n. 耐久性,耐用性
fabrication [ˌfæbriˈkeiʃən] n. 制作
alloy [ˈæləi] n. 合金
manganese [ˌmæŋgəˈniːz] n. 锰
ductility [dʌkˈtiliti] n. 延展性
machinability [məʃiːnəˈbiliti] n. 可加工性
phosphorus [ˈfɔsfərəs] n. 磷

chromium [ˈkrəumjəm] n. 铬
molybdenum [məˈlibdinəm] n. 钼
vanadium [vəˈneidiəm] n. 钒
austenitic [ˌɔːstəˈnitik] a. 奥氏体的
ferritic [fəˈritik] a. 铁素体的
martensitic [ˌmɑːtinˈzitik] a. 马氏体的
temper [ˈtempə] n. 回火

## NOTES

1) The other elements affect hardenability, toughness, corrosion resistance, machinability, and strength retention at high temperatures.

其他元素影响硬度、韧性、防腐蚀性、可加工性以及高温下强度保持性。

2) Although most steel alloys contain less than 1.0% carbon, it is included in the designation because of its effect on the properties of steel.

尽管大多数合金钢中碳的含量不足1.0%,但由于它会影响钢的特性,因此,合金钢的牌号中要包含碳的含量。

3) Whereas most uses of tool steels are related to the field of manufacturing engineering, they are also pertinent to machine design where the ability to maintain a keen edge under abrasive conditions is required.

尽管大部分工具钢都用在与制造工程相关的领域,然而,在腐蚀环境下,需要保持边缘锋利时,也与机床设计有关。

4) Also, some tool steels have rather high shock resistance which may be desirable in machine components such as parts for mechanical clutches, pawls, blades, guides for moving materials and clamps.

同样,一些工具钢也具有比较高的抗冲击能力,这种抗冲击能力对机床零件是很有利的,如机床离合器、棘爪、刀刃等零件,移动部件中的导向装置以及夹具。

## EXERCISES

1. After reading the text above, summarize the main ideas in oral.

2. Fill in the blanks with proper words or phrases according to the text (note the proper tense).

(1) If wear is a potential problem, low-carbon steels can be c_____ to increase the carbon content in the very outer surface of the part and to improve the combination of properties.

(2) Austenitic stainless steels f_____ the AISI 200 and 300 series.

(3) The high carbon content provides better wear properties s_____ applications requiring durable cutting edges and for applications where surfaces are s_____ constant abrasion.

(4) The numerous varieties of tool steel materials have been c_____ seven general types.

(5) Since d_____ decreases with increasing carbon content, selecting a suitable steel involves some c_____ between strength and ductility.

(6) The term "tool steels" r_____ a group of steels typically used for cutting tools, punches, dies, shearing blades, chisels and similar uses.

3. Translate the following phrases into Chinese according to the text.
(1) have a very effect on          (2) corrosion resistance
(3) heat treatment                 (4) fall into
(5) be subjected to                (6) tensile strength

4. Translate the following phrases into English according to the text.
(1) 分类                           (2) 结构钢
(3) 与……有关                      (4) 屈服点
(5) 抗腐蚀                         (6) 淬火不锈钢

5. Write a 100-word summary according to the text.

## READING MATERIAL

The final properties of steels are dramatically affected by the way the steels are produced. Some processes involve mechanical working, such as rolling to a particular shape or drawing through the dies. In machine design, many bar-shaped parts, shafts, wire and structural members are produced in these ways. But most machine parts, particularly those carrying heavy loads, are heat-treated to produce high strength with acceptable toughness and ductility.

Carbon steel bar and sheet forms are usually delivered in the as-rolling condition, that is, they are rolled at an elevated temperature that eases the rolling process. The rolling can also be done cold to improve strength and surface finish. Cold-drawn bar and wire have the highest strength of the worked forms, along with a very good surface finish. However, when a material is designated to be as-rolled, it should be assumed that it was hot-rolled.

## 1. Heat Treating

Heat treating is the process in which steel is modified its properties by different elevated temperatures. Of the several processes available, those most used for machine steels are annealing, normalizing, through-hardening (quench and temper), and case hardening.

Figure 1.3 shows the temperature-time cycles for these heat treating processes. The symbol RT indicates normal room temperature, and LC refers to the lower critical temperature at which the ferrite transformation begins during the heating of the steel. At the upper critical temperature (UC), the transformation is complete. These temperatures vary with the composition of the steel. For most medium-carbon (0.30%—0.50%) steels, UC is approximately 1 500 °F (822°C). References giving detailed heat treating process data should be consulted.

1) Annealing

Full annealing (Figure 1.3(a)) is performed by heating the steel above the upper critical temperature and holding it until the composition is uniform. Then the steel is cooled very slowly in the furnace until its temperature is below the lower critical temperature. Slow cooling to room temperature outside the furnace completes the process. This treatment produces a soft, low-strength form of the material, free of significant internal stresses. Parts are frequently cold-formed or machined in the annealed condition.

Stress relief annealing (Figure 1.3 (b)) is often used following welding, machining, or cold forming to relieve residual stresses and thereby minimize subsequent distortion. The steel is heated to approximately 1 000 °F to 1 200 °F (540°C—650°C), held to achieve uniformity, and then slowly cooled in still air to room temperature.

2) Normalizing

Normalizing (Figure 1.3 (c)) is similar to annealing, but at a higher temperature, above the transformation range where austenite is formed, approximately 1 600 °F (870°C). The result is a uniform internal structure in the steel and somewhat higher strength than annealing produces. Machinability and toughness are usually improved over the as-rolled condition.

## 2. Through-Hardening and Quenching and Tempering

Through-hardening (Figure 1.3(d)) is accomplished by heating the steel to above the transformation range where austenite forms and then rapidly cooling it in a quenching medium. The rapid cooling causes the formation of martensite, the hard and strong form of steel. The

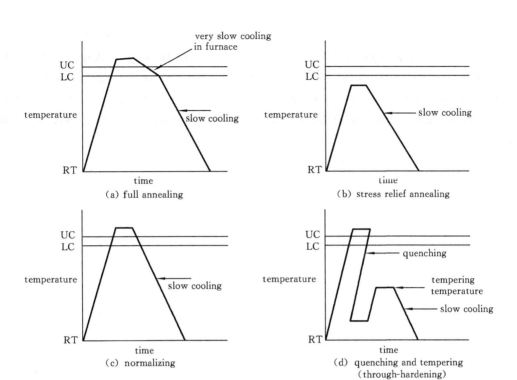

**Figure 1.3  Heat treatments for steels**

properties of the martensite forms depends on the alloy's composition. An alloy containing a minimum of 80% of its structure in the martensite form over the entire cross section has high hardenability. This is an important property to look for when selecting a requiring high strength and hardness steel. The common quenching media are water, brine, and special mineral oils. The selection of a quenching medium depends on the required cooling rate. Most machine steels use either oil or water quenching.

Tempering is usually performed immediately after quenching and involves reheating the steel from a temperature of 400 °F to 1 300 °F (200℃ — 700℃) and then slowly cooling it in air to room temperature. This process modifies the steel's properties. Tensile strength and yield strength decrease with increasing tempering temperature, whereas ductility improves, as indicated by an increase in the percent elongation. Thus, the designer can tailor the properties of the steel to meet specific requirements. Furthermore, the steel in its as-quenched condition has high internal stresses and is usually quite brittle. Machine parts should normally be tempered at 700 °F (370℃) or higher after quenching.

## 3. Case Hardening

In many cases, many parts require only moderate strength although the surface must have a very high hardness. In gear teeth, for example, high surface hardness is necessary to resist wearing as the mating teeth come into contact several million times during the expected life of the gears. At each contact, a high stress happens at the surface of the teeth. In this condition, case hardening is used. The surface (or case) of the part is given a high hardness to a depth of perhaps 0.010 in to 0.040 in (0.25 mm—1.00 mm), although the interior of the part (the core) is affected only slightly, if at all. The advantage of surface hardening is that as the surface receives the required wear-resisting hardness, the core of the part remains in a more ductile form which is resistant to impact and fatigue. The most used processes of case hardening are flame hardening, induction hardening, carburizing, nitriding, cyaniding, carbonitriding.

# Lesson 3  Plastics and Composite Materials

## TEXT

Plastics include a wide variety of materials formed of large molecules called polymers. Thousands of different plastics are created by combining different chemicals to form long molecular chains.

One method of classifying plastics is by the terms thermoplastic and thermosetting. In general, the thermoplastic materials can be formed repeatedly by heating or molding because their basic chemical structure is unchanged from its initial linear form. Thermosetting plastics do undergo some changes during forming and result in a structure in which the molecules are cross-linked and formed a network of interconnected molecules. Some designers recommend the terms "linear" and "cross-linked" in place of the more familiar thermoplastic and thermosetting.

Listed next are several thermoplastics and several thermosets that are used for load-carrying parts.

### 1. Thermoplastics

**Nylon**: Good strength, wear resistance, and toughness, wide range of possible properties depending on fillers and formulations. Used for structural parts, mechanical devices such as gears and bearings, and parts needing wear resistance.

**Acrylonitrile-butadiene-styrene (ABS)**: Good impact resistance, rigidity, moderate strength. Used for housings, helmets, cases, appliance parts, pipe, and pipe fittings.

**Polycarbonate**: Excellent toughness, impact resistance, and dimensional stability. Used for cams, gears, housings, electrical connectors, food processing products, helmets, pump and meter parts.

**Acrylic**: Good weather resistance and impact resistance, can be made with excellent transparency or translucent or opaque with color. Used for glazing, lenses, signs, and housings.

**Polyvinyl chloride (PVC)**: Good strength, weather resistance, and rigidity. Used for pipe, electrical conduit, small housings, ductwork, and moldings.

**Polyimide**: Good strength and wear resistance; very good retention of properties at elevated temperatures up to 500 °F. Used for bearings, seals, rotating vanes, and electrical parts.

**Acetal**: High strength, stiffness, hardness, wear resistance, low friction, good weather resistance and chemical resistance. Used for gears, bushings, sprockets, conveyor parts, and plumbing products.

**Polyurethane elastomer**: A rubberlike material with exceptional toughness and abrasion resistance, good heat resistance and resistance oils. Used for wheels, rollers, gears, sprockets, conveyor parts, and tubing.

**Thermoplastic polyester resin**: Polythylene terephthalate (PET) resin with fibers of glass and/or mineral. Very high strength and stiffness, excellent resistance to chemicals and heat, excellent dimensional stability, and good electrical properties. Used for pump parts, housings, electrical parts, motor parts, auto parts, oven handles, gears, sprockets, and sporting goods.

**Polyetherester elastomer**: Flexible plastic with excellent toughness and resilience, high resistance to creep, impact, and fatigue under flexure, good chemical resistance. Remains flexible at low temperatures and retains good properties at moderately elevated temperatures. Used for seals, belts, pump diaphragms, protective boots, tubing, springs, and impact absorbing devices. High modulus grades can be used for gears and sprockets.

## 2. Thermosets

**Phenolic**: High rigidity, good moldability and dimensional stability, very good electrical properties. Used for load-carrying parts in electrical equipment, switch gear, terminal strips, small housings, handles for appliances and cooking utensils, gears, and structural and mechanical parts. Alkyd, allyl, and amino thermosets have properties and uses similar to those of the phenolics.

**Polyester**: Known as fiber glass when reinforced with glass fibers; high strength and stiffness, good weather resistance. Used for housings, structural shapes, and panels.

## 3. Composite Materials

Composite materials are composed of two or more different materials that act together to produce properties that are different from, and generally superior to, those of the individual components. Typical composites include a polymeric resin matrix material with fibrous reinforcing material dispersed within it. Some advanced composites have a metal matrix.

Designers can tailor the properties of composite materials to meet the specific needs of a particular application by the selection of several variables that determine the properties of the final product. The factors under the designer's control are the following:

- Matrix resin or metal
- Type of reinforcing fibers
- Amount of fiber contained in the composite
- Orientation of the fibers
- Overall thickness of the material
- Orientation of the layers relative to each other
- Combination of two or more types of composites or other materials into a composite structure

Typically, the filler is a strong, stiff material, whereas the matrix has a relatively low density. When the two materials are bonded together, much of the load-carrying ability of the composite is produced by the filler material. The matrix serves to hold the filler in a favorable orientation which is relative to the manner of loading and to distribute the loads to the filler. The result is a somewhat optimized composite that has high strength and high stiffness with low weight.

### 4. Matrix Materials

The following are among the more frequently used matrix materials:
- Thermoplastic polymers   Polyethylene, nylon, polypropylene, polystyrene, polyamides
- Thermosetting polymers   Polyester, epoxy, phenolic polyimide
- Ceramics and glass
- Carbon and graphite
- Metals   Aluminum, magnesium, titanium

### 5. Forms of Filler Materials

Many forms of filler materials are used:
- Continuous fiber strand
- Chopped strands in short lengths (0.75 mm to 50 mm or 0.03 in to 2.00 in)
- Roving   A group of parallel strands
- Woven fabric made from roving or strands
- Metal filaments or wires
- Solid or hollow microspheres
- Metal, glass, or mica flakes
- Single-crystal whiskers of material such as graphite, silicon carbide, and copper.

# NEW WORDS AND EXPRESSIONS

molecule ['mɔlikju:l] n. 分子
polymer ['pɔlimə] n. 聚合体
thermoplastic [,θə:məu'plæstik] a. 热塑性的
thermosetting [,θə:məu'setiŋ] a. 热固性的
acrylonitrile-butadiene-styrene (ABS) 丙烯腈-丁二烯-苯乙烯
polyimide [,pɔli'imaid] n. 聚酰亚胺
polycarbonate [,pɔli'kɑ:bənit] n. 聚碳酸酯

polyvinyl chloride (PVC) 聚氯乙烯
acrylic [ə'krilik] n. 丙烯酸
acetal ['æsitæl] n. 乙缩醛
polyurethane elastomer 聚氨酯橡胶
thermoplastic polyester resin (PET) 热塑性的聚酯树脂
polyetherester elastomer 聚醚酯橡胶

# NOTES

1) Thermosetting plastics do undergo some changes during forming and result in a structure in which the molecules are cross-linked and formed a network of interconnected molecules.

成型期间，热固性塑料结构的确要发生一些改变，造成分子交叉链接，分子之间形成一种网络。

2) Designers can tailor the properties of composite materials to meet the specific needs of a particular application.

设计人员可以调整复合材料的特性，使之适合特殊使用场合的特殊要求。

tailor...to...使……适合……的要求（需要、条件等）

3) When the two materials are bonded together, much of the load-carrying ability of the composite is produced by the filler material.

当两种材料结合在一起时，复合材料的承载能力取决于填充材料。

4) The matrix serves to hold the filler in a favorable orientation which is relative to the manner of loading and to distribute the loads to the filler.

基料的作用在于使填充料在相对于载荷保持有利的定位，并将载荷分散到填充料上。

# EXERCISES

1. After reading the text above, summarize the main ideas in oral.

2. Fill in the blanks with proper words or phrases according to the text (note the proper tense).

（1）Designers can t_____ the properties of composite materials to m_____ the specific needs of a particular application by the selection of several variables that d_____ the properties of the final product.

（2）The result is a somewhat o_____ composite that has high strength and high stiffness with low weight.

（3）When the two materials are b_____ together, much of the load-carrying ability of the composite is produced by the filler material.

（4）Composite materials a_____ two or more different materials that act together to produce properties that are different from, and generally s_____, those of the individual components.

（5）Some designers recommend the terms "linear" and "cross-linked" i_____ the more familiar thermoplastic and thermosetting.

3. Translate the following phrases into Chinese according to the text.

（1）composite structure　　　　　　（2）organic and inorganic materials
（3）glass fiber　　　　　　　　　　（4）chemical resistance
（5）filler material　　　　　　　　（6）in place of
（7）moderate strength

4. Translate the following phrases into English according to the text.

（1）分子链　　　　　　　　　　　　（2）尺寸稳定性
（3）玻璃纤维　　　　　　　　　　　（4）复合材料
（5）取代

5. Write a 100-word summary according to the text.

# READING MATERIAL

## 1. Processing of Composites

One method that is frequently used to produce composite products is first to place layers of sheet-formed fabrics on a form having the desired shape and then to impregnate the fabric with wet resin. Each layer of fabric can be adjusted in its orientation to produce special properties of the finished article. After the lay-up and resin impregnation are completed, the entire system is subjected to heat and pressure while a curing agent reacts with the base resin to produce cross-linking that binds all of the elements into a three-dimensional, unified structure. The polymer binds to the fibers and holds them in their preferred position and orientation during use.

An alternative method of fabricating composite products starts with a process of preimpregnating the fibers with the resin material to produce strands, tape, braids, or sheets. The resulting form, called a pre-preg, can then be stacked into layers or wound onto a form to produce the desired shape and thickness. The final step is the curing cycle as described for the wet process.

Polyester-based composites are often produced as sheet-molding compounds (SMC) in which preimpregnated fabric sheets are placed into a mold and shaped and cured simultaneously under heat and pressure. Large body panels for automotive applications can be produced in this manner.

Pultrusion is a process in which the fiber reinforcement is coated with resin as it is pulled through a heated die to produce a continuous form in the desired shape. This process is used to produce rod, tubing, structural shapes (I-beams, channels, angles, and so on), tees, and hat sections used as stiffeners in aircraft structures.

Filament winding is used to make pipe, pressure vessels, rocket motor cases, instrument enclosures, and odd-shaped containers. The continuous filament can be placed in a variety of patterns, including helical, axial, and circumferential, to produce desired strength and stiffness characteristics.

## 2. Advantages of Composites

Designers typically seek to produce products that are safe, strong, stiff, lightweight, and highly tolerant of the environment. Composites often excel in meeting these objectives when compared with alternative materials such as metals, wood, and unfilled plastics. Two parameters that are used to compare materials are specific strength and specific modulus, defined as follows.

Specific strength is the ratio of the tensile strength of a material to its specific weight.

Specific modulus is the ratio of the modulus of elasticity of a material to its specific weight.

Because the modulus of elasticity is a measure of the stiffness of a material, the specific modulus is sometimes called specific stiffness.

Although obviously not a length, both of these quantities have the unit of length, derived from the ratio of the units for strength or modulus of elasticity and the units for specific weight. In the U. S. Customary System, the units for tensile strength and modulus of elasticity are $lb/in^2$, whereas specific weight is in $lb/in^3$. Thus, the unit for specific strength or specific modulus is inches. In the SI, strength and modulus are expressed in $N/m^2$ (pascal), whereas specific weight is in $N/m^3$. Then the unit for specific strength or specific modulus is meters.

Advantages of composites can be summarized as follows:

- Specific strengths for composite materials can range, as high as five times, those of high-strength steel alloys.
- Specific modulus values for composites materials can be as high as eight times those for steel, aluminum, or titanium alloys.
- Composite materials typically perform better than steel or aluminum in applications where cyclic loads can lead to the potential for fatigue failure.
- Where impact loads and vibrations are expected, composites can be specially formulated with materials that provide high toughness and a high level of damping.
- Some composites have much lighter wear resistance than metals.
- Careful selection of the matrix and filler materials can provide superior corrosion resistance.
- Dimensional changes due to changes in temperature are typically much less for composites than for metals.
- Because composite material have properties that are highly directional, designers can tailor the placement of reinforcing fibers in directions that provide the required strength and stiffness under the specific loading conditions to be encountered.
- Composite structures can often be made in complex shapes in one piece, thus reducing the number of parts in a product and the number of fastening operations required. The elimination of joints typically improves the reliability of such structures as well.
- Composite structures are typically made in their final form directly or in a near-net shape, thus reducing the number of secondary operations required.

# Lesson 4 | Gears

## TEXT

Gears are toothed, cylindrical wheels used for transmitting motion and power from one rotating shaft to another. The teeth of a driving gear mesh accurately in the spaces between teeth on the driven gear. The driving teeth push on the driven teeth, exerting a force perpendicular to the radius of the gear. Thus, a torque is transmitted, and because the gear is rotating, power is also transmitted.

### 1. Spur Gear Geometry Involute Tooth Form

The most widely used spur gear tooth form is the full-depth involute form. Its characteristic shape is shown in Figure 1.4.

The involute is one of a class of geometric curves called conjugate curves. When two such gear teeth are in mesh and rotating, there is a constant angular velocity ratio between them. From the moment of initial contact to the moment of disengagement, the speed of the driving gear is in a constant proportion to the speed of the driven gear. The resulting action of the two gears is very smooth.

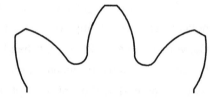

Figure 1.4  Involute-tooth form

Otherwise there would be speeding up or slowing down during the engagement, with the resulting accelerations causing vibration, noise, and dangerous torsional oscillations in the system.

An involute curve by taking a cylinder and wrapping a string around its circumference can be seen. Tie a pencil to the end of the string. Then start with the pencil tight against the cylinder, and hold the string taut. Move the pencil away from the cylinder while keeping the string taut. The curve drawed is an involute.

The circle represented by the cylinder is called the base circle. Notice that at any position on the curve, the string represents a line tangent to the base circle and, at the same time, perpendicular to the involute. Drawing another base circle along the same centerline in such a position that the resulting involute is tangent to the first one, it demonstrates that at the point of contact, the two lines tangent to the base circles are coincident and will stay in the same position as the base circles rotate. This is what happens when two gear teeth are in mesh.

It is a fundamental principle of kinematics, the study of motion, that if the line drawn perpendicular to the surfaces of two rotating bodies at the point of contact always crosses the centerline between the two bodies at the same place, the angular velocity ratio of the two bodies will be constant. This is a statement of gearing. As demonstrated here, the gear teeth made in the involute-tooth form obey the law.

## 2. Helical Gear Geometry

Helical and spur gears are distinguished by the orientation of their teeth. On spur gears, the teeth are straight and are aligned with the axis of the gear. On helical gears, the teeth are inclined at an angle with the axis, that angle being called the helix angle. If the gear was very wide, it would appear that the teeth wind around the gear blank in a continuous, helical path. However, practical considerations limit the width of the gears so that the teeth normally appear to be merely inclined with respect to the axis. Figure 1.5 shows two examples of commercially available helical gears.

Figure 1.5  Helical gears

The forms of helical gear teeth are very similar to those discussed for spur gears. The basic task is to account for the effect of the helix angle.

## 3. Helix Angle

The helix for a given gear can be either left-hand or right-hand. The teeth of a right-hand helical gear would appear to lean to the right when the gear is lying on a flat surface. Conversely, the teeth of a left-hand helical gear would lean to the left. In normal installation, helical gears would be mounted on parallel shafts. To achieve this arrangement, it is required that one gear should be of the right-hand design and that the other be left-hand with an equal helix angle. If both gears in mesh are of the same hand, the shafts will be at 90 degrees to each other. Such gears are called crossed helical gears.

The parallel shaft arrangement for helical gears is preferred because it results in a much higher power-transmitting capacity for a given size of gear than the crossed helical arrangement.

The main advantage of helical gears over spur gears is smoother engagement because a given tooth assumes its load gradually instead of suddenly. Contact starts at one end of a tooth near the tip and progresses across the face in a path downward across the pitch line to the lower flank of the tooth, where it leaves engagement. Simultaneously, other teeth are coming into engagement before a given tooth leaves engagement, with the result that a larger average number of teeth are engaged and are sharing the applied loads compared with a spur gear. The lower average load per tooth allows a greater power transmission capacity for a given size of gear, or a smaller gear can be designed to carry the same power.

The main disadvantage of helical gears is that an axial thrust load is produced as a natural result of the inclined arrangement of the teeth. The bearings that hold the shaft carrying the helical gear must be capable of reacting against the thrust load.

## NEW WORDS AND EXPRESSIONS

involute ['invəluːt] n. 渐开线　　　　　　mesh [meʃ] v. 啮合

perpendicular [ˌpəːpenˈdikjulə] *a.* 垂直的
torque [tɔːk] *n.* 扭矩
engagement [inˈgeidʒmənt] *n.* 啮合
spur gear 直齿轮，正齿轮
helical gear 斜齿轮
bevel gear 锥齿轮
axial thrust load 轴向推力
helix angle 螺旋角
conjugate curves 共轭曲线

## NOTES

1) The driving teeth push on the driven teeth, exerting a force perpendicular to the radius of the gear.

主动轮齿推动从动轮齿运动，产生一个垂直于齿轮半径方向的力。

2) Otherwise there would be speeding up or slowing down during the engagement, with the resulting accelerations causing vibration, noise, and dangerous torsional oscillations in the system.

若情况并非如此，啮合时，时而加速、时而减速，产生的加速度会引起系统振动、噪声以及危险的扭转摆动。

3) It is a fundamental principle of kinematics, the study of motion, that if the line drawn perpendicular to the surfaces of two rotating bodies at the point of contact always crosses the centerline between the two bodies at the same place, the angular velocity ratio of the two bodies will be constant.

研究运动的运动学的一条基本原理是，如果在接触点垂直于两个定轴转动物体的直线总是过两物体的中心线，则两物体的角速度保持常数。

4) The parallel shaft arrangement for helical gears is preferred because it results in a much higher power-transmitting capacity for a given size of gear than the crossed helical arrangement.

对斜齿轮优先安排平行轴安装，因为对于一定尺寸的齿轮，平行轴安装可比交错轴安装传递更大的功率。

## EXERCISES

1. After reading the text above, summarize the main ideas in oral.

2. Fill in the blanks with proper words or phrases according to the text (note the proper tense).

(1) The teeth of a driving gear m_____ accurately in the spaces between teeth on the driven gear.

(2) Helical and spur gears are d_____ by the orientation of their teeth.

(3) When two such gear teeth are in m_____ and rotating, there is a constant angular velocity ratio between them.

(4) From the moment of initial contact to the moment of disengagement, the speed of the driving gear is i_____ the speed of the driven gear.

(5) On spur gears, the teeth are straight and a_____ the axis of the gear.

(6) The driving teeth push on the driven teeth, exerting a force p_____ the radius of the gear.

3. Translate the following phrases into Chinese according to the text.

(1) account for          (2) be aligned with
(3) perpendicular (to)   (4) be in mesh
(5) tangent to           (6) speed up
(7) in proportion to

4. Translate the following phrases into English according to the text.

(1) 减速        (2) 与……成正比
(3) 螺旋角      (4) 啮合
(5) 接触点      (6) 与……相比

5. Write a 100-word summary according to the text.

# READING MATERIAL

## Types of Gears

Several kinds of gears having different tooth geometries are in common use. To acquaint you with the general appearance of some, their basic descriptions are given here.

Spur gears have teeth that are straight and arranged parallel to the axis of the shaft that carries the gear. The curved shape of the faces of the spur gear teeth has a special geometry called an involute curve. This shape makes it possible for two gears to operate together with smooth, positive transmission of power.

The teeth of helical gears are arranged so that they lie at an angle with respect to the axis of the shaft. The angle, called the helix angle, can be virtually any angle. Typical helix angle range from approximately 10° to 30°, but angles up to 45° are practical. The helical teeth operate more smoothly than equivalent spur gear teeth, and stresses are lower. Therefore, a smaller helical gear can be designed for a given power-transmitting capacity than a spur gear. One of the disadvantages of helical gears is that an axial force, called a thrust force, is generated in addition to the driving force that acts tangent to the basic cylinder on which the teeth are arranged. The designer must consider the thrust force when selecting bearing that will hold the shaft during operation. Shafts carrying helical gears are typically arranged parallel to each other. However, a special design, called crossed helical gears, has 45° helix angles, and the shafts operate 90° to each other.

Bevel gears have teeth that are arranged as elements on the surface of a cone. The teeth of straight bevel gears appear to be similar to spur gear teeth, but they are tapered, being wider at the outside and narrower at the top of the cone. Bevel gears typically operate on shafts that are 90° to each other. Indeed, this is often the reason for specifying bevel gears in a drive system. Specially designed bevel gears can operate on shafts that are at some angel other than 90°. When bevel gears are made with teeth that form a helix angle similar to that in helical gears, they are called spiral bevel gears. They operate more smoothly than straight bevel gears and can be made smaller for a given power transmission capacity. When both bevel gears in a pair have the same number of teeth, they are called miter gears and are used only to change the axes of the shaft to 90 degrees. No speed change occurs.

A rack is a straight gear that moves linearly instead of rotating. When a circular gear is mated with a rack, the combination is called a rack and pinion drive. You may have heard that term applied to the steering mechanism of a car or to a part of other machinery.

A worm and its mating worm gear operate on shafts that are at 90 degrees to each other. They typically accomplish a rather large speed reduction ratio compared with other types of gears. The worm is the driver, and the worm gear is the driven gear. The teeth on the worm appear similar to screw threads, and, indeed, they are often called threads rather than teeth. The teeth of the worm gear can be straight like spur gear teeth, or they can be helical. Often the shape of the tip of the worm gear teeth is enlarged to partially wrap around the threads of the worm to improve the power transmission capacity of the set. One disadvantage of the worm/worm gear drive is that it has a somewhat lower mechanical efficiency than most other kinds of gears because there is extensive rubbing contact between the surfaces of the worm threads and the sides of the worm gear teeth.

Think of examples of gears in actual equipment. Describe the operation of the equipment, particularly the power transmission system. Sometimes, of course, the gears and the shafts are enclosed in housing, making it difficult for you to observe the actual gears. Perhaps you can find a manual for the equipment that shows the drive system. Try to answer the following questions:

(1) What was the source of the power, an electric motor, a gasoline engine, a steam turbine, or a hydraulic motor? Were the gears operated by hand?

(2) How were the gears arranged together, and how were they attached to the driving source and the driven machine?

(3) Was there a speed change? Can you determine how much of a change?

(4) Were there more than two gears in the drive system?

(5) What types of gears were used?

(6) What materials were gears made from?

(7) How were the gears attached to the shafts that supported them?

(8) Were the shafts for mating gears aligned parallel to each other, or were they perpendicular to one another?

(9) How were the shafts themselves supported?

(10) Was the gear transmission system enclosed in housing?

# Lesson 5 | Keys, Couplings and Seals

## TEXT

A key is the machinery component placed at the interface between a shaft and the hub of a power-transmitting element for the purpose of transmitting torque (see Figure 1.6 (a)). The key is demountable to facilitate assembly and disassembly of the shaft system. It is installed in an axial groove machined into the shaft, called a keyseat. A similar groove in the hub of the power-transmitting element is usually called a keyway, but it is more properly also a keyseat. The key is typically installed into the shaft keyseat first; then the hub keyseat is aligned with the key, and the hub is slid into position.

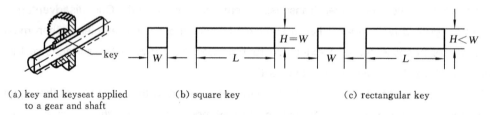

(a) key and keyseat applied to a gear and shaft    (b) square key    (c) rectangular key

**Figure 1.6   Parallel keys**

### 1. Square and Rectangular Parallel Keys

The most common type of key for shafts up to 6.5 inches in diameter is the square key, as illustrated in Figure 1.6 (b). The rectangular key (illustrated in Figure 1.6 (c)) is recommended for larger shafts and is used for smaller shafts where the shorter height can be tolerated. Both the square and the rectangular keys are referred to as parallel keys because the top, bottom and the sides of the key are parallel.

The keyseats in the shaft and the hub are designed so that exactly one-half of the height of the key is bearing on the side of the shaft keyseat and the other half on the side of the hub keyseat.

### 2. Couplings

The term coupling refers to a device used to connect two shafts together at their ends for the purpose of transmitting power. There are two general types of couplings: rigid and flexible.

1) Rigid Couplings

Rigid couplings are designed to draw two shafts together tightly so that no relative motion can occur between them. This design is desirable for certain kinds of equipment in which precise alignment of two shafts is required and can be provided. In such cases, the coupling must be designed to be capable of transmitting the torque in the shafts.

A typical rigid coupling is shown in Figure 1.7, in which flanges are mounted on the ends of each shaft and are drawn together by a series of bolts. The load path is then from the driving shaft to its flange, through the bolts, into the mating flange, and out to the driven shaft. The torque places the bolts in shear. The total shear force on the bolts depends on the radius of the bolt circle and the torque.

Rigid couplings should be used only when the alignment of the two shafts can be maintained very accurately, not only at the time of installation but also during operation of the machines. If significant angular, radial, or axial misalignment

Figure 1.7  Rigid coupling

occurs, stresses that are difficult to predict and that may lead to early failure due to fatigue will be induced in the shafts. These difficulties can be overcome by the use of flexible couplings.

2) Flexible Couplings

Flexible couplings are designed to transmit torque smoothly while permitting some axial, radial, and angular misalignment. The flexibility is such that when misalignment does occur, parts of the coupling move with little or no resistance. Thus, no significant axial or bending stresses are developed in the shaft.

Many types of flexible couplings are available commercially. Each of them is designed to transmit a given limiting torque. The manufacturer's catalog lists the design data from which you can choose a suitable coupling. Remember that torque equals power divided by rotational speed. So for a given size of coupling, as the speed of rotation increases, the amount of power that the coupling can transmit also increases, although not always in direct proportion. Of course, centrifugal effects determine the upper limit of speed.

### 3. Seals

Seals are an important part of machine design in situations where the following conditions apply:

● Contaminants must be excluded from critical areas of a machine.

● Lubricants must be contained within a space.

● Pressurized fluids must be contained within a component such as a valve or a hydraulic cylinder.

Some of the parameters affecting the choice of the type of sealing system, the materials used, and the details of its design are as follows:

● The nature of the fluids to be contained or excluded.

● Pressures on both sides of the seal.

● The nature of any relative motion between the seal and the mating components.

● Temperatures on all parts of the sealing system.

● The degree of sealing required  Is some small amount of leakage permissible?

● The life expectancy of the system.

- The nature of the solid materials against which the seal must act: corrosion potential, smoothness, hardness, wear resistance.
- Ease of service for replacement of worn sealing elements.

The number of designs for sealing systems is virtually limitless, and only a brief overview will be presented here. Often, designers rely on technical information provided by manufacturers of complete sealing systems or specific sealing elements. Also, in critical or unusual situations, testing of a proposed design is advised.

# NEW WORDS AND EXPRESSIONS

key [kiː] n. 键
keyseat n. 键槽
hub [hʌb] n. 轮毂
contaminant [kən'tæminənt] n. 杂质
lubricant ['luːbrikənt] n. 润滑剂

leakage ['liːkidʒ] n. 泄漏,渗漏
rigid coupling 刚性联轴器
flexible coupling 柔性联轴器
hydraulic cylinder 液压缸
sealing system 密封系统

# NOTES

1) A key is the machinery component placed at the interface between a shaft and the hub of a power-transmitting element for the purpose of transmitting torque.
键是一种置于轴与传递动力的轮毂之间的机械零件,用于传递转矩。

2) The rectangular key is recommended for larger shafts and is used for smaller shafts where the shorter height can be tolerated.
对于较大的轴,推荐采用矩形键,当高度较低的一边允许时,可用于较小的轴。

3) This design is desirable for certain kinds of equipment in which precise alignment of two shafts is required and can be provided.
对于某些设备而言,当两轴要求具有精确的对中性时,这种设计才是令人满意的。

4) A typical rigid coupling in which flanges are mounted on the ends of each shaft and are drawn together by a series of bolts.
典型的刚性联轴器每根轴的末端装上凸缘并用螺栓连在一起。

# EXERCISES

1. After reading the text above, summarize the main ideas in oral.
2. Fill in the blanks with proper words or phrases according to the text (note the proper tense).
   (1) The key is d_____ to facilitate assembly and disassembly of the shaft system.
   (2) This design is desirable for certain kinds of equipment in which precise a_____ of two shafts is required and can be provided.
   (3) Often, designers r_____ technical information provided by manufacturers of

complete sealing systems or specific sealing elements.

(4) Of course, c_____ determine the upper limit of speed.

(5) The term coupling r_____ a device used to connect two shafts together at their ends for the purpose of transmitting power.

(6) If significant angular, radial, or axial m_____ occurs, stresses that are difficult to predict and that may lead to early failure due to f_____ will be induced in the shafts.

3. Translate the following phrases into Chinese according to the text.

(1) be aligned with  (2) refer to
(3) depend on  (4) lead to
(5) exclude from  (6) life expectancy

4. Translate the following phrases into English according to the text.

(1) 刚性联轴器  (2) 柔性联轴器
(3) 平行键  (4) 密封系统
(5) 相对运动  (6) 抗磨损性

5. Write a 100-word summary according to the text.

# READING MATERIAL

## Fasteners

A fastener is a device used to connect or join two or more components. Literally hundreds of fastener types and variations are available. The most common are threaded fasteners referred to by many names, among them are bolts, screws, nuts, studs, lag screws, and set screws.

A bolt is a threaded fastener designed to pass through holes in the mating members and to be secured by tightening a nut from the end opposite the head of the bolt. A screw is a threaded fastener designed to be inserted through a hole in one member to be joined and into a threaded hole in the mating member. The threaded hole may have been preformed, for example, by tapping, or it may be formed by the screw itself as it is forced into the material. Machine screws, also called cap screws, are precision fasteners with straight-threaded bodies that are turned into tapped holes.

A popular type of machine screw is the socket head cap screw. The usual configuration has a cylindrical head with a recessed hex socket. Also readily available are flat head styles for countersinking to produce a flush surface, button head styles for a low profile appearance, and shoulder screws providing a precision bearing surface for location or pivoting.

1) Thread Forms

For a screw to function there must be two mating parts, one with an internal thread and the other with an external thread. The internal threads can be tapped into a part, such as a cast housing or, more commonly, inside a nut. Whenever possible, the selection of a thread should be standard to improve interchangeability for maintenance or replacement.

Thread forms defines the shape of the thread. The thread features introduced in the previous section were illustrated on a unified thread form. Regardless, these definitions are applicable to all thread forms. The most popular thread forms include unified, metric, square, and ACME threads.

2) Unified Threads

Unified threads are the most common threads used on fasteners and small mechanisms. They are also commonly used for positioning mechanisms. The dimensions of a unified thread have been standardized. Unified threads are designated as either coarse pitch (UNC) or fine pitch (UNF). A standard unified thread is specified by the size, threads per inch, and coarse or fine pitch. Standard thread designations would appear as

10-32 UNF

1/2-13 UNC

3) Metric Threads

Metric thread forms are also described as sharp, triangular shapes, but with a flat root. However, the standard dimensions are convenient metric values and coordinated through the International Organization for Standardization (ISO). A standard metric thread is specified by an "M" metric designation, the nominal major diameter, and pitch. A standard thread designation would appear as

M10 × 1.5

4) Square Threads

Square threads, as the name implies, are a square, flat-top thread. They are strong and are originally designed to transfer power. Although they efficiently transfer large loads, these threads are difficult to machine with perpendicular sides. The square threads have been generally replaced by Acme threads.

5) Acme Threads

Acme threads are similar to square threads, but with sloped sides. They are commonly used when rapid movement is required or large forces are transmitted. This thread is the most common form used in screw mechanisms for industrial machines. Advantages are low cost and ease of manufacture. Disadvantages include low efficiencies, as will be discussed later, and difficulty in predicting service life.

6) Ball Screws

Ball screws have also been designated to convert rotary motion of either the screw or nut into relatively slow linear motion of the mating member along the screw axis. However, a ball screw has drastically less friction than a traditional screw configuration. The sliding contact between the screw and nut has been replaced with rolling contact of balls in grooves along the screw. Thus a ball screw requires less power to drive a load.

The operation of a ball screw is smooth because the rolling balls eliminate the "slip-stick" motion caused by the friction of a traditional screw and nut. However, because of the low friction of a ball screw, a brake must usually be used to hold in place.

Look in your car, particularly under the hood in the engine compartment. If you can also

## Lesson 5  Keys, Couplings and Seals

look the chassis to see where fasteners are used to hold different components onto the frame or some other structural member.

Look also at bicycles, lawn and garden equipment, grocery carts, display units in a store, hand tools, kitchen appliances, toys, exercise equipment, and furniture. If you have access to a factory, you should be able to identify hundreds or thousands of examples. Try to get some insight about where certain types of fasteners are used and for what purposes.

# Lesson 6  Rolling Contact Bearings

## TEXT

The purpose of a bearing is to support a load while permitting relative motion between two elements of a machine. The term rolling contact bearings refers to the wide variety of bearings that use spherical balls or some other type of roller between the stationary and the moving elements. The most common type of bearing supports a rotating shaft, resisting purely radial loads or a combination of radial and axial (thrust) loads. Some bearings are designed to carry only thrust loads. Most bearings are used in applications involving rotation, but some are used in linear motion applications.

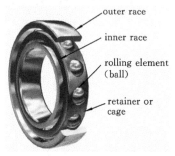

Figure 1.8  Single-row, groove ball bearing

The components of a typical rolling contact bearing are the inner race, the outer race, and the rolling elements. Figure 1.8 shows the common single-row, deep-groove ball bearing. Usually the outer race is stationary and is held by the housing of the machine. The inner race is pressed onto the rotating shaft and thus rotates with it. Then the balls roll between the outer and inner races. The load path is from the shaft, to the inner race, to the balls, to the outer race, and finally to the housing. The presence of the balls allows a very smooth, low-friction rotation of the shaft. The typical coefficient of friction for a rolling contact bearing is approximately 0.001 to 0.005. These values reflect only the rolling elements themselves and the means of retaining them in the bearing.

### 1. Types of Rolling Contact Bearing

Here we will discuss several different types of rolling contact bearings and the applications in which each is typically used.

Radial loads act toward the center of the bearing along a radius. Such loads are typical of those created by power transmission elements on shafts such as spur gears, V-belt drives, and chain drives. Thrust loads are those that act parallel to the axis of the shaft. The axial components of the forces on helical gears, worms and wormgears, and bevel gears are thrust loads. Also, bearings supporting shafts with vertical axes are subjected to thrust loads due to the weight of the shaft and the elements on the shaft as well as from axial operating forces. Misalignment refers to the angular deviation of the axis of the shaft at the bearing from the true axis of the bearing itself. An excellent rating for misalignment in Table 1.1 indicates that the bearing can accommodate up to 4.0° of angular deviation. A bearing with a fair rating can withstand up to 0.15°, while a poor rating indicates that rigid shafts with less than 0.05° of misalignment are required. Manufacturers' catalogs should be consulted for specific data.

Table 1.1  Comparison of bearing types

| Bearing types | Radial load capacity | Thrust load capacity | Misalignment capability |
|---|---|---|---|
| Single-row, deep-groove ball | Good | Fair | Fair |
| Double-row, deep-groove ball | Excellent | Good | Fair |
| Angular contact | Good | Excellent | Poor |
| Cylindrical roller | Excellent | Poor | Fair |
| Needle | Excellent | Poor | Poor |
| Spherical roller | Excellent | Fair/good | Excellent |
| Tapered roller | Excellent | Excellent | Poor |

1) Single-Row, Deep-Groove Ball Bearing

The inner race is typically pressed on the shaft at the bearing seat with a slight interference fit to ensure that it rotates with the shaft. The spherical rolling elements, or balls, roll in a deep groove in both the inner and the outer races. The spacing of the balls is maintained by retainers or "cages". While designed primarily for radial load-carrying capacity, the deep groove allows a fairly sizable thrust load to be carried. The thrust load would be applied to one side of the inner race by a shoulder on the shaft. The load would pass across the side of the groove, through the ball, to the opposite side of the outer race, and then to the housing. The radius of the ball is slightly smaller than the radius of the groove to allow free rolling of the balls. The contact between a ball and the race is theoretically at a point, but it is actually a small circular area because of the deformation of the elements. Because the load is carried on a small area, very high local contact stresses occur. To increase the capacity of a single-row bearing, a bearing with a greater number of balls, or larger balls operating in larger-diameter races should be used.

2) Double-Row, Deep-Groove Ball Bearing

Adding a second row of balls (Figure 1.9) increases the radial load-carrying capacity of the deep-groove type of bearing compared with the single-row design because more balls share the load. Thus, a greater load can be carried in the same space, or a given load can be carried in a smaller space. The greater width of double-row bearings often adversely affects the misalignment capability.

3) Angular Contact Ball Bearing

One side of each race in an angular contact bearing is higher to allow the accommodation of greater thrust loads compared with the standard single-row, deep-groove bearing. Figure 1.10 shows the preferred angle of the resultant force (radial and thrust loads combined), with commercially available bearings having angles of 15° to 40°.

## 2. Bearing Materials

The load on a rolling contact bearing is exerted on a small area. The resulting contact stresses are quite high, regardless of the type of bearing. Contact stresses of approximately

Figure 1.9  Double-row, deep-groove ball bearing

Figure 1.10  Angular contact ball bearing

300 000 psi are not uncommon in commercially available bearings. To withstand such high stresses, the balls, rollers, and races are made from a very hard, high-strength steel or ceramic.

Rolling elements and other components can be made from ceramic materials such as silicon nitride. Although the cost is higher than that of steels, ceramics offer significant advantages. The light weight, high strength, and high temperature capability make them desirable for aerospace, engine, military, and other demanding applications.

## NEW WORDS AND EXPRESSIONS

spherical ['sferikəl] *a*. 球的,球形的
retainer [ri'teinə] *n*. 保持架
ceramic [si'ræmik] *n*. 陶瓷
rolling contact bearing 滚动接触轴承
inner race 内圈
outer race 外圈

radial loads 径向载荷
axial loads 轴向载荷
deep-groove ball bearing 深沟球轴承
angular contact ball bearing 角接触球轴承
silicon nitride 氮化硅

## NOTES

1) The term rolling contact bearings refers to the wide variety of bearings that use spherical balls or some other type of roller between the stationary and the moving elements.

滚动接触轴承是指在静止元件与运动元件之间使用球或其他类型滚动体的、种类繁多的轴承。

2) Misalignment refers to the angular deviation of the axis of the shaft at the bearing from the true axis of the bearing itself.

偏斜是指轴在轴承上的中心线与轴承自身中心线的角度偏差。

3) A bearing with a fair rating can withstand up to 0.15°, while a poor rating indicates that rigid shafts with less than 0.05° of misalignment are required.

较高等级的轴承最高可以承受 0.15° 的偏斜,而较低等级的则要求刚性轴的偏斜小于 0.05°。

4) The inner race is typically pressed on the shaft at the bearing seat with a slight interference fit to ensure that it rotates with the shaft.

一般，内圈压到轴承座上的轴上，二者为过盈配合，以确保同轴一起转动。

# EXERCISES

1. After reading the text above, summarize the main ideas in oral.
2. Fill in the blanks with proper words or phrases according to the text (note the proper tense).

(1) The load on a rolling contact bearing i_____ a small area.

(2) The components of a typical rolling contact bearing are the i_____, the o_____, and the r_____.

(3) Also, bearings supporting shafts with vertical axes _____ thrust loads due to the weight of the shaft and the elements on the shaft as well as from axial operating forces.

(4) One side of each race in an angular contact bearing is higher to allow the _____ of greater thrust loads _____ the standard single-row, deep-groove bearing.

(5) A bearing with a fair rating can w_____ up to 0.15°, while a poor rating indicates that rigid shafts with less than 0.05° of m_____ are required.

(6) The outer race is _____ and is held by the housing of the machine.

3. Translate the following phrases into Chinese according to the text.

(1) resultant force (2) linear motion
(3) angular deviation (4) axial component
(5) interference fit (6) ceramic material

4. Translate the following phrases into English according to the text.

(1) 内圈 (2) 外圈
(3) 保持架 (4) 深沟球轴承
(5) 角接触轴承 (6) 接触应力

5. Write a 100-word summary according to the text.

# READING MATERIAL

## Practical Considerations in the Application of Bearings

1) Lubrication

The functions of lubrication in a bearing unit are as follows:

i) To provide a low-friction film between the rolling elements and the races of the bearing and at points of contact with cages, guiding surfaces, retainers, and so on.

ii) To protect the bearing components from corrosion.

iii) To help dissipate heat from the bearing unit.

iv) To carry heat away from the bearing unit.

ⅴ) To help dispel contaminants and moisture from the bearing.

Rolling contact bearing are usually lubricated with either grease oil. Under normal ambient temperatures (approximately 70 ℉) and relatively slow speeds (under 500 rpm), grease is satisfactory. At higher speeds or higher ambient temperatures, oil lubrication applied in a continuous flow is required, possibly with external cooling of the oil.

Oils used in bearing lubrication are usually clean, stable mineral oils. Under lighter loads and lower speeds, light oil is used. Heavier loads and/or higher speeds require heavier oils up to SAE30. A recommended upper limit for lubricant temperature is 160 ℉. The choice should be maintained at the operating temperature of the lubricant in the bearing. Manufacturer's recommendations should be sought.

In some critical applications such as bearings in jet engines and very-high-speed devices, lubricating oil is pumped under pressure to an enclosed housing for the bearing where the oil is directed at the rolling elements themselves. A controlled return path is also provided. The temperature of the oil in the sump is monitored and controlled with heat exchangers or refrigeration to maintain oil viscosity within acceptable limits. Such systems provide reliable lubrication and ensure the removal of heat from the bearing.

Greases used in bearings are mixtures of lubricating oils and thickening agents, usually soaps such as lithium or barium. The soaps act as carriers for the oil which is drawn out at the point of need within the bearing. Additives to resist corrosion or oxidation of the oil itself are sometimes added. Classifications of greases specify the operating temperatures to which the greases will be exposed, as defined by the American Bearing Manufacturers' Association (ABMA).

2) Installation

It has already been stated that most bearings should be installed with a light interference fit between the bore of the bearing and the shaft to preclude the possibility of rotation of the inner race of the bearing with respect to the shaft. Such a condition would result in uneven wear of the bearing elements and early failure. To install the bearing then requires rather heavy forces applied axially. Care must be exercised so that the bearing is not damaged during installation. The installation force should be applied directly to the inner race of the bearing.

If the force were applied through the outer race, the load would be transferred through the rolling elements to the inner race. Because of the small contact area, it is likely that such transfer of forces would overstress some element, exceeding the static load capacity. Brinelling would result, along with the noise and rapid wear that accompany this condition. For large bearings it may be necessary to heat the bearing to expand its diameter in order to keep the installation forces within reason. Removal of bearings intended for reuse requires similar precautions. Bearing pullers are available to facilitate this task.

3) Preloading

Some bearings are made with internal clearances that must be taken up in a particular direction to ensure satisfactory operation. In such cases, preloading must be provided, usually in the axial direction. On horizontal shafts, springs are typically used, with axial adjustment of the spring deflection sometimes provided to adjust the amount of preload. When space is limited, the use of Belleville washers is desirable because they provide high forces with small deflections. Shims can be used to adjust the actual deflection and preload obtained. On vertical shafts the weight of the shaft assembly itself may be sufficient to provide the required preload.

4) Sealing

When the bearing is to operate in dirty or moist environments, special shields and seals are usually specified. They can be provided on either or both sides of the rolling elements. Shields are typically metal and are fixed to the stationary race, but they remain clear of the rotating race. Seals are made of elastomeric materials and do contact the rotating race. Bearings fitted with both seals and shields and precharged at the factory with grease are sometimes called permanently lubricated. Although such bearings are likely to give many years of satisfactory service, extreme conditions can produce a degradation of the lubricating properties of the grease. The presence of seals also increases the friction in a bearing. Sealing can be provided outside the bearing in the housing or at the shaft/housing interface. On high-speed shafts, a labyrinth seal, consisting of a noncontacting ring around the shaft with a few thousandths of an inch radial clearance, is frequently used. Grooves, sometimes in the form of a thread, are machined in the ring. The relative motion of the shaft with respect to the ring creates the sealing action.

5) Limiting Speeds

Most catalogs of mechanical engineering list the limitation of speed for each bearing. It may result in excessively high operating temperatures due to friction between the cages supporting the rolling elements, if exceeding the limitations. Generally, the limiting speed is lower for larger bearings than for smaller bearings. Also, a given bearing will have a lower limiting speed as loads increase. With special care, either in the fabrication of the bearing cage or in the lubrication of the bearing, bearings can be operated at higher speeds than those listed in the catalogs. The manufacturer should be consulted in such applications. The use of ceramic rolling elements with their lower mass can work in higher limiting speeds.

# Lesson 7 | Belt and Chain Drives

## TEXT

Belts and chains represent the major types of flexible power transmission elements. Rotary power is developed by the electric motor, but motors typically operate at too high a speed and deliver too low a torque to be appropriate for the final drive application. Remember, for a given power transmission, the torque is increased in proportion to the amount that rotational speed is reduced. The high speed of the motor makes belt drives somewhat ideal for that first stage of reduction. A smaller drive pulley is attached to the motor shaft, while a larger diameter pulley is attached to a parallel shaft that operates at a correspondingly lower speed. Pulleys for belt drives are also called sheaves.

In general, belt drives are applied where the rotational speeds are relatively high, as on the first stage of speed reduction from an electric motor or engine. The linear speed of a belt is usually 2 500 ft/min to 6 500 ft/min, which results in relatively low tensile forces in the belt. At lower speeds, the tension in the belt becomes too large for typical belt cross sections, and slipping may occur between the sides of the belt and the sheave or pulley. At higher speeds, dynamic effects such as centrifugal forces, belt whip, and vibration reduce the effectiveness of the drive and its life. A speed of 4 000 ft/min is generally recommended. Some belt designs employ high-strength, reinforcing strands, and some cogged designs that engage matching grooves in the pulleys to enhance their ability to transmit the high forces at low speeds. These designs compete with chain drives in many applications.

### 1. Types of Belt Drives

A belt is a flexible power transmission element that seats on a set of pulleys or sheaves. When the belt is used for speed reduction, the typical case, the smaller sheave is mounted on the high-speed shaft, such as the shaft of an electric motor. The larger sheave is mounted on the driven machine.

The belt is installed around the two sheaves while the center distance between them is reduced. Then the sheaves are moved apart, placing the belt in a rather high initial tension. When the belt is transmitting power, friction causes the belt to grip the driving sheave, increasing the tension on one side, called the "tight side". The tensile force in the belt exerts a tangential force on the driven sheave, and thus a torque is applied to the driven shaft. The opposite side of the belt is still under tension, but at a smaller value. Thus, it is called the "slack side".

Many types of belts are available, such as flat belts, grooved or cogged belts, standard V-belts, double-angle V-belts, and others. See Figure 1.11 for examples.

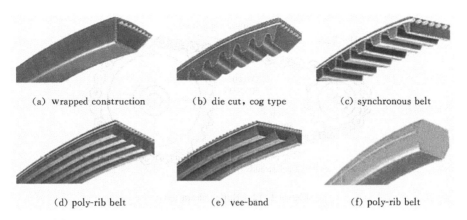

(a) wrapped construction  (b) die cut, cog type  (c) synchronous belt

(d) poly-rib belt  (e) vee-band  (f) poly-rib belt

Figure 1.11  Examples of belt construction

The flat belt is the simplest type, that often made from leather or rubber-coated fabric. The sheave surface is also flat and smooth, and the driving force is therefore limited by the pure friction between the belt and the sheave. Some designers prefer flat belts for delicate machinery because the belt will slip if the torque tends to rise to a level high enough to damage the machine.

Synchronous belts, sometimes called timing belts (see Figure 1.11 (c)), ride on sprocket having mating grooves into which the teeth on the belt seat. This is a positive drive, limited only by the tensile strength of the belt and the shear strength of the teeth.

Some cog belts, such as that shown in Figure 1.11 (b), are applied to standard V-grooved sheaves. The cogs give the belt greater flexibility and higher efficiency compared with standard belts. They can operate on smaller diameters sheaves.

A widely used type of belt, particularly in industrial drives and vehicular applications, is the V-belt drive, shown in Figure 1.11 (e). The V-shape causes the belt to wedge tightly into the groove, increasing friction and allowing high torques to be transmitted before slipping occurs. Most belts have high-strength cords positioned at the pitch diameter of the belt cross section to increase the tensile strength of the belt. The cords, made from natural fibers, synthetic strands, or steel, are embedded in a firm rubber compound to provide the flexibility needed to allow the belt to pass around the sheave. Often an outer fabric cover is added to give the belt good durability.

## 2. Chain Drives

A chain is a power transmission element made as a series of pin-connected links. The design provides for flexibility while enabling the chain to transmit large tensile forces.

When transmitting power between rotating shafts, the chain engages mating toothed wheels, called sprockets. Figure 1.12 shows a typical chain drive.

The most common type of chain is the roller chain, in which the roller on each pin provides exceptionally low friction between the chain and the sprockets.

The average tensile strengths of the various chain sizes are also listed in Table 1.2. These data can be used for very low speed drives or for applications in which the function of the chain

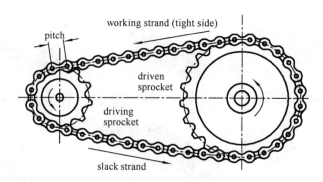

Figure 1.12  Roller chain drive

is to apply a tensile force or to support a load. It is recommended that only 10% of the average tensile strength be used in such applications. For power transmission, the rating of a given chain size as a function of the speed of rotation must be determined.

Table 1.2  Roller chain sizes

| Chain number | Pitch (in) | Roller diameter | Roller width | Link plate thickness | Average tensile strength (lb) |
|---|---|---|---|---|---|
| 35 | 3/8 | None | — | 0.050 | 2 100 |
| 41 | $\frac{1}{2}$ | 0.306 | 0.250 | 0.050 | 2 000 |
| 40 | $\frac{1}{2}$ | 0.312 | 0.312 | 0.060 | 3 700 |
| 50 | $\frac{5}{8}$ | 0.400 | 0.375 | 0.080 | 6 100 |
| 60 | $\frac{3}{4}$ | 0.469 | 0.500 | 0.094 | 8 500 |
| 80 | 1 | 0.626 | 0.625 | 0.125 | 14 500 |
| 100 | $1\frac{1}{4}$ | 0.750 | 0.750 | 0.156 | 24 000 |
| 120 | $1\frac{1}{2}$ | 0.875 | 1.000 | 0.187 | 34 000 |
| 140 | $1\frac{3}{4}$ | 1.000 | 1.000 | 0.219 | 46 000 |
| 160 | 2 | 1.125 | 1.250 | 0.250 | 58 000 |
| 180 | $2\frac{1}{4}$ | 1.406 | 1.406 | 0.281 | 80 000 |
| 200 | $2\frac{1}{2}$ | 1.562 | 1.500 | 0.312 | 95 000 |
| 240 | 3 | 1.875 | 1.875 | 0.375 | 130 000 |

# NEW WORDS AND EXPRESSIONS

rotary ['rəutəri] *a.* 旋转的　　　　　　sheave [ʃi:v] *n.* 带轮
pulley ['puli] *n.* 滑轮　　　　　　　　groove [gru:v] *n.* 凹槽

pin [pin] *n.* 销子
sprocket ['sprɔkit] *n.* 链轮
linear speed 线速度
centrifugal force 离心力
belt whip 带抖动

flat belt 平带
synchronous belt 同步带
cog belt 嵌齿带
V-belt drive V 型带传动

# NOTES

1) Rotary power is developed by the electric motor, but motors typically operate at too high a speed and deliver too low a torque to be appropriate for the final drive application.

回转动力尽管由电动机供给，然而，一般的电动机由于转速过高、传递转矩过低，无法成为最终的驱动装置。

2) A smaller drive pulley is attached to the motor shaft, while a larger diameter pulley is attached to a parallel shaft that operates at a correspondingly lower speed.

较小的带轮作为驱动轮，安装在电动机轴上，而较大的带轮安装在输出速度相对较低的平行轴上。

3) Some designers prefer flat belts for delicate machinery because the belt will slip if the torque tends to rise to a level high enough to damage the machine.

对于精密机械，一些设计人员偏爱平带，这是因为当转矩超过一定值对机器造成损坏时，平带会打滑。

4) These data can be used for very low speed drives or for applications in which the function of the chain is to apply a tensile force or to support a load.

当链条低速运动或链条主要用来提供拉力或支撑负载时，就可以使用这些抗拉强度的数据。

# EXERCISES

1. After reading the text above, summarize the main ideas in oral.

2. Fill in the blanks with proper words or phrases according to the text (note the proper tense).

(1) Remember, for a given power transmission, the torque is increased i_____ the amount that rotational speed is reduced.

(2) S_____, sometimes called timing belts, ride on sprocket having mating grooves into which the teeth on the belt seat.

(3) The high speed of the motor makes belt drives somewhat i_____ for that first stage of reduction.

(4) Some belt designs e_____ high-strength, reinforcing strands, and some cogged designs that engage m_____ grooves in the pulleys to e_____ their ability to transmit the high forces at low speeds.

(5) The V-shape causes the belt to w_____ tightly into the groove, increasing

friction and allowing high torques to be transmitted before s_____ occurs.

3. Translate the following phrases into Chinese according to the text.
(1) be attached to          (2) result in
(3) compete with            (4) exert a force on
(5) be appropriate for      (6) be embedded in

4. Translate the following phrases into English according to the text.
(1) V-型带传动              (2) 转动速度
(3) 带轮直径                (4) 松边
(5) 链传动                  (6) 滚子链

5. Write a 100-word summary according to the text.

# READING MATERIAL

## 1. Chains

As with belts, chain drives are used to transmit rotational motion and torque from one shaft to another, smoothly, quietly, and inexpensively. Chain drives provide the flexibility of a belt drive with the positive engagement feature of a gear drive. Therefore, chain drives are well suited for applications with large distances between the respective shafts, slow speed, and high torque.

Compared to other forms of power transmission, chain drives have the following advantages:

● They are less expensive than gear drives.

● They have no slippage, as with belts, and provide a more efficient power transmission.

● They have flexible shaft center distances, whereas gear drives are restricted.

● They are more effective at lower speeds than belts.

● They have lower loads on the shaft bearing because initial tension is not required as with belts.

● They have a longer service life and do not deteriorate with factors such as heat, oil, or age, as do belts.

● They require little adjustment, whereas belts require frequent adjustment.

## 2. Types of Chains

Chains are made from a series of interconnected links. Many types of chain designs are commercially available and are listed here.

(1) A roller chain is the most common type of chain used for power transmission. Large roller chains are rated to over 600 hp. The roller chain design provides quiet and efficient operation but must be lubricated.

(2) A multiple-strand roller chain uses multiple standard roller chains as parallel strands. It increases the power capacity of the chain drive.

(3) An offset sidebar roller chain is less expensive than a roller chain but it has slightly less power capability. It also has an open construction that lets it to withstand dirt and contaminants, which can wear out other chains. These chains are often used on construction equipment.

(4) An inverted tooth, silent chain is the most expensive chain to manufacture. It can be efficiently used in applications that require high-speed, smooth, and quiet power transmission. Lubrication is required to keep these chains in reliable operation. They are common in machine tools, pumps, and power drive units.

### 3. Design of Chain Drives

The rating of chain for its power transmission capacity considers three modes of failure: (1) fatigue of the link plates due to the repeated application of the tension in the tight side of the chain, (2) impact of the rollers as they engage the sprocket teeth, and (3) galling between the pins of each link and the bushings on the pins.

The ratings are based on empirical data with a smooth driver and a smooth load (service factor = 1.0) and with a rated life of approximately 15 000 h. The important variables are the pitch of the chain, the size and the rotational speed of the smaller sprocket. Lubrication is critical to the satisfactory operation of a chain drive. Manufacturers recommend the type of lubrication method for given combinations of chain size, sprocket size, and speed. These are typical of the types of data available for all chain sizes in manufacturers' catalogs. Notice these features of the data:

(1) The ratings are based on the speed of the smaller sprocket and an expected life of approximately 15 000 hours.

(2) For a given speed, the power capacity increases with the number of teeth on the sprocket. Of course, the larger the number of teeth, the larger the diameter of the sprocket. Note that the use of a chain with a small pitch on a large sprocket produces the quieter drive.

(3) For a given sprocket size (a given number of teeth), the power capacity increases with increasing speed up to a point; then it decreases. Fatigue due to the tension in the chain governs at the low to moderate speeds; impact on the sprockets governs at the higher speeds. Each sprocket size has an absolute upper-limit speed due to the onset of galling between the pins and the bushings of the chain. This explains the abrupt drop in power capacity to zero at the limiting speed.

(4) The ratings are for a single strand of chain. Although multiple strands do increase the power capacity, they do not provide a direct multiple of the single-strand capacity. Multiply the capacity in Table1.2 by the following factors.

Two strands: Factor = 1.7

Three strands: Factor = 2.5

Four strands: Factor = 3.3

(5) The ratings are for a service factor of 1.0. Specify a service factor for a given application in manufacturers' catalog.

## 4. Lubrication

It is essential that adequate lubrication should be provided for chain drives. There are numerous moving parts within the chain, along with the interaction between the chain and the sprocket teeth. The designer must define the lubricant properties and the method of lubrication.

(1) Lubricant Properties. Petroleum-based lubricating oil similar to engine oil is recommended. Its viscosity must enable the oil to flow readily between chain surfaces that move relative to each other while providing adequate lubrication action. The oil should be kept clean and free of moisture.

(2) Method of Lubrication. The American Chain Association recommends three different types of lubrication depending on the speed of operation and the power being transmitted.

Type A. Manual or drip lubrication: For manual lubrication, oil is applied copiously with a brush or a spout can, at least once every 8 h of operation. For drip feed lubrication, oil is fed directly onto the link plates of each chain strand.

Type B. Bath or disc lubrication: The chain cover provides a sump of oil into which the chain dips continuously. Alternatively, a disc or a slinger can be attached to one of the shafts to lift oil to a trough above the lower strand of chain. The trough then delivers a stream of oil to the chain. The chain itself, then, does not need to dip into the oil.

Type C. Oil stream lubrication: An oil pump delivers a continuous stream of oil on the lower part of the chain.

# Lesson 8  CAD

## TEXT

Computer-aided design (CAD) involves the use of computers to create design drawings and product models. Computer-aided design is usually associated with interactive computer graphics, known as a CAD system. Computer-aided design systems are powerful tools and are used in the design and geometric modeling of components and products.

Drawings are generated at workstations, and the design is displayed continuously on the monitor in different colors for its various components. The designer can easily conceptualize the part designed on the graphics screen and can consider alternative designs or modify a particular design to meet specific design requirements. Using powerful software such as CATIA (computer-aided three-dimensional interactive applications), the design can be subjected to engineering analysis and can identify potential problems, such as excessive load, deflection, or interference at mating surfaces during assembly. Information (such as a list of materials, specifications, and manufacturing instructions) is also stored in the CAD database. Using this information, the designer can analyze the manufacturing economics of alternatives.

### 1. Exchange Specifications

Because of the availability of a variety of CAD systems with different characteristics supplied by different vendors, effective communication and exchange of data between these systems are essential. Drawing exchange format (DEX) was developed for use with Autodesk and basically has become a standard because of the long-term success of this software package. DEX is limited to transfer geometry information only. Similarly, stereolithography (STL) formats are used to export three-dimensional geometries, initially only to rapid prototyping system, but recently, it has become a format for data exchange between different CAD systems.

The necessity for a single, neutral format for better compatibility and for the transfer of more information than geometry alone is currently filled mainly by initial graphics exchange specification (IGES). This is used for translation in two directions (in and out of a system) and is also widely used for translation of three-dimensional line and surface data. Because IGES is evolving, there are many variations of IGES.

Another useful format is a solid-model-based standard called the Product Data Exchange Specification (PDES), which is based on the Standard for the Exchange of Product Model Data (STEP) developed by the International Standard Organization. PDES allows information on shape, design, manufacturing, quality assurance, testing, maintenance, etc., to be transferred between CAD systems.

## 2. Elements of CAD Systems

The design process in a CAD system consists of the four stages described in this section.

1) Geometric modeling

In geometric modeling, a physical object or any of its parts is described mathematically or analytically. The designer first constructs a geometric model by giving commands that create or modify lines, surfaces, solids, dimensions, and text. Together, these propose an accurate and complete two or three dimensional representation of the object. The results of these commands are displayed and can be moved around on the screen, and any section desired can be magnified to view details. These data are stored in the database contained in computer memory.

The octree representation of a solid object is shown in Figure 1.13. It is a three-dimensional analog to pixels on a television screen. Just as any area can be broken down into quadrants, any volume can be broken down into octants, which are then identified as solid, void, or partially filled. Partially filled voxels (from volume pixels) are broken into smaller octants and are reclassified. With increasing resolution, exceptional part detail is achieved. This process may appear to be somewhat cumbersome, but it allows for accurate description of complex surfaces. It is used particularly in biomedical applications, such as for modeling bone geometries.

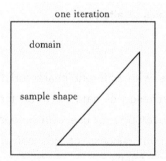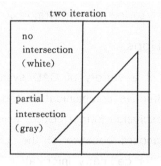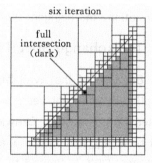

**Figure 1.13**

The octree representation of a solid object. Any volume can be broken down into octants, which are then identified as solid, void or partially filled. Shown is a two-dimensional version (or quadtree) for the representation of shapes in a plane.

2) Design analysis and optimization

After the geometric features of a particular design have been determined, the design is subjected to an engineering analysis. This phase may consist of analyzing (for example) stresses, strains, deflections, vibrations, heat transfer, temperature distribution, or dimensional tolerances. Various sophisticated software packages are available, each having the capabilities to compute these quantities accurately and rapidly.

Because of the relative ease with which such analysis can now be done, designers increasingly are willing to analyze a design more thoroughly before it moves on to production. Experiments and measurements in the field nonetheless may be necessary to determine the actual effects of loads, temperature, and other variables on the designed components.

3) Design review and evaluation

An important design stage is design review and evaluation used to check for any interference between various components. This is done in order to avoid difficulties during assembly or in use of the part and to determine whether moving members (such as linkages) are going to operate as intended. Software is available with animation capabilities to identify potential problems with moving members and other dynamic situations. During the design review and evaluation stage, the part is dimensioned and toleranced precisely to the full degree required for manufacturing it.

4) Documentation and drafting

After the preceding stages have been completed, the design is reproduced by automated drafting machines for documentation and reference. At this stage, detailed and working drawing also are developed and printed. The CAD system is also capable of developing and drafting sectional views of the part, scaling the drawings, and performing transformations in order to present various views of the part.

## NEW WORDS AND EXPRESSIONS

conceptualize [kən'septjuəlaiz] v. 概念化
pixel ['piksəl] n. 像素
octant ['ɔktənt] n. 八分圆
tolerance ['tɔlərəns] v. 给(机器部件等)规定公差　n. 公差
computer-aided design(CAD) 计算机辅助设计
interactive computer graphics 交互式计算机绘图
octree representation 八叉树表示方法
drawing exchange format 图形交换格式
Autodesk 美国电脑软件公司，生产计算机辅助设计软件，如 AutoCAD, 3D Studio 等。
stereolithography 光固化快速成型
geometric modeling 几何建模
quadtree 四叉树
initial graphics exchange specification 初始图形交换标准

## NOTES

1) The designer can easily conceptualize the part designed on the graphics screen and can consider alternative designs or modify a particular design to meet specific design requirements.

设计人员可以不费力气地在图形屏幕上获得想要设计的零件概念，并能考虑几种可能的设计方案，或者修正某种设计来满足具体的设计要求。

2) Just as any area can be broken down into quadrants, any volume can be broken down into octants, which are then identified as solid, void, or partially filled.

正如任何面积可以分解为四等份一样，任何体积也可以分解为八等份，然后作为实体、空穴或部分填充进行识别。

句中，由 which 引导的非限定从句修饰前面的内容。

3) During the design review and evaluation stage, the part is dimensioned and toleranced precisely to the full degree required for manufacturing it.

在设计评审与评估阶段，零件被最大程度地标注准确尺寸并规定公差，以满足制造要求。

dimension 与 tolerance 在本句中作动词，分别解释为"标注所需尺寸"和"规定公差"。

4) The CAD system is also capable of developing and drafting sectional views of the

part, scaling the drawings, and performing transformations in order to present various views of the part.

CAD 系统也能够生成零件剖视草图并进行缩放、绘制，同时也可以进行转换以呈现零件的各种剖面。

# EXERCISES

1. After reading the text above, summarize the main ideas in oral.
2. Fill in the blanks with proper words or phrases according to the text (note the proper tense).

(1) Computer-aided design is usually a_____ interactive computer graphics, known as a CAD system.

(2) The CAD system is also c_____ developing and drafting sectional views of the part, s_____ the drawings, and p_____ transformations in order to present various views of the part.

(3) During the design review and evaluation stage, the part is d_____ precisely to the full degree required for manufacturing it.

(4) After the geometric features of a particular design h_____, the design is subjected to an engineering analysis.

(5) Just as any area can be b_____ quadrants, any volume can be broken down into octants, which are then identified as solid, void, or partially filled.

(6) The designer can easily c_____ the part designed on the graphics screen and can consider a_____ designs or modify a particular design to meet specific design requirements.

3. Translate the following phrases into Chinese according to the text.
(1) allow for                (2) be capable of
(3) be broken down into     (4) be based on
(5) be associated with      (6) consist of

4. Translate the following phrases into English according to the text.
(1) 几何建模              (2) 几何特征
(3) 软件包                (4) 设计评审
(5) 设计优化              (6) 八叉树表示方法

5. Write a 100-word summary according to the text.

# READING MATERIAL

## CAD Model Development for Automotive Components

CAD models are used extensively for a great variety of tasks. In the automotive industry, for example, it is especially important to have a detailed CAD model of a particular component in the product database in order to ensure that all of those who will be working on it have all of the data they need to perform their tasks. Special care is taken to build very precise CAD models of the automobile components that passengers will see and interact with on a regular basis. Examples of such components are outer-body panels, handles, seats, and the instrument panel. The quality of the visible (class I) surfaces has a major impact on overall vehicle quality and customer perception of the look and feel of the automobile.

1) Two-dimensional concept sketches

Stylists with a background and experience in industrial design and/or art first develop two-dimensional concepts through a series of sketches. These sketches most frequently are drawn by hand, although software may be used instead, especially if the stylist starts with a photograph or a scanned drawing that needs to be modified. Concept sketches provide an overall feel for the aesthetics of the object and frequently are very detailed and show texture, color, and where individual surfaces on a vehicle should meet.

Most often, stylists are given a set of packaging constraints, such as (a) how the component should be assembled with other components, (b) what the size of the component should be, and (c) what the size and shape of any structure lying behind the visible surfaces should be. The time involved in producing a series of such concept sketches for an individual component or a set of components typically ranges from a few days to several weeks.

2) Three-dimensional surface model

As a concept is being reviewed and refined, several very accurate surface models of the component are constructed. To start the surface model, a computer-controlled optical scanner scans a conceptualized clay model, producing a cloud-of-points organized along the scan lines. Depending on the size of the component, a point cloud may consist of hundreds of thousands to millions of points. The point cloud is read into point-processing software (such as Paraform or ICEM surf) to further organize the points and filter out noise. Scanning can take anywhere from several hours to a day to be completed. If, however, a digital three-dimensional clay model of the component is already available, it is converted into a point cloud organized into scan lines without the need for physical scanning and point-cloud post-processing.

Next, the scan lines from the point cloud are used to construct mathematical surfaces using software, such as ICEM Surf and Alias/Wavefront StudioTools. To construct the surfaces, first freeform NURBS curves that interpolate or approximate the scan lines are constructed. A NURBS surface patch then is fit through the curves. An individual surface patch models a small region of a single component's face. Several patches are constructed and jointed smoothly at common edges to form the entire face.

Faces join each other at common edges to model an entire component. A great deal of experience is required to determine how to divide a face into a collection of patches that can be fit with the simplest low-order surfaces possible and still meet smoothly at common boundaries. A surfacing specialist performs this task in conjunction with the stylist to ensure that the surfaces are of high quality and that they capture the stylist's intent. A single component may take as long as a week to model.

Surface models are passed along to the various downstream departments to be used for tooling design, feasibility checks, analysis, and for the design of non-visible (class II) surfaces. As the design evolves, the dimensional tolerances on the surfaces are tightened gradually.

When designing outer-body panels, a major milestone is finalizing what is called first flange and fillet, in which the edges of the body panels are turned under or hemmed to provide a flange to connect to the inner panel. The shape of the flange and fillet affects the overall aesthetics and shape of the body panel; hence, their careful design is important. After the shape of the fillet and flange had been decided, the inner-panel designs can be completed.

3) Surface verification

Once the final surface model, which must be verified and evaluated for surface quality and aesthetics, is completed NC tool paths are generated automatically from the surfaces, either from within the surfacing software or through specialized machining software. The tool paths then are used to CNC machine surfaces in clay. If the component is small, instead of machining a clay model, an STL file can be generated and the mock-up can be built on a rapid prototyping machine. It takes anywhere from several hours to several days to machine a component and perform any hand finishing that may be required.

Clay models can be coated with a thin layer of latex material and painted to make them look more realistic and to help evaluate surface quality. The coating may be modified to improve surface smoothness between patches or to change the way light reflects off the surface of the model. All changes made to the clay must be translated back to the digital surface model, either through rescanning and refitting the surface patches or by tweaking the shape of the existing patches.

4) Solid-model construction

After the surface model is finalized, it is used to develop a solid model. For sheet-metal components (such as body panels), body specialists offset the surfaces to form a solid. For other components (such as instrument panels, door handles, or wheels), they add manufacturing features to the surface models (such as flanges, bosses, and ribs). They collaborate with the manufacturers to determine what features must be added and where they should be placed to ensure that the component can be fabricated from the desired material at the target cost.

In the process of making a solid model, it may be discovered that the surface model must be modified because of (a) changes in packaging constraints, (b) the component failing to meet minimal manufacturing requirements, or (c) surfaces not matching up properly at common edges with the appropriate smoothness. These changes are communicated back to the surface modeler and the stylist so that the surfaces can be modified and re-verified. Finally, the solid model is entered into a product database where it is then available to suppliers and engineers for further analysis and manufacturing.

# Lesson 9  Extruding

## TEXT

In extrusion the workpiece is pushed against the deforming die while it is being supported in a container against uncontrolled deformation. The process, therefore, offers the possibility of heavy deformations coupled with a wide choice of extruded cross sections.

Extruding is classified as hot extrusion and cold extrusion. Hot extrusion of metal is another process used in the plastic shaping of metals. It consists of heating a billet of suitable metal or alloy to its proper extruding temperature, and placing it in the cylinder of an extruding press, where pressure exerted by a moving piston or ram forces the plastic metal through a die of the required shape. The metals are brought to temperatures near their melting points by the time they are ready to be forced through the die openings. Extruded parts are correctly shaped within close tolerances. Their surfaces are clean and smooth, and their mechanical properties are high. If some of these parts were made by rolling, they could not be rolled.

Pneumatic-mechanical machines have been used to extrude a wide range of materials. Copper and its alloys, aluminum alloys, and steels have all been extruded on this equipment. Extrusion of refractory metals by these machines has been shown to be very promising. Reductions of 40 to 1 on tungsten have been made in a single pass. One serious drawback is the high velocity of the extruded piece which is encountered when this equipment is used for extruding. Initially, the extrusion leaves the die orifice at a high velocity and immediately begins to decelerate. As the length of the extrusion increases, its mass increases. When, and if, the force due to deceleration equals the tensile strength of the extruded material, separation results. This may repeat during the extrusion of one blank, resulting in two or more pieces. In view of this drawback, it is possible to make an extrusion of good quality but limited in length. By maintaining a given amount of energy in the striking ram and lowering its velocity, a longer extrusion can be produced without defects.

These machines can extrude materials which would be very difficult for conventional equipment, or would require conventional machines of enormous size because of the energy requirements.

While hot deformation is often typical of primary processes, the hot extrusion of shapes, particularly of nonferrous materials, offers such a wide scope for custom design that this process can justifiably be regarded as a secondary manufacturing technique.

Cold extrusion of metals is employed for the plastic shaping of metals, as is hot extrusion. The two processes are much the same, except that in cold extrusion, the metals worked possess the plasticity necessary for successful forming without the application of heat. Usually, these metals have a high degree of ductility. Cold extrusion is accomplished by any of several methods, among which the process of extrusion down and the impact process are widely employed.

The method of extrusion down consists of forcing a thick-walled, cup-shaped blank through a die. The operation is carried out at high speeds on an ordinary crank press, the mass of metal in work being comparatively small. A crank press is actuated by one or more cranks. The crank-throw controls the stroke of the press. Examples of products extruded by this process are light, thin-walled, seamless tubes and small cartridge cases.

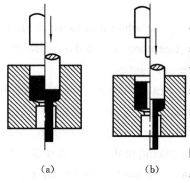

**Figure 1.14  Extrusion**

Small copper tubes and cartridge cases may also be extruded by the method, merely by dropping a flat blank of specified diameter and thickness in a suitable die, and forcing it through the opening of the die with a punch as shown in Figure 1.14(a). Similar products of other soft metals may be extruded by this method.

The impact or extrusion consists of dropping a flat blank of specified diameter and thickness in the die cavity, and then delivering a single powerful blow with the punch. This forces the thin metal to squirt up around the punch, as shown in Figure 1.14(b).

The purpose of cold extrusion is mostly that of producing a finished part.

In most instances, the residue (butt) in the container becomes an integral part of the finished product.

## NEW WORDS AND EXPRESSIONS

abrasion [əˈbreiʒən] n. 磨去，磨蚀，剥蚀
profile [ˈprəufail] n. 外形，轮廓
brittle [ˈbritl] a. 易碎的，脆弱的
slender [ˈslendə] a. 微薄的
delicate [ˈdelikit] a. 精密的
rigorous [ˈrigərəs] a. 严格的
residual [riˈzidjuəl] a. 残留的
nontraditional [ˌnɔntrəˈdiʃənəl] a. 非传统的
unconventional [ˈʌnkənˈvenʃənəl] a. 非常规的
fuel-injection nozzle 喷油嘴
residual stresses 残余应力

## NOTES

1) The metal are brought to temperatures near their melting points by the time they are ready to be forced through the die openings.

到金属将被挤压过模腔时，它已经加热到接近其熔点。

2) Extrusion of refractory metals by these machines has been shown to be very promising.

用这种机器冲压难熔金属的方法已显示出是很有前景的。

句中动词不定式 to be very promising 是用来补充说明主语 extrusion 的。我们称此不定式为主语补足语。

3) These machines can extrude materials which would be very difficult for conventional equipment, or would require conventional machines of enormous size because of the energy requirements.

这种机器能够冲压用普通设备很难完成的材料挤压或者是出于能量的要求需要巨型的普通机器才能进行冲压。

定语从句中的谓语动词所用的时态形式很特殊。英语中常用过去时来表示与现在情况相反的一些假设。如上面句中 would be 和 would require 就表示与现在情况相反的假设。

## EXERCISES

1. After reading the text above, summarize the main ideas in oral.
2. Fill in the blanks with proper words or phrases according to the text (note the proper tense).
   (1) Extruding is c_____ hot extrusion and cold extrusion.
   (2) The method of extrusion down c_____ forcing a t_____, c_____ through a die.
   (3) Pneumatic-mechanical machines h_____ extrude a wide range of materials.
   (4) As the length of the extrusion increases, its mass i_____.
   (5) Extruded parts a_____ correctly shaped within c_____.
   (6) Extrusion of r_____ metals by these machines h_____ to be very promising.
3. Translate the following phrases into Chinese according to the text.
   (1) refractory metals            (2) plastic shaping of metals
   (3) pneumatic-mechanical machines    (4) extruded parts
   (5) close tolerances
4. Translate the following phrases into English according to the text.
   (1) 在挤压过程中              (2) 铝容易被挤压
   (3) 塑性变形                  (4) 加工硬化
   (5) 难熔金属                  (6) 抗张强度
5. Write a 100-word summary according to the text.

## READING MATERIAL

### The Extrusion Process

To initiate extrusion, a cylindrical billet is inside a container and is pushed against a die held in place by a firm support. The press force is applied to the punch and, after the billet has upset to fill out the container, the product emerges through the die. Initially, deformation is non-steady-state but once the product has emerged, steady-state conditions prevail until close to the end of extrusion when continuous material flow is again disturbed. In direct or forward extrusion, the product emerges in the same direction as the movement of the punch, while in indirect (reverse or back) extrusion the product travels against the movement of the punch. By definition, piercing in a container may be regarded as a case of back extrusion.

Extrusion may be carried out without a lubricant, and then the material seeks a flow pattern that results in minimum energy expenditures. With a die of flat face the material cannot follow the very sharp directional changes that would be imposed on it. Instead, the corner between the die face and container is filled out by a stationary, dead-metal zone and material flow takes place by shearing along the surface of this zone. Thus, the extruded product acquires a completely freshly formed surface which is highly desirable in materials such as aluminum extruded at hot-working temperatures. In cold-working it is much better to apply a very effective lubricant to assure complete sliding on the die face. Accordingly, the die is now provided with a conical entrance zone that, ideally, corresponds to the angle of minimum-energy flow. A similar situation prevails in the hot extrusion of steel with glass as a lubricant. Even though the die has a flat face, the glass pad applied to it melts off to give a die shape of optimum profile.

The movement of the punch must be stopped before the conical die entry is touched or, in unlubricated extrusion, before material from the dead-metal zone is moved, since this would create internal defects. When the purpose of extrusion is to produce a bar of uniform cross section, the remaining material is scrap which is removed by taking it out with the die. After the butt is cut off, the extrusion can be extricated from the die, and the die is returned for inspection, conditioning, and reuse. When, however, the purpose of extrusion is to produce a finished component, with the butt forming the head of the component, it is customary to eject the extrusion by pushing it back through the extrusion die and lifting it out from the container. Since ejector actuation can be mechanically synchronized with the punch movement, high production rates are achieved, provided, of course, that the extruded product is strong enough to take the ejection force.

# Part II

# Manufacturing

# Part 1

## Manufacturing

# Lesson 10  Lathe, Shaper, Grinding and Milling Machine

## TEXT

### 1. Lathes and Lathe Operations

Lathes are generally considered to be the oldest machine tools. Although woodworking lathes were originally developed during the period 1000-1 B.C., metalworking lathes with lead screws were not built until the late 1700s. The most common lathe (Figure 2.1) was originally called engine lathe because it was powered with overhead pulleys and belts from nearby engines. Today these lathes are set up with individual electric motors.

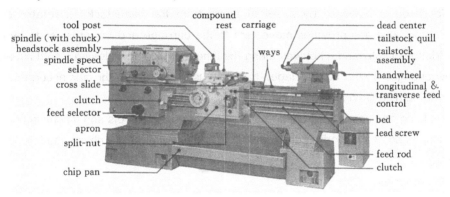

Figure 2.1  Components of a typical lathe

1) Lathe Components

Lathes are equipped with a variety of components and accessories. The basic components of a common lathe are described below.

i) Bed

The bed supports all major components of the lathe. Beds have a large mass and are rigidly built, usually from gray or nodular cast iron. The top portion of the bed has two ways, with various cross-sections, that are hardened and machined for wear resistance and dimensional accuracy during use.

ii) Carriage

The carriage, or carriage assembly, slides along the ways and consists of an assembly of the cross-slide, tool post, and apron. The cutting tool is mounted on the tool post, usually with a compound rest that swivels for tool positioning and adjustment. The cross-slide moves radially in and out, controlling the radial position of the cutting tool in operations such as facing. The apron is equipped with mechanisms for both manual and mechanized movement of the carriage and the cross-slide by means of the lead screw.

iii) Headstock

The headstock is fixed to the bed and is equipped with motors, pulleys, and V-belts that supply power to the spindle at various rotational speeds. The speeds can be set through manually-controlled selectors. Most headstocks are equipped with a set of gears, and some have various drives to provide a continuously variable speed range to the spindle. Headstock have a hollow spindle to which workholding devices, such as chucks and collets, are attached, and long bars or tubing can be fed through for various turning operations.

iv) Tailstock

The tailstock, which can slide along the ways and be clamped at any position, supports the other end of the workpiece. It is equipped with a tailstock center that may be fixed (dead tailstock center) or may be free to rotate with the workpiece (live tailstock center). Drills and reamers can be mounted on the tailstock quill (a hollow cylindrical part with a tapered hole) to drill axial holes in the workpiece.

v) Feed Rod and Lead Screw

The feed rod is powered by a set of gears from the headstock. It rotates during the operation of the lathe and provides movement to the carriage and the cross-slide by means of gears, a friction clutch, and a keyway along the length of the rod. Closing a split nut around the lead screw engages it with the carriage. It is also used for cutting threads accurately.

vi) Workholding Devices

Workholding devices are particularly important in machine tools and machining operations. In a lathe, one end of the workpiece is clamped to the spindle by a chuck, collet, face plate, or mandrel.

vii) Accessories

Several devices are available as accessories and attachments for lathes. Among these devices are the following:

Carriage and cross-slide stop with various designs to stop the carriage at a predetermined distance along the bed.

Devices for turning parts with various tapers or radii.

Milling, sawing, gear-cutting, and grinding attachments, and various attachments for boring, drilling, and thread cutting.

2) Lathe Turning

In a typical turning, the workpiece is clamped by any workholding devices described. Long and slender parts should be supported by a steady rest and follow rest placed on the bed, otherwise, the part will deflect under the cutting forces. These rests are usually equipped with three adjustable fingers or rollers, which support the workpiece while allowing it to rotate freely. Steady rests are clamped directly on the ways of the lathe, whereas follow rests are clamped on the carriage and travel with it.

The cutting tool, attached to the tool post, which is driven by the lead screw, removes material by traveling along the bed. A right-hand tool travels toward the headstock, and a left-hand tool toward the tailstock. Facing cutting are done by moving the tool radially with the cross-slide, and clamping the carriage for better dimensional accuracy.

## 2. Milling Machine and Milling

Milling includes a number of highly versatile machining operations capable of producing a variety of configurations (Figure 2.2) with the use of a milling cutter, a multitoothed cutter that produces a number of chips in one revolution.

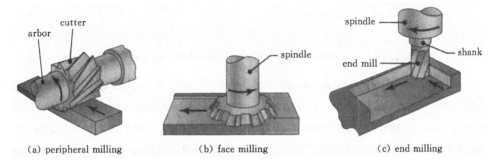

(a) peripheral milling  (b) face milling  (c) end milling

**Figure 2.2  Milling Operations**

1) Milling Operations

i) Slab Milling

In slab milling, also called peripheral milling, the axis of cutter rotation is parallel to the workpiece surface to be machined (Figure 2.2(a)). The cutter, generally made of high-speed steel, has a number of teeth along its circumference, each tooth acting like a single-point cutting tool called a plain mill.

ii) Face Milling

In face milling, the cutter is mounted on a spindle having an axis of rotation perpendicular to the workpiece surface (Figure 2.2(b)). Because of the relative motion between the cutting teeth and the workpiece, a face-milling cutter leaves feed marks on the machined surface similar to those left by turning operations. Note that surface roughness of the workpiece depends on insert corner geometry and feed per tooth.

iii) End Milling

Flat surfaces as well as various profiles can be produced by end milling. The cutter in end milling is shown in Figure 2.2(c). It has either straight or tapered shanks for smaller and larger cutter sizes, respectively. The cutter usually rotates on an axis perpendicular to the workpiece, although it can be tilted to machine-tapered surfaces.

In conventional milling, also called up milling, the maximum chip thickness is at the end of the cut (Figure 2.3(a)). The advantages to conventional milling are that (a) tooth engagement is not a function of workpiece surface characteristics, and (b) contamination or scale on the surface does not affect tool life. This is the more common method of milling. The cutting process is smooth, provided that the cutter teeth are sharp. However, there may be a tendency for the tool to chatter and the workpiece has a tendency to be pulled upward, necessitating proper clamping.

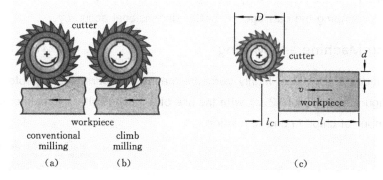

Figure 2.3 Schematic illustration of conventional milling and climb milling

In climb milling, also called down milling, cutting starts at the surface of the workpiece, where the chip is at its thickest (Figure 2.3(b)). The advantage is that the downward component of the cutting forces holds the workpiece in place, particularly for slender parts. Because of the resulting high-impact forces when the teeth engage the workpiece, however, this operation must have a rigid setup, and backlash must be eliminated in the table feed mechanism. Climb milling is recommended, in general, for maximum cutter life in using computer numerical controlled (CNC) machine tools.

2) Types of Milling Machine

i) Column-and-Knee Type Machines

Used for general-purpose milling, column-and-knee type machines are the most common milling machines. The spindle on which the milling cutter is mounted may be horizontal for slab milling, or vertical for face and end milling, boring, and drilling operations. The basic components of these machines are as follows:

A work table, on which the workpiece is clamped using T-slots. The table moves longitudinally relative to the saddle.

A saddle, which supports the table and moves in the transverse direction.

A knee, which supports the saddle and gives the table vertical movement so that the depth of cut can be adjusted.

An overarm in horizontal machines, which is adjustable to accommodate different arbor lengths.

A head, which contains the spindle and cutter holders. In vertical machines, the head may be fixed or it can be vertically adjustable, and it can be swiveled in a vertical plane on the column for cutting tapered surfaces.

ii) Bed-Type Machines

In bed-type machines, the work table is mounted directly on the bed, which replaces the knee and can move only longitudinally. These milling machines are not as versatile as other types, but they have great stiffness and are used for high-production work. The spindles may be horizontal or vertical, and of duplex or triplex types—that is, with two or three spindles, respectively, for the simultaneous machining of two or three workpiece surfaces.

iii) Other Types of Milling Machines

Planer-type milling machines, which are similar to bed-type machines, are equipped with several heads and cutters to mill various surfaces. They are used for heavy workpieces and are more efficient than planers when used for similar purposes. Rotary-table machines are similar to vertical milling machines and are equipped with one or more heads for face-milling operations.

Various milling-machine components are being rapidly replaced by computer numerical control machines. These machine tools are versatile and capable of milling, drilling, boring, and tapping with repetitive accuracy.

## NEW WORDS AND EXPRESSIONS

lathe [leið] n. 车床
accessory [æk'sesəri] n. 附件
carriage ['kæridʒ] n. （车床的）拖板，[机]滑[刀、车、台]架
apron ['eiprən] n. [机]挡板，溜板
chuck [tʃʌk] n. 卡盘，夹盘
collet ['kɔlit] n. [机]筒夹，夹头
mandrel ['mændril] n. [机]心轴
circumference [sə'kʌmfərəns] n. 圆周，周围
contamination [kən,tæmi'neiʃən] n. 污染，污染物
necessitate [ni'sesiteit] v. 成为必要

perpendicular [,pə:pen'dikjulə] a. 垂直的，正交的
arbor ['ɑ:bə] n. 支持切割工具的条棒；刀轴
cast iron 铸铁
cross-slide 横向拖板
lead screw 丝杠
feed rod 光杆，分配杆，进给杆
slab milling 平面铣法，阔面铣削
up milling 仰铣，对向铣，逆铣
down milling 顺铣，同向铣切
depth of cut 切削深度

## NOTES

1) The apron is equipped with mechanisms for both manual and mechanized movement of the carriage and the cross-slide by means of the lead screw.

溜板箱上安装有一些机械装置，通过丝杠来实现刀架（或托板）和横托板的手动或机动的运动。

be equipped with 装（配）备，安装；来自于 equip sth. with（用……装备，使装（具）备）的被动语态。by means of 依靠，通过……手段。

2) It rotates during the operation of the lathe and provides movement to the carriage and the cross-slide by means of gears, a friction clutch, and a keyway along the length of the rod. Closing a split nut around the lead screw engages it with the carriage. It is also used for cutting threads accurately.

它（光杠）在车床的操作过程中旋转，并通过齿轮、摩擦离合器和沿着光杠长度方向上的键槽的配合为刀架（或托板）和横拖板提供运动。将一个劈开的螺母与丝杠啮合，使得丝杠与刀架（或拖板）啮合。这同样被用于螺纹的精确加工。

第一句是一个并列句，It 为主语，根据上文可知它指光杠，后接并列谓语 rotates 和 provides 及各自的宾语部分。

第二句中动名词短语 Closing a split nut around the lead screw 作主语，engages 为其谓语部分，it 指丝杠。engage with 意指"（齿轮等）与……啮合，搭合"。

3) Because of the resulting high-impact forces when the teeth engage the workpiece, however, this operation must have a rigid setup, and backlash must be eliminated in the table feed mechanism.

然而，由于当齿与工件啮合时导致的高冲击力，此操作必须要有一个刚性的安装支撑，并且必须消除工作台进给机构的后冲。

4) The spindle on which the milling cutter is mounted may be horizontal for slab milling, or vertical for face and end milling, boring, and drilling operations.

在阔面铣削中，铣刀安装轴是水平安装的，而在端面铣削和端铣、镗削和钻孔加工中铣刀安装轴是垂直安装的。

5) Because of the relative motion between the cutting teeth and the workpiece, a face-milling cutter leaves feed marks on the machined surface similar to those left by turning operations.

由于在切削刀齿和工件之间的相对运动，端（面）铣（削）刀具在加工表面上留下的进给痕迹类似于在车削加工中的痕迹。

face-milling 端（面）铣（削），turning 车削。

## EXERCISES

1. After reading the text above, summarize the main ideas in oral.

2. Fill in the blanks with proper words or phrases according to the text (note the proper tense).

（1）The most common lathe was originally called e_____ because it was powered with overhead p_____ and b_____ from nearby engines.

（2）Lathes are equipped with a variety of components and accessories. The basic components of a common lathe are b_____, c_____, h_____, t_____, f_____, w_____ and a_____.

（3）Steady rests are clamped directly o_____ of the lathe, whereas follow rests are clamped o_____ and travel with it.

（4）According to the direction that the cutter fed to the workpiece, the milling action can be divided into u_____ and d_____.

（5）Milling operations include p_____, f_____ and e_____.

（6）The basic components of milling machines are included w_____, s_____, k_____, o_____, and h_____.

3. Translate the following phrases into Chinese according to the text.

（1）engine lathe （2）compound rest

（3）wear resistance and dimensional accuracy

(4) an axis perpendicular to the workpiece
(5) face milling    (6) column-and-knee type machines
(7) boring, and drilling operations    (8) be mounted on the tailstock quill
4. Translate the following phrases into English according to the text.
(1) 主轴    (2) 溜板箱
(3) 拖板    (4) 周铣法
(5) 光杠和丝杠    (6) 高冲击力
(7) 螺纹切削加工
5. Write a 100-word summary according to the text.

# READING MATERIAL

## 1. Planing and Shaping

Planing is a relatively simple cutting operation by which flat surfaces, as well as various cross-sections with grooves and notches, are produced along the length of the workpiece. Planing is usually done on large workpieces—as large as 25 m × 15 m (75 ft × 40 ft).

In a planer, the workpiece is mounted on a table that travels along a straight path. A horizontal cross-rail, which can be moved vertically along the ways in the column, is equipped with one or more tool heads. The cutting tools are attached to the heads, and machining is done along a straight path. Because of the reciprocating motion of the workpiece, elapsed noncutting time during the return stroke is significant.

Consequently, these operations are neither efficient nor economical, except for low-quantity production. The efficiency of the operation can be improved by equipping planers with tool holders and tools that cut in both directions of table travel.

In order to prevent tool cutting edges from chipping when they rub along a workpiece during the return stroke, tools are either tilted away or lifted mechanically or hydraulically. Because of the length of the workpiece, it is essential to equip cutting tools with chip breakers. Otherwise, the chips produced can be very long, interfering with the operation as well as becoming a safety hazard.

Shaping is used to machine parts, which is much like planing, unless the parts are smaller. Cutting by shaping is basically the same as by planing. In a horizontal shaper, the tool travels along a straight path, and the workpiece is stationary. The cutting tool is attached to the tool head, which is mounted on the ram.

The ram has a reciprocating motion. In most machines, cutting is done during the forward movement of the ram (push cut). But in others, it is done during the return stroke of the ram (draw cut). Vertical shapers (slotters) are used to machine notches, keyways, and dies. Because of low production rates, only special-purpose shapers, such as gear shapers, are in common use today.

## 2. Grinding Operations and Machines

Grinding is carried out with a variety of wheel-workpiece configurations. The selection of a grinding process for a particular application depends on part shape and size, ease of fixturing, and the production rate required.

The basic types of grindings—surface, cylindrical, internal, and centerless grinding—are described in this section. The relative movement of the wheel may be along the surface of the workpiece (traverse grinding, through feed grinding, cross-feeding), or it may be radially into the workpiece (plunge grinding). Surface grinders are comprised the largest percentage of grinders used in industry, followed by bench grinders (usually with two wheels at each end of the spindle), cylindrical grinders, and tool and cutter grinders. The least common are internal grinders.

Grinding machines are available for various workpiece geometries and sizes. Modern grinding machines are computer controlled, with features such as automatic workpiece loading and unloading, clamping, cycling, gaging, dressing, and wheel shaping. Grinders can also be equipped with probes and gages for determining the relative position of the wheel and workpiece surfaces as well as with tactile sensing features whereby diamond dressing-tool breakage, if any, can readily be detected during the dressing cycle.

1) Surface Grinding

Surface grinding involves grinding flat surfaces and is one of the most common grinding operations. Typically, the workpiece is secured on a magnetic chuck attached to the work table of the grinder. Nonmagnetic materials generally are held by vises, special fixtures, vacuum chucks, or double-sided adhesive tapes.

A straight wheel is mounted on the horizontal spindle of the grinder. Traverse grinding occurs as the table reciprocates longitudinally and feeds laterally after each stroke. In plunge grinding, the wheel is moved radially into the workpiece, as it is grinding a groove.

2) Cylindrical Grinding

In cylindrical grinding, also called center-type grinding, the external cylindrical surfaces and shoulders of the workpiece are ground. Typical applications include crankshaft bearings, spindles, pins, bearing rings, and rolls for rolling mills.

The rotating cylindrical workpiece reciprocates laterally along its axis. In grinders used for large and long workpieces, the grinding wheel reciprocates; called a roll grinder, it is capable of grinding rolls as large as 1.8 m (72 in.) in diameter for rolling mills.

The workpiece in cylindrical grinding is held between centers or in a chuck, or it is mounted on a faceplate in the headstock of the grinder. For straight cylindrical surfaces, the axes of rotation of the wheel and workpiece are parallel. Separate motors drive the wheel and workpiece at different speeds. Long workpieces with two or more diameters are also ground on cylindrical grinders. Cylindrical grinding can produce shapes (form grinding and plunge grinding) in which the wheel is dressed to the form to be ground.

In universal grinders, both the workpiece and the wheel axes can be moved and swiveled around a horizontal plane, permitting the grinding of tapers and other shapes. These machines

## Lesson 10 Lathe, Shaper, Grinding and Milling Machine

are equipped with computer controls, reducing labor and producing parts accurately and repetitively.

3) Internal Grinding

In internal grinding, a small wheel is used to grind the inside diameter of the part, such as to bushings and bearing races. The workpiece is held in a rotating chuck and the wheel rotates at 30 000 rpm or higher. Internal profiles can also be ground with profile-dressed wheels that move radially into the workpiece. The headstock of internal grinders can be swiveled on a horizontal plane to grind tapered holes.

4) Centerless Grinding

Centerless grinding is a high-production process for continuously grinding cylindrical surfaces in which the workpiece is supported not by centers (hence the term "centerless") or chucks, but by a blade. Typical parts made by centerless grinding are roller bearings, piston pins, engine valves, camshafts, and similar components. This continuous production process requires little operator skill.

In internal centerless grinding, the workpiece is supported between three rolls and is internally ground. Typical applications are sleeve-shaped parts and rings.

# Lesson 11  Numerical Control

## TEXT

### 1. Introduction

One of the most fundamental concepts in the area of advanced manufacturing technologies is numerical control (NC).

Controlling a machine tool using a punched tape or stored program is known as numerical control (NC). NC has been defined by the Electronic Industries Association (EIA) as "a system in which actions are controlled by the direct insertion of numerical data at some point. The system must automatically interpret at least some portion of this data". The numerical data required to produce a part is known as a part program.

A numerical control machine tool system contains a machine control unit (MCU) and the machine tool itself (Figure 2.4). The MCU is further divided into two elements: the data processing unit (DPU) and the control loops unit (CLU). The DPU processes the coded data from the tape or other media and passes information on the position of each axis, required direction of motion, feed rate, and auxiliary function control signals to the CLU. The CLU operates the drive mechanisms of the machine, receives feed back signals concerning the actual position and velocity of each of the axes, and signals of the completion of operation. The DPU sequentially reads the data. When each line has completed execution as noted by the CLU, another line of data is read.

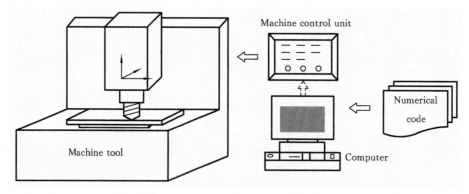

Figure 2.4  Numerical control system

Geometric and kinematic data are typically fed from the DPU to the CLU and CLU then governs the physical system based on the data from the DPU.

Numerical control was developed to overcome the limitation of human operators, and it has done so. Numerical control machines are more accurate than manually operated machines, they can produce parts more uniformly, they are faster, and the long-run tooling costs are lower. The development of NC led to the development of several other innovations in manufacturing technology:

- Electric discharge machining
- Laser-cutting
- Electron beam welding

Numerical control has also made machine tools more versatile than their manually operated predecessors. An NC machine tool can automatically produce a wide variety of parts, each involving an assortment of widely varied and complex machining processes. Numerical control has allowed manufacturers to undertake the production of products that would not have been feasible from an economic perspective using manually controlled machine tools and processes.

## 2. Principles of NC Machines

An NC machine can be controlled through two types of circuits: open-loop and closed-loop. In the open-loop system (Figure 2.5(a)), the signals are sent to the servomotor by the controller, but the movements and final positions of the worktable are not checked for accuracy.

The closed-loop system (Figure 2.5(b)) is equipped with various transducers, sensors, and counters that measure accurately the position of the worktable. Through feedback control, the position of the worktable is compared against the signal. Table movements terminate when the proper coordinates are reached. The closed-loop system is more complicated and more expensive than the open-loop system.

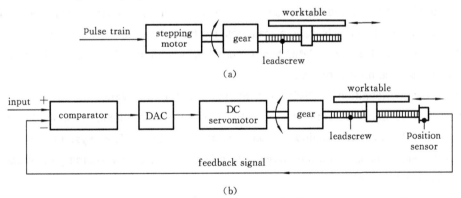

Figure 2.5 Schematic illustration of (a) an open-loop and (b) a closed-loop control system for an NC machine

## 3. Types of Control Systems

There are two basic types of control systems in numerical control, point-to-point and contouring.

(1) In a point-to-point system, also called positioning, each axis of the machine is driven separately by leadscrews and, depending on the type of operation, at different velocities. The

machine moves initially at maximum velocity in order to reduce nonproductive time, but decelerates as the tool approaches its numerically defined position. Thus, in an operation such as drilling (or punching a hole), the positioning and cutting take place sequentially.

After the hole is drilled or punched, the tool retracts upward and moves rapidly to another position, and the operation is repeated. The path followed from one position to another is important in only one respect. It must be chosen to minimize the time of travel, for better efficiency. Point-to-point systems are used mainly in drilling, punching, and straight milling operations.

(2) In a contouring system (also known as a continuous path system), the positioning and the operations are both performed along controlled paths but at different velocities. Because the tool acts as it travels along a prescribed path, accurate control and synchronization of velocities and movements are important. The contouring system is typically used on lathes, milling machines, grinders, welding machinery, and machining centers.

## 4. Computer Numerical Control

In the next step of the development of numerical control, the control hardware (mounted on the NC machine) was converted to local computer control by software. Two types of computerized systems were developed: direct numerical control and computer numerical control.

In direct numerical control (DNC), as originally conceived and developed in the 1960s, several machines are directly controlled, step by step, by a central mainframe computer. In this system, the operator has access to the central computer through a remote terminal. In this way, the handling of tapes and the need for a separate computer on each machine are eliminated. With DNC, the status of all machines in a manufacturing facility can be monitored and assessed from the central computer. However, DNC has a crucial disadvantage. If the computer shuts down, all the machines become inoperative.

A more recent definition of DNC (now meaning distributed numerical control) covers the use of a central computer serving as the control system over a number of individual computer numerical control machines having onboard microcomputers. This system provides large memory and computational capabilities and offers flexibility while overcoming the disadvantage of direct numerical control.

Computer numerical control is a system in which a control microcomputer is an integral part of a machine or a piece of equipment (onboard computer). The part program may be prepared at a remote site by the programmer, and it may incorporate information obtained from drafting software packages and from machining simulations, in order to ensure that the part program is bug free. The machine operator can, however, easily and manually program onboard computers. The operator can modify the programs directly, prepare programs for different parts, and store the programs.

Because of the availability of small computers having a large memory, microprocessor(s), and program-editing capabilities, CNC systems are widely used today. The availability of low-cost programmable controllers also played a major role in the successful implementation of CNC in manufacturing plants.

Some advantages of CNC over conventional NC systems are the following:

● Increased flexibility—the machine can produce a specific part, followed by other parts with different shapes, at reduced cost;

● Greater accuracy—computers have a higher sampling rate and faster operation; and

● More versatility—editing and debugging programs, reprogramming, and plotting and printing part shape are simpler.

## NEW WORDS AND EXPRESSIONS

auxiliary [ɔːgziljəri] a. 辅助的；副的，备用的
kinematic [ˌkainiˈmætik] a. [物]运动学的
tooling [ˈtuːliŋ] n. 给机床配备成套工具，工艺装置
discharge [disˈtʃɑːdʒ] n. 放电，卸下
assortment [əˈsɔːtmənt] n. 分类，分配，种类
transducer [trænsˈdjuːsə] n. 传感器，变换器
terminate [ˈtəːmineit] vt. 使结束，限定
retract [riˈtrækt] v. 缩回，取消，撤销
synchronization [ˌsiŋkrənaiˈzeiʃən] n. 同时（性）；[物]同步，同期
mainframe [ˈmeinfreim] n. [计]主机，主计算机
terminal [ˈtəːminl] n. 终点站，终端
assess [əˈses] vt. 评估，评定
versatility [ˌvəːsəˈtiləti] n. 多功能性，通用性
punch [pʌntʃ] vt. 冲孔，打孔
numerical control (NC) 数字控制，数值控制

## NOTES

1) NC has been defined by the Electronic Industries Association (EIA) as "a system in which actions are controlled by the direct insertion of numerical data at some point. The system must automatically interpret at least some portion of this data".

美国电子工业协会对数字控制所下的定义为"一种各项工作都由在各点上直接插入的数字来控制的系统。该系统必须至少能够自动解释这些数字中的部分。"

EIA（美国电子工业协会）广泛代表了设计生产电子元件、部件、通信系统和设备的制造商以及工业界、政府和用户的利益，在提高美国制造商的竞争力方面起到了重要的作用。

该句引号中的前一句为 as 的宾语从句。

2) The CLU operates the drive mechanisms of the machine, receives feed back signals concerning the actual position and velocity of each of the axes, and signals of the completion of operation.

控制单元操作机床的机械驱动装置，接收关于每个轴的实际位置和速度的反馈信号，并且发出控制信号完成操作。

CLU 为本句的主语，后带三个动词作并列谓语。第二个分句中的 feed back signals 为动词宾语，concerning 引导的现在分词短语对其进行修饰。第三个分句中的 signal 为动词，表示"发出信号"，与前两个动词时态相同，构成并列谓语。

3) Numerical control has allowed manufacturers to undertake the production of products

that would not have been feasible from an economic perspective using manually controlled machine tools and processes.

数字控制使得制造者们可以承担产品的加工,其产品的加工从经济的观点上看使用人工控制机床和加工过程是不太可行的。

that 引导的定语从句对名词短语 production of products 进行修饰。

from an economic perspective 从经济的观点出发,从经济的角度来看

4) The path followed from one position to another is important in only one respect. It must be chosen to minimize the time of travel, for better efficiency.

由一点到另一点的路径很重要,这只是一个方面。为了更高效,必须选择移动时间最短的路径。

respect 在本文中的含义为"方面,着眼点"。例如:

in one respect 在一个方面,在一点上

in all respects (= in every respect)无论从哪方面(哪一点)来看,在各方面

in no respect 无论在哪方面(哪一点)都不是……,完全不是……

5) A more recent definition of DNC (now meaning distributed numerical control) covers the use of a central computer serving as the control system over a number of individual computer numerical control machines having onboard microcomputers.

最近对 DNC(现在表示分布式数字控制)的定义涵盖了"使用主计算机作为控制系统,来管理大量的带有机载微型计算机的独立的计算机数控机床"的含义。

serving as 为现在分词短语,作 a central computer 的定语。

having onboard microcomputers 为现在分词短语作定语,修饰前面的名词短语。

onboard a. 随车携带的,机载的

6) The part program may be prepared at a remote site by the programmer, and it may incorporate information obtained from drafting software packages and from machining simulations, in order to ensure that the part program is bug free.

零件程序由编程者事先准备好,该程序应结合由绘图软件包和加工仿真中获得的信息,从而确保零件没有程序缺陷。

part program 零件程序

remote site 遥远的地方,在这里指"应事先编写好,不在现场"的含义。

bug free 没有程序缺陷。bug 程序缺陷,电脑系统或者程序中存在的任何一种破坏正常运转能力的问题或者缺陷。

## EXERCISES

1. After reading the text above, summarize the main ideas in oral.

2. Fill in the blanks with proper words or phrases according to the text (note the proper tense).

(1) A numerical control machine tool system contains a m_____ and the m_____. The MCU is further divided into two elements: the d_____ and the c_____.

(2) An NC machine can be controlled through two types of circuits: o_____ and

c_____.

(3) The closed-loop system is equipped with various t_____, s_____, and c_____ that measure accurately the position of the worktable. Through f_____, the position of the worktable is compared against the signal. Table movements terminate when the p_____ are reached.

(4) There are two basic types of control systems in numerical control, p_____ and c_____. The first systems are used mainly in d_____, p_____, and s_____ operations. The second system is typically used on l_____, m_____, g_____, w_____, and m_____.

(5) DNC means d_____, in that several machines are directly controlled by a c_____.

(6) CNC means c_____ in which a c_____ is an integral part of a machine or a piece of equipment (onboard computer). Because of the availability of s_____, m_____, and p_____ capabilities, CNC systems are widely used today.

3. Translate the following phrases into Chinese according to the text.

(1) the control loops unit (CLU)　　(2) geometric and kinematic data
(3) the long-run tooling costs　　(4) electric discharge machining
(5) point-to-point control system　　(6) computer numerical control (CNC)
(7) synchronization of velocities and movements

4. Translate the following phrases into English according to the text.

(1) 数据处理单元　　(2) 进给速度
(3) 轮廓控制系统　　(4) 分布式数控
(5) 闭环系统　　(6) 加工中心
(7) 零件程序编写　　(8) 变换器、传感器和计数器

5. Write a 100-word summary according to the text.

# READING MATERIAL

## 1. Machining Centers

Machining centers have been defined as multifunction CNC machines with automatic tool-changing capabilities and rotating tool magazine. Since their introduction in the late 1950s, they have become one of the most common of all cutting machines. Increased productivity and versatility are major advantages of machining centers. The ability to perform drilling, turning, reaming, boring, milling, contouring, and threading operations on a single machine eliminates the need for a number of individual machine tools, thus reducing capital equipment and labor requirements. One relatively unskilled operator can often attend two machining centers and sometimes more. Most workpieces can be completed on a single machining center, often with one setup.

Additional savings result from reduced materials handling, fixture costs, and floor space requirements. Substantial time conventionally spent moving work from machine to machine is saved, and throughput is much faster. Also, in-process inventory, represented by skids of workpieces normally seen at several machines, is replaced by work at only one machine.

Most machining centers maintain close, consistently repetitive tolerances, resulting in higher quality parts, as well as reduced inspection costs and scrap. In particular, the relationships of machined features on the several faces of a workpiece are more easily held within tolerances. Changeover from the production of one workpiece to another can be done quickly.

Actual machining time on machining centers can be two or more times better than that of single-purpose, manually operated machine tools. Estimates of increases in productivity per man-hour range from 300% to 500% or more, especially on applications requiring many tools and frequent changeover.

While machining centers have a higher initial cost than many other machine tools, annual return on investment has been conservatively estimated to be about 30%. Smaller, compact models now available make these machines affordable even to small job shops. Accuracy that can be maintained and the reliability of the machines and their controls have been continuously improved.

## 2. Types, Construction, and Operations Performed

Machining centers, just like turning centers, are classified as either vertical or horizontal machining centers. Vertical machining centers continue to be widely accepted and used, primarily for flat parts and where three-axis machining is required on a single part face such as in mold and die work. Horizontal machining centers are also widely accepted and used, particularly with large, boxy, and heavy parts and because they lend themselves to easy and accessible pallet shuttle transfer when used in a cell of FMS application.

Universal machining centers are more recent developments and are equipped with both vertical and horizontal spindles. They have a variety of features and are capable of machining all surfaces of a workpiece.

Machining center innovations and developments have brought about the following improvements:

- Improved flexibility and reliability
- Increased feeds, speeds, and overall machine construction and rigidity
- Reduced loading, tool-changing, and other non-cutting time
- Greater MCU (machine control unit) capability and compatibility with systems
- Reduced operator involvement
- Improved safety features and less noise

These improvements, driven by increased productivity demands and intense competition among machine tool suppliers, have created part-hungry machine tools able to machine workpieces to exacting tolerances accurately and consistently.

By today's definition, a machining center must include an automatic tool changer. Tool-storage and tool-change mechanisms vary among the diversified machine tool suppliers, such as front, side, or top mounted. The advantages of having tool stored away from the working spindle include less contamination from flying chips and better protection for an operator changing tools during machining. The double-ended, 180-degree indexing arm continues to be the most popular approach, although various designs of the tool gripping and clamping mechanisms will vary among builders.

More cutting tools are needed with modern machining centers, which means more tool storage capacity is required. Machining requirements for cells and systems demand that backup tools be available on-line to replace a broken tool or a worn-out tool before it breaks. Tools stored at machining centers fit into individual pockets of a machine tool's magazine or tool matrix. Pocket designs vary, ranging from simple holes cut into a disk-shaped carrousel to individually machined pockets assembled into a chain to interconnected plastic pockets.

Both random and sequential tool selection are used on machining centers, although random is by far the most predominant type used on modern machining centers. Random tooling refers to the capability of selecting any tool from the machine tool matrix at any time. With advanced machine tool and control capabilities, cutting tools may be selected, in any order, used more than once, and placed back in a different pocket from which they were originally selected, and the CNC unit will remember their new location.

# Lesson 12  Rapid-Prototyping Operations

## TEXT

### 1. Introduction

In the development of a new product, there is invariably a need to produce a single example or prototype of a designed part or system before the allocation of large amounts of capital to new production facilities or assembly lines. The main reasons for this need are that the capital cost is very high and the production tooling takes considerable time to prepare. Consequently, a working prototype is needed for design evaluation and troubleshooting before a complex product or system is ready to be produced and marketed.

An iterative process naturally occurs when (a) errors are discovered or (b) more efficient or better design solutions are gleaned from the study of an earlier-generation prototype. The main problem of this approach, however, is that the production of a prototype can be extremely time consuming. Tooling can take several months to prepare, and the production of a single complicated part by conventional manufacturing operations can be very difficult. Furthermore, while waiting for a prototype to be prepared, facilities and staff still generate costs.

An even more important concern is the speed with which a product flows from concept to a marketable item. In a competitive marketplace, it is well known that products that are introduced before those of their competitions are generally more profitable and enjoy a larger share of the market. At the same time, there are important concerns regarding the production of high-quality products to market quickly.

A technology which considerable speeds the iterative product-development process is the concept and practice of rapid prototyping(RP) which is also called solid freeform fabrication.

Rapid-prototyping processes can be classified into three major groups: subtractive, additive, and virtual. As the names imply, subtractive processes involve material removal from a workpiece that is larger than the final part. Additive processes build up a part by adding material incrementally to produce the part. Virtual processes use advanced computer-based visualization technologies.

Almost all materials can be used through one or more rapid-prototyping operations. Polymers are the workpiece material most commonly used today, followed by ceramics and metals. However, new processes are being introduced continually, and, thus, existing processes and materials are improved.

## 2. Subtractive Processes

Making a prototype traditionally has involved a series of processes using a variety of tooling and machines, and it usually takes anywhere from weeks to months, depending on part complexity and size. This approach requires skilled operators using material removal by machining and finishing operations—one by one—until the prototype is completed. To speed this process, subtractive processes increasingly use computer-based technologies, such as:

- Computer-based drafting packages, which can produce three-dimensional representations of parts.
- Interpretation software, which can translate the CAD file into a format usable by manufacturing software.
- Manufacturing software, which is capable of planning the operations required to produce the desired shape.
- Computer numerical control machinery with the capabilities necessary to produce the parts.

When a prototype is required only for the purpose of shape verification, a soft material (usually a polymer or a wax) is used as the workpiece in order to reduce or avoid any machining difficulties. The material intended for use in the actual application also can be machined, but this operation may be more time consuming, according to the machinability of the material. According to part complexity and machining capabilities, prototypes can be produced in a matter of from a few days to a few weeks. Subtractive systems can take many forms that are similar in approach to the manufacturing cells. Operators may or may not be involved, although the handling of parts is usually a human task.

## 3. Additive Processes

Additive rapid-prototyping operations all build parts in layers. They consist of stereo lithography, fused-deposition modeling, ballistic-particle manufacturing, three-dimensional printing, selective laser sintering and laminated-object manufacturing. In order to visualize the methodology used, it is beneficial to think of constructing a loaf of bread by stacking and bonding individual slices on top of each other. All of the processes described in this section build parts slice-by-slice. The main difference between the various additive processes lies in the method of producing the individual slices, which are typically 0.1 mm to 0.5 mm thick and can be thicker for some systems.

All additive operations require elaborate software. As an example, note the solid part shown in Figure 2.6(a). The first step is to obtain a CAD file description of the part. The computer then constructs slices of the three-dimensional part (Figure 2.6(b)). Each slice is analyzed separately, and a set of instructions is compiled in order to provide the rapid-prototyping machine with detailed information regarding the manufacture of the part. Figure 2.6(d) shows the paths of the extruder in one slice, using the fused-deposition-modeling operation.

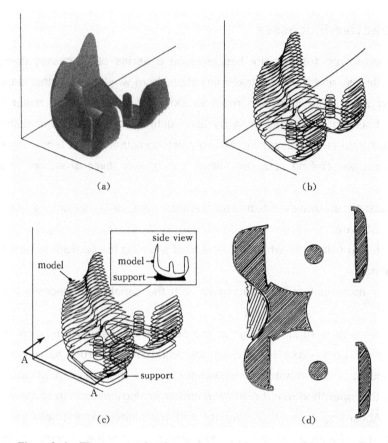

Figure 2.6 The computational steps in producing a stereolithography file

This approach requires operator input in the setup of the proper computer files and in the initiation of the production process. Following this stage, the machines generally operate unattended and provide a rough part after a few hours. The part then is subjected to a series of manual finishing operations (such as sanding and painting) in order to complete the rapid-prototyping process.

It should be recognized that the setup and finishing operations are very labor intensive and that the production time is only a portion of the time required to obtain a prototype. In general, however, additive processes are much faster than subtractive processes, taking as little as a few minutes to a few hours to produce a part.

### 4. Virtual Prototyping

Virtual prototyping is a purely software form of prototyping and uses advanced graphics and virtual-reality environments to allow designers to examine a part. In a way, this technology is used by common, conventional CAD packages to render a part so that the designer can observe and evaluate the part as it is drawn. However, virtual-prototyping systems should be recognized as extreme cases of rendering detail.

The simplest forms of systems use complex software and three-dimensional graphics routines to allow viewers to change the view of the parts on a computer screen. More complicated versions will use virtual-reality headgear and gloves with appropriate sensors to let the user observe a computer-generated prototype of the desired part in a completely virtual environment.

Virtual prototyping has the advantage of the instantaneous rendering of parts for evaluation, but the more advanced systems are costly. Because familiarity with software interfaces is a necessary prerequisite to their application, these systems have very steep learning curves. Furthermore, many manufacturing and design practitioners prefer a physical prototype to evaluate, rather than a video-screen rendering. They often perceive virtual-reality prototypes to be inferior to mechanical prototypes, even though designers debug as many or more errors in the virtual environment.

There have been some important examples of complicated products which have been produced without any physical prototype whatsoever (paperless design). Perhaps the best-known example is the Boeing 777 aircraft, where mechanical fits and interferences were evaluated on a CAD system and the difficulties were corrected before manufacture of the first production model.

## NEW WORDS AND EXPRESSIONS

allocation [ˌæləuˈkeiʃən] n. 分配，安置
considerable [kənˈsidərəbl] a. 相当大的，相当多的
iterative [ˈitərətiv] a. 重复的，反复的
subtractive [səbˈtræktiv] a. 减去的，负的
additive [ˈæditiv] a. 附加的，添加的
verification [ˌverifiˈkeiʃən] n. 确认，查证，作证
wax [wæks] n. 蜡，蜡状物
slice [slais] n. 薄片，部分，片段
elaborate [iˈlæbərət] a. 精心制作的
prerequisite [ˈpriːˈrekwizit] n. 先决条件
RP(rapid prototyping) 快速成型法，快速成型

solid freeform fabrication 实体自由成型制造
subtractive process 脱除过程
stereo lithography (SL) 光固化立体造型
fused deposition modeling 熔融沉积造型
ballistic-particle manufacturing 喷粒法制造，弹道粒子制造
three dimensional printing 三维印刷
selective laser sintering 选区激光烧结
laminated-object manufacturing 叠层制造
virtual-prototyping 虚拟原型制作，虚拟样机技术

## NOTES

1) In the development of a new product, there is invariably a need to produce a single example or prototype of a designed part or system before the allocation of large amounts of capital to new production facilities or assembly lines.

在新产品的开发过程中，在为新生产设备或装配线投入大量资金前，总是需要制造出所设计零件或系统的、单个的样件或样机。

该句主句部分为典型的 there be 结构，不定式短语 to produce 修饰前面的名词 need，before... 为时间状语。

invariably *ad.* 不变地，总是

assembly line 装配线

2) In a competitive marketplace, it is well known that products that are introduced before those of their competitions are generally more profitable and enjoy a larger share of the market.

众所周知,在充满竞争的市场中,通常先于同类竞争产品被推广是非常有利可图的,而且将占领更大的市场份额。

该句中,it 为形式主语,真正的主语为第一个 that 引导的从句(该从句中 products 为主语,are more profitable and enjoy a larger share of the market 为并列的谓语结构),第二个 that 引导的定语从句对 products 进行修饰。

enjoy a larger share of the market 占有更大的市场份额

3) According to part complexity and machining capabilities, prototypes can be produced in a matter of from a few days to a few weeks.

根据零件的复杂性和加工性能的不同,样机在大约几天到几星期内可以被加工出来。

a matter of (a)大约,大概。例:a matter of ten minutes 大约十分钟。

(b)……的问题。例:a matter of course 当然的事，a matter of opinion 看法不同的问题。

4) In order to visualize the methodology used, it is beneficial to think of constructing a loaf of bread by stacking and bonding individual slices on top of each other.

为了使所采用的方法形象化(为了说明所采用的方法),可以想象一下从每一片面包的顶部堆或压上其他的面包片来构成一条面包的方法,这对你的理解很有帮助。

think of 考虑，关心，想起，想象

5) Each slice is analyzed separately, and a set of instructions is compiled in order to provide the rapid-prototyping machine with detailed information regarding the manufacture of the part.

每一层单独分析,并对整套指令编译从而为快速造型机床提供详细的零件制造的信息。

regarding *prep.* 关于，有关

例:regarding the future of reform 关于改革的前途。

6) Furthermore, many manufacturing and design practitioners prefer a physical prototype to evaluate, rather than a video-screen rendering.

而且,许多生产者和设计者更喜欢用物理样机来评价设计,而不喜欢电脑屏幕上的(虚拟样机的)演示。

prefer ... rather than ... 宁愿(愿意)……而不愿……

# EXERCISES

1. After reading the text above, summarize the main ideas in oral.

2. Fill in the blanks with proper words or phrases according to the text (note the proper tense).

(1) A working prototype is needed for d_____ and t_____ before a complex product or system is ready to be produced and marketed.

(2) Rapid-prototyping processes can be classified into three major groups: s_____, a_____, and v_____.

(3) Almost all materials can be used through one or more rapid-prototyping operations. P_____ are the workpiece material most commonly used today, followed by c_____ and m_____.

(4) According to p_____ and m_____, prototypes can be produced in a matter of from a few days to a few weeks.

(5) Additive rapid-prototyping operations all build parts in l_____. They consist of s_____, f_____, b_____, t_____, s_____ and l_____.

(6) Virtual prototyping is a purely s_____ form of prototyping and uses a_____ and v_____ to allow designers to examine a part.

3. Translate the following phrases into Chinese according to the text.

(1) RP (rapid-prototyping) operation  (2) virtual-reality environment
(3) subtractive process  (4) finishing operation
(5) virtual prototyping  (6) three-dimensional graphics routine
(7) design evaluation and troubleshooting  (8) the setup of the proper computer files

4. Translate the following phrases into English according to the text.

(1) 装配线  (2) 反复的产品开发过程
(3) 可视化技术  (4) 解释软件
(5) 材料机械加工性  (6) 光固化立体造型
(7) 实体零件  (8) 物理样机

5. Write a 100-word summary according to the text.

# READING MATERIAL

## Rapid-Prototyping and Manufacturing

### 1. What Is RP & M?

Manufacturing community is facing two important challenging tasks: (1) substantial reduction of product development time; and (2) improvement on flexibility for manufacturing small batch size products and a variety of types of products. Computer-aided design and manufacturing (CAD and CAM) have significantly improved the traditional production design and manufacturing. However, there are a number of obstacles in true integration of computer-aided design with computer-aided manufacturing for rapid development of new products. Although substantial research has been done in the past for computer-aided design and manufacturing integration, such as feature recognition, CNC programming and process planning, the gap between CAD and CAM remains unfilled in the following aspects.

1) Rapid creation of 3-D models and prototypes.
2) Cost-effective production of patterns and moulds with complex surfaces.

To substantially shorten the time for developing patterns, moulds, and prototypes, some manufacturing enterprises have started to use Rapid Prototyping (RP) methods for complex patterns making and component prototyping. Over the past few years, a variety of new rapid manufacturing technologies, generally called Rapid Prototyping and Manufacturing (RP&M), have emerged the technologies developed include Stereo Lithography (SL), Selective Laser Sintering (SLS), Fused Deposition Modeling (FDM), Laminated Object Manufacturing (LOM), and Three Dimensional Printing (3-D Printing). These technologies are capable of directly generating physical objects from CAD databases. They have a common important feature. The prototype part is produced by adding materials rather than removing materials, that is, a part is first modeled by a geometric modeler such as a solid modeler, and then is mathematically sectioned (sliced) into a series of parallel cross-section pieces. For each piece, the curing or binding paths are generated. These curing or binding paths are directly used to instruct the machine for producing the part by solidifying or binding a line of material. After a layer is built, a new layer is built on the previous one in the same way. Thus, the model is built layer by layer from bottom to top. In summary, the rapid prototyping activities consist of two parts: data preparation and model production.

## 2. Current Application Areas of RP&M

Although RP&M technologies are still at their early stage, a large number of industrial companies, such as Texas Instruments, Inc., Chrysler Corporation, Amp Inc. and Ford Motor Co., have benefited from applying the technologies to improve their product development in the following three aspects.

1) Design engineering

i) Visualization

Conceptual models are very important in product design. Designers use CAD to generate computer representations of their design concepts. However, no matter how well engineers can interpret blueprints and how excellent CAD images of complex objects are, it is still very difficult to visualize exactly what the actual complex products will look like. Some errors may still escape from the review of engineers and designers. The touch of the physical objects can reveal unanticipated problems and sometimes spark a better design. With RP&M, the prototype of a complex part can be built in short time, therefore engineers can evaluate a design very quickly.

ii) Verification and optimization

Improving product quality is always an important issue of manufacturing. With the traditional method, developing of prototypes to validate or optimize a design is often time consuming and costly. In contrast, an RP&M prototype can be produced quickly without substantial tooling and labor cost. Consequently, the verification of design concepts becomes simple: the product quality can be improved within the limited time frame and with affordable cost.

ⅲ) Iteration

Just like the automotive industry, manufacturers often put new product models into market. With RP&M technology, it is possible to go through multiple design iterations within a short time and to reduce the model development time substantially.

2) Manufacturing

We can use the RP&M prototype for producibility studies. By providing a physical product at an earlier design stage, we can speed up process planning and tooling design. In addition, by accurately describing complex geometry, the prototype can help reduce problems in interpreting the blueprints on the shop floor. Another application is tooling development for moulds. The prototypes can also be used as master patterns for castings.

3) Marking

To assist product sales, a prototype can be used to demonstrate the concept, design ideas, as well as the company's ability to produce it. The reality of the physical model illustrates the feasibility of the design. Also, the prototype can be used to gain customers' feedback for design modifications so that the final product will meet customers' requirements. Meeting customers' demands in a timely manner is the key to penetrating the market in today's economy. RP&M technologies have the potential to ensure that quality products are developed quickly for two major reasons: there are almost no restrictions on geometrical shapes; and the layered manufacturing allows a direct and very simple interface from CAD to CAM which almost completely eliminates the need for computer-aided process planning.

## 3. Advantages

Developments in rapid prototyping began in the mid-1980s. The advantages of this technology include the following:

● Physical models of parts produced from CAD data files can be manufactured in a matter of hours and allow the rapid evaluation of manufacturability and design effectiveness. In this way, rapid prototyping serves as a very important tool for visualization and for concept verification.

● With suitable materials, the prototype can be used in subsequent manufacturing operations to produce the final parts. In this way, rapid prototyping itself serves as an important manufacturing technology.

● Rapid-prototyping operations can be applied to produce actual tooling for manufacturing operations (rapid tooling). In this way, one can obtain tooling in a matter of a few days.

# Lesson 13 | Fabrication of Micro-electromechanical Devices and Systems (MEMS)

## TEXT

### 1. Introduction

The devices dealt with the manufacture of integrated circuits and products that operate purely on electrical or electronic principles, called microelectronic devices. These semiconductor-based devices often have the common characteristic of extreme miniaturization. A large number of devices exist that are mechanical in nature and are of a similar size as microelectronic devices. A micromechanical device is a product that is purely mechanical in nature and has dimensions between a few millimeters and atomic length scales, such as some very small gears and hinges.

Micro-electromechanical devices (MEMS device) are products that combine mechanical and electrical or electronic elements at these very small length scales. Micro-electromechanical systems (MEMS) are micro-electromechanical devices that also incorporate an integrated electrical system into one product. Common examples of micromechanical devices are all types of sensors. Micro-electromechanical systems are rarer, but typical examples are airbag sensors and digital micromirror devices.

Many of the materials and manufacturing methods and systems also apply to the manufacture of micro-electromechanical devices and systems. However, it should be noted that microelectronic devices are semiconductor based, whereas micro-electromechanical devices and portions of MEMS do not have this material restriction. This allows the use of many more materials and the development of processes suitable for these materials. Regardless, silicon often is used because several highly advanced and reliable manufacturing processes have been developed for microelectronic applications. This lesson emphasizes the manufacturing processes that are applicable specifically to micro-electromechanical devices and systems, but it should be realized that processes and concepts, such as lithography, metallization, etching, coating, and packaging, are still applied.

### 2. Micromachining of MEMS Devices

In the manufacture of MEMS devices, lithography and etching can be used to obtain two-dimensional or two-and-one-half-dimensional features on wafer surfaces. However, three-dimensional features often are required. The production of features ranging from micrometers to millimeters is called micromachining. The use of anisotropic-etching techniques allows the

*Lesson 13  Fabrication of Micro-electromechanical Devices and Systems (MEMS)*

fabrication of devices with well-defined walls and high aspect ratios. For this reason, some single-crystal silicon MEMS devices have been fabricated.

One of the recognized difficulties associated with using silicon for MEMS devices is the high adhesion encountered at small length scales and the associated rapid wear. Most commercial devices are designed to avoid friction, for example, by using flexing springs instead of bushings, however, this complicates the designs and makes some MEMS devices not feasible. Significant research now is being conducted to identify materials and lubricants that provide reasonable life and performance. Silicon carbide, diamond, and metals (such as aluminum, tungsten, and nickel) are being studied as potential MEMS materials.

Lubricants also have been investigated. For example, it is known that surrounding the MEMS devices in silicone oil practically eliminates adhesive wear, but it also limits the performance of the device. Self-assembling layers of polymers also are being investigated, as well as novel and new materials with self-lubricating characteristics. However, the tribology (such as friction, wear, and lubrication) of MEMS devices remains the main technological barrier to their widespread use.

1) Bulk micromachining

Until the early 1980s, bulk micromachining was the most common method of machining at micrometer scales. This process uses orientation-dependent etches on single-crystal silicon. This approach depends on etching down into a surface and stopping on certain crystal faces, doped regions, and etchable films to form a desired structure. As an example of this process, consider the fabrication of the silicon cantilever shown in Figure 2.7. Using the masking techniques, a rectangular patch of the *n*-type silicon substrate is changed to *p*-type silicon through boron doping. Etchants such as potassium hydroxide will not be able to remove heavily boron-doped silicon, hence this patch will not be etched.

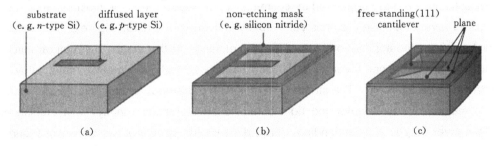

Figure 2.7  Schematic illustration of bulk micromachining

A mask then is produced, such as with silicon nitride on silicon. When etched with potassium hydroxide, the undoped silicon will be removed rapidly, while the mask and the doped patch essentially will be unaffected. Etching progresses until the (111) planes are exposed in the *n*-type silicon substrate; they undercut the patch, leaving a suspended cantilever as shown.

　i) Diffuse dopant in desired pattern.

　ii) Deposit and pattern masking film.

　iii) Orientation-dependent etching (ODE) leaves behind a freestanding structure.

2) Surface micromachining

Bulk micromachining is very useful for producing very simple shapes. It is restricted to single-crystal materials, since polycrystalline materials will not machine at different rates in different directions when using wet etchants. Many MEMS applications require the use of other materials, so alternatives to bulk micromachining are needed. One of such alternatives is surface micromachining. The basic steps in surface micromachining are illustrated in Figure 2.8 for silicon devices. A spacer or sacrificial layer is deposited onto a silicon substrate coated with a thin dielectric layer (called an isolation or buffer layer).

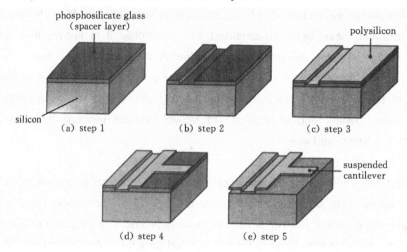

Figure 2.8  Schematic illustration of the steps in surface micromachining
(a) deposition of a phosphosilicate glass (PSG) spacer layer;(b) etching of spacer layer;
(c) deposition of polysilicon;(d) etching of polysilicon;(e) selective wet etching of PSG, leaving the silicon substrate and deposited polysilicon unaffected.

Phosphosilicate glass deposited by chemical vapor deposition is the most common material for a spacer layer, because it etches very rapidly in hydrofluoric acid. Figure 2.8(b) shows the spacer layer after the application of masking and etching. At this stage, a structural thin film is deposited onto the spacer layer, and the film can be polysilicon, metal, metal alloy, or a dielectric (Figure 2.8(c)). The structural film is then patterned, usually through dry etching in order to maintain vertical walls and tight dimensional tolerances. Finally, wet etching of the sacrificial layer leaves a free-standing, three-dimensional structure, as shown in Figure 2.8 (e). It should be noted that the wafer must be annealed to remove the residual stresses in the deposited metal before it is patterned. If this is not done, the structural film will severely warp once the spacer layer is removed.

# NEW WORDS AND EXPRESSIONS

semiconductor ['semikən'dʌktə] n. [物] 半导体

hinge [hindʒ] n. 铰链,转轴

silicon ['silikən] n. [化]硅,硅元素

metallization [ˌmetəlai'zeiʃən] n. 镀金属(法);金属喷镀

## Lesson 13  Fabrication of Micro-electromechanical Devices and Systems (MEMS)

etching ['etʃiŋ] n. 蚀刻法
coating ['kəutiŋ] n. 涂层,镀覆
packaging ['pækidʒiŋ] n. 组装(法),封装(技术)
wafer ['weifə] n. [电子学] 晶片
anisotropic [ə,naisəu'trɔpik] a. [物]各向异性的
adhesion [əd'hi:ʒən] n. 黏着,附着,黏附力
tribology [trai'bɔlədʒi] n. 摩损学
mask [mɑ:sk] n. [电子]掩模
dope [dəup] v. [电子学]加入掺杂剂
patch [pætʃ] n. 金属补片,碎片
hydroxide [hai'drɔksaid,-sid] n. 氢氧化物,羟化物
nitride ['naitraid] n. [化]氮化物
cantilever ['kæntili:və] n. 悬臂
polycrystalline [,pɔli'kristəlain] a. 多晶体的,多(结)晶的
dielectric [,daii'lektrik] n. 电介质,绝缘体
phosphosilicate [,fɔsfə'silikeit] n. 磷硅酸盐
hydrofluoric ['haidrəflu(:)'ɔrik] a. [化]含氟化氢的,氢氟酸的
anneal [ə'ni:l] n. 退火
microelectromechanical system 微型机电系统
bulk micromachining 体微加工技术
surface micromachining 表面微加工技术

# NOTES

1) A micromechanical device is a product that is purely mechanical in nature and has dimensions between a few millimeters and atomic length scales, such as some very small gears and hinges.

微机械装置本质上是一种纯机械的产品,其尺寸在几个毫米到原子大小范围内,比如一些非常小的齿轮和铰链。

in nature 实际上,本质上

2) This lesson emphasizes the manufacturing processes that are applicable specifically to microelectromechanical devices and systems, but it should be realized that processes and concepts, such as lithography, metallization, etching, coating, and packaging, are still applied.

本课的重点在于可应用于微机电装置和系统的加工技术,但同时应认识到,如光刻、镀金属、蚀刻、镀覆和封装的技术及概念仍在应用。

applicable to 适用于,可应用于,对……很合适

etch 蚀刻,利用化学反应或物理撞击作用将材料移除的技术

package 封装:①对元器件等进行固定、连接及保护的物理处理方法(或过程)。②封装的类型和方法(取决于热耗散和尺寸等因素)。用此种方式即可放置经过精制的半导体芯片。封装类型可以是塑料型、陶瓷型、陶瓷双列直插型或其他类型。

3) The use of anisotropic-etching techniques allows the fabrication of devices with well-defined walls and high aspect ratios. For this reason, some single-crystal silicon MEMS devices have been fabricated.

各向异性蚀刻技术使得微机电装置的制造具有平滑的蚀刻侧壁和高的高深宽比的特点。由此,一些单晶硅微机电装置已经(采用此项技术)被加工出来。

well-defined walls 平滑的蚀刻侧壁

high aspect ratios 高的高深宽比

4) This process uses orientation-dependent etches on single-crystal silicon. This

approach depends on etching down into a surface and stopping on certain crystal faces, doped regions, and etchable films to form a desired structure.

此过程(体微加工)是在单晶硅上采用定向蚀刻技术。这种方法通过蚀刻至某一表面,并且在到达某晶面、掺杂区后停止,形成蚀刻薄膜,从而构造出所希望的结构。

orientation-dependent etch 定向蚀刻

crystal face 晶面

doped region 掺杂区

etchable film 蚀刻薄膜

专业提示:一些微机电组件在制造过程中需要蚀刻较大量的 Si 基材,如压力传感器即为一例,即通过蚀刻晶背形成深的孔洞,但未蚀穿正面,在正面形成一层薄膜。

5) When etched with potassium hydroxide, the undoped silicon will be removed rapidly, while the mask and the doped patch essentially will be unaffected. Etching progresses until the (111) planes are exposed in the *n*-type silicon substrate; they undercut the patch, leaving a suspended cantilever as shown.

当用氢氧化钾蚀刻时,未掺杂质的硅会被快速去除掉,而掩膜和掺杂区本质上不受影响。蚀刻一直进行到 111 晶面露出 N 型硅基底。该过程对薄片进行底切,从而产生如图所示的悬浮的悬梁。

(111) plane 111 晶面,就是在 a,b,c 三个晶轴上的截长都相等的晶面。

undercut 底切

6) Bulk micromachining is very useful for producing very simple shapes. It is restricted to single-crystal materials, since polycrystalline materials will not machine at different rates in different directions when using wet etchants.

体微加工技术对加工非常简单的形状十分有用。它局限于单晶硅材料,因为当使用湿蚀刻剂时,多晶材料不能在不同方向上以不同的速度进行加工。

wet etchant 湿蚀刻剂。就湿蚀刻作用而言,对某一特定被蚀刻的材料,通常可以找到一种可快速有效蚀刻,而且不致蚀刻其他材料的蚀刻剂。

# EXERCISES

1. After reading the text above, summarize the main ideas in oral.

2. Fill in the blanks with proper words or phrases according to the text (note the proper tense).

(1) Microelectronic devices dealt with the manufacture of i_____ that operate purely on e_____ or e_____ principles. Micromechanical devices are purely m_____ in nature and have dimensions between a few m_____ and a_____ scales. Microelectromechanical devices combine m_____ and e_____ or e_____ elements at these very small length scales.

(2) Microelectronic devices are s_____ based, whereas microelectromechanical devices and portions of MEMS allow the use of m_____ and the d_____ suitable for these materials. S_____, d_____, and m_____ (such as aluminum, tungsten, and nickel) are being studied as potential MEMS materials.

*Lesson 13  Fabrication of Micro-electromechanical Devices and Systems （MEMS）*

(3) The tribology (f_____, w_____, and l_____) of MEMS devices remains the main technological barrier to their widespread use.

(4) Bulk micromachining uses o_____ on single-crystal silicon. It is restricted to s_____, since p_____ materials will not machine at different rates in different directions when using wet etchants. So s_____ instead of bulk micromachining.

3. Translate the following phrases into Chinese according to the text.

(1) integrated circuit  (2) microelectronic device
(3) single-crystal silicon  (4) dry etch
(5) barrier to one's widespread use  (6) doped region
(7) spacer layer  (8) orientation-dependent etches
(9) self-assembling layers of polymers  (10) well-defined walls and high aspect ratios

4. Translate the following phrases into English according to the text.

(1) 微机电系统  (2) 单晶硅
(3) 各向异性蚀刻  (4) 掺杂区域
(5) 自润滑特性  (6) 晶面
(7) 湿蚀刻  (8) 表面微加工技术
(9) 残余应力  (10) 尺寸公差

5. Write a 100-word summary according to the text.

# READING MATERIAL

## Micro-electromechanical Device and System

### 1. Evolution of MEMS

The next ambitious goal is to fabricate monolithic or integrated chips that can not only sense (with microsensors) but also actuate (with microactuators), that is, to create a microsystem that encompasses the information-processing triptych. The technology employed to make such a microsystem is commonly referred to as MST. Figure 2.9 provides an overview of MST together with some of the application areas. Working to achieve this goal started in the late 1980s, and there has been enormous effort to fabricate micro-electromechanical systems (MEMS) using MST.

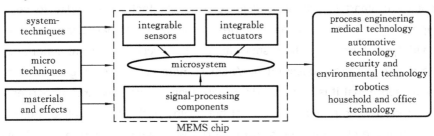

Figure 2.9  An overview of microsystems technology and the elements of a MEMS chip

A MEMS is a device made from extremely small parts (i.e. microparts).

Early efforts focused upon silicon technology and resulted in a number of successful micromechanical devices, such as pressure sensors and ink-jet printer nozzles. Yet, these are, perhaps, more accurately described as devices rather than as MEMS. The reason for the relatively slow emergence of complete MEMS has been the complexity of the manufacturing process.

One attractive solution to the development of MEMS is to make all the techniques compatible with silicon processing. In other words, conventional complementary metal oxide semiconductor (CMOS) processing is combined with a pre-CMOS or post-CMOS MST.

The present MEMS market is relatively staid and mainly consists of some simple optical switches for the communications industry, pressure sensors, and inertial sensors for the automotive industry. This current staidness contrasts with the potential for MEMS, which is enormous. The major growth areas are identified as microfluidics and photonics and communications. However, there have been some exciting developments in methods to fabricate true three-dimensional structures on the micron scale. To meet these challenges, certain industries have moved away from the use of silicon to the use of glasses and plastics, and the emergence of chips in biotechnology that include microfluidic system, which can truly be regarded as MEMS devices is indicated.

## 2. MEMS Devices

Silicon micromachining techniques are used to fabricate various micromechanical structures and many of these form micromechanical actuators. These include microvalves, micropumps, microgears, and so on.

MEMS devices can be considered as smart devices because they integrate sensors with actuators (i.e. a smart microsystem), but the degree of integration can vary significantly.

There are many different types of MEMS devices being made today, but two of the most exciting ones are used in optical and chemical instrumentation. The former is sometimes referred to as micro-optoelectromechanical system (MOEMS), and this is being driven by the optical telecommunications and biotechnology industries.

## 3. Smart Sensors and MEMS

The adjective smart is widely used in science and technology today to describe many different types of artefacts. Its meaning varies according to its particular use. For example, there is a widespread use of the term smart material, although functional material is also used and may be a more accurate description. A smart material may be regarded as an "active" material in the sense that it is being used for more than just its structural properties. The latter is normally referred to as a passive material but could, perhaps, be called a dumb material. The classical example of a so-called smart material is a shape memory alloy (SMA), such as NiTi. This material undergoes a change from its martensitic to austenitic crystalline phase and back when thermally cycled. The associated volumetric change induces a stress and so this

## Lesson 13  Fabrication of Micro-electromechanical Devices and Systems (MEMS)

type of material can be used in various types of microactuator and micro-electromechanical system (MEMS) devices. Another example of a smart material is a magnetostrictive one, which is a material that changes its length under the influence of an external magnetic field. This type of smart material can be used to make, for example, a strain gauge on microsensors.

The term "smart" is also applied in the field of structures. However, a smart structure is, in general, neither a small structure nor one made of silicon. In this case, as we shall see later on, the term really implies a form of intelligence and is applied to civil buildings and bridges. A classic example of a smart structure is that of a building that contains a number of motion sensors together with an active damping system. Therefore, the building can respond to changes in its environment (e.g. wind loading) and modify its mechanical response appropriately (e.g. through its variable damping coefficient). Perhaps, a more familiar way that engineers would describe this type of structure is one with a closed-loop control system.

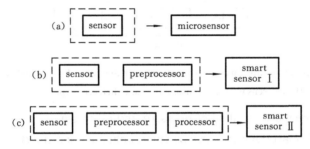

Figure 2.10  Basic concept of integrating the processing elements with an integrated sensor (microsensor) to make different types of smart sensor

The term "smart sensor" was first coined in the 1980s by electrical engineers and became associated with the integration of a silicon sensor with its associated microelectronic circuitry. Figure 2.10 shows the basic concept of a smart sensor in which a silicon sensor or microsensor (i.e. integrated sensor) is integrated with either a part or all of its associated processing elements (i.e. the preprocessor and/or the main processing unit). These devices are referred to here, for convenience, as smart sensor types I and II. For example, a silicon thermodiode could be integrated with a constant current circuit to make a simple three-terminal voltage supply (+5 V DC), ground and output (0 to 5 V DC) smart device. Of course, this is a trivial example and barely deserves the title of smart. Nowadays, the term tends to imply a higher degree of integration, such as the integration of an eight-bit microcontroller or microprocessor. It would be referred to here as a type II smart sensor. When the technologies and processes employed to make the microsensor are incompatible with the microprocessor, it is possible to make a hybrid rather than a true smart chip. In this case, the term smart is sometimes used in a less formal sense, but hybrid would be a more accurate term.

The integration of part (type I) or all (type II) of the processing element with the microsensor in order to create a smart sensor is highly desirable when one or more of the following conditions are met.

- Integration reduces the unit manufacturing cost of the device.

- Integration substantially enhances the performance.
- The device would not work at all without integration.

These prerequisites make integration feasible when there is either a large potential market (i.e. millions or more units per year) demanding that the unit cost be kept low, or there is a specialized "added value" market that can absorb the higher unit costs associated with smaller chip runs. Sometimes, these so-called market drivers are combined to define a performance-prince (PP) indicator.

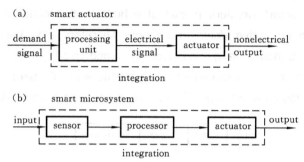

Figure 2.11　Basic architecture of (a) a smart actuator and (b) a smart microsystem (or MEMS) sensor (microsensor) to make different types of smart sensor

The successful commercialization of pressure and other smart sensors has led to a whole host of other types of smart devices, such as smart actuators and smart interfaces. Figure 2.11 gives a schematic representation of both a smart actuator and a smart microsystem. Of course, a MEMS device is one type of smart microsystem because a microsystem need not involve an electromechanical component.

# Lesson 14　CAM

## TEXT

### 1. Introduction

Computer-aided manufacturing involves the use of computers and computer technology to assist in all the phases of manufacturing a product, including process and production planning, machining, scheduling, management, and quality control. Because of the benefits, computer-aided design and computer-aided manufacturing are often combined into CAD/CAM systems, show as Figure 2.12.

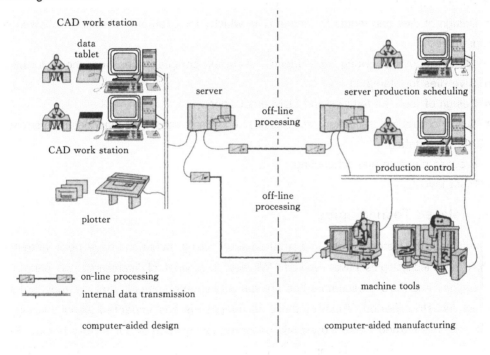

Figure 2.12　Information flow chart in CAD/CAM application

This combination allows the transfer of information from the design stage into the stage of planning for the manufacture of a product, without the need to reenter the data on part geometry manually. The database developed during CAD is stored, then it is processed further, by CAM, into the necessary data and instructions for operating and controlling production machinery, material-handling equipment, and automated testing and inspection for product quality.

In machining operations, an important feature of CAD/CAM is its capability to describe the tool path for various operations, such as NC turning, milling, and drilling. The instructions (programs) are computer generated, and they can be modified by the programmer to optimize the tool path. The engineer or technician can then display and visually check the tool path for possible tool collisions with clamps, fixtures, or other interferences.

The tool path can be modified at any time, to accommodate other part shapes to be machined. CAD/CAM systems are also capable of coding and classifying parts into groups that have similar shapes, using alphanumeric coding.

The emergence of CAD/CAM has had a major impact on manufacturing, by standardizing product development and by reducing design effort, tryout, and prototype work. It has made possible significantly reduced costs and improved productivity. The two-engine Boeing 777 passenger airplane, for example, was designed completely by computer (paperless design), with 2 000 workstations linked to eight computers. The plane is constructed directly from the developed (an enhanced CATIA system) CAD/CAM software and no prototypes or mockups were built, which were required for previous models. The cost for this development was on the order of $6 billion.

Some typical applications of CAD/CAM are as follows:

● Programming for NC, CNC, and industrial robots.

● Design of dies and molds for casting, in which, for example, shrinkage allowances are preprogrammed.

● Dies for metalworking operations, such as complex dies for sheet forming and progressive dies for stamping.

● Design of tools ad fixtures and EDM electrodes.

● Quality control and inspection—for instance, coordinate-measuring machines programmed on a CAD/CAM workstation.

● Process planning and scheduling.

● Plant layout.

## 2. Related Technologies

Throughout the history of our industrial society, many inventions have been patented and the whole new technologies have evolved. Whitney's concept of interchangeable parts, Watt's steam engine, and Ford's assembly line are but a few developments that are most noteworthy during our industrial period. Each of these developments has impacted manufacturing as we know it, and has earned these individuals deserved recognition in our history books. Perhaps the single development that has impacted manufacturing more quickly and significantly than any previous technology is the digital computer.

Since the advent of computer technology, manufacturing professionals have wanted to automate the design process and use the database developed therein for automating manufacturing processes. Computer-aided design/computer-aided manufacturing (CAD/CAM), when successfully implemented, should remove the "wall" that has traditionally existed between the designs and manufacturing components.

CAD/CAM means using computers in the design and manufacturing processes. Since the advent of CAD/CAM, other terms have developed.

● Computer graphics(CG).

- Computer-aided engineering (CAE).
- Computer-aided design and drafting (CADD).
- Computer-aided process planning (CAPP).

These spin-off terms all refer to specific aspects of the CAD/CAM concept, CAD/CAM itself is a broader, more inclusive term. It is at the heart of automated and integrated manufacturing.

A key goal of CAD/CAM is to produce data that can be used in manufacturing a product while developing the database for the design of that product. When successfully implemented, CAD/CAM involves the sharing of a common database between the designs and manufacturing components of a company.

Interactive computer graphics (ICG) plays an important role in CAD/CAM. Through the use of ICG, designers develop a graphic image of the product being designed while storing the data that electronically make up the graphic image. The graphic image can be presented in a two-dimensional (2-D), three-dimensional (3-D), or solids format. ICG images are constructed using such basic geometric characters as points, lines, circles, and curves. Once created, these images can be easily edited and manipulated in a variety of ways including enlargements, reductions, rotations, and movements.

An ICG system has three main components: ①hardware, which consists of the computer and various peripheral devices; ② software, which consists of the computer programs and technical manuals for the system (the popular ICG software are used in CAD/CAM at present includes AutoCAD, CADKEY, Pro/E, UG, I-DEAS an CATIA etc.); ③the human designer, the most important of the three components.

A typical hardware configuration for an ICG system includes a computer, a display terminal, a disk drive unit for floppy diskettes, a hard disk, or both; and input/output devices such as a keyboard, plotter, and printer. These devices, along with the software, are the tools modern designers use to develop and document their designs.

The ICG systems could enhance the design process by allowing the human designer to focus on the intellectual aspects of the design process, such as conceptualization and making judgment-based decisions. The computer performs tasks for which it is better suited, such as mathematical calculations, storage and retrieval of data, and various repetitive operations such as crosshatching.

## NEW WORDS AND EXPRESSIONS

reenter [ˌriːˈentə(r)] v. 再次进来,再次进入
database [ˈdeitəbeis] n. [计]数据库,资料库
instruction [inˈstrʌkʃən] n. [计]指令,指示,程序
optimize [ˈɔptimaiz] vt. 使最优化
collision [kəˈliʒən] n. 碰撞,冲突
clamp [klæmp] n. 夹子,夹具,夹钳

fixture [ˈfikstʃə] n. [机]装置器,工作夹具
interference [ˌintəˈfiərəns] n. [物]干扰,干涉
alphanumeric [ˌælfənjuːˈmerik] a. 字母数字混合编制的
tryout [ˈtraiˌaut] n. 示范性试验,尝试
prototype [ˈprəutətaip] n. 原型(体),样机(品)

mockup [mɔkʌp] n. 实体模型
shrinkage [ˈʃrinkidʒ] n. [物]缩减量
allowance [əˈlauəns] n. [机](加工)余量,公差
stamp [stæmp] v. 压印,冲压
electrode [iˈlektrəud] n. 电极
patent [ˈpeitənt, ˈpætənt] n. 专利权,专利品
intellectual [ˌintiˈlektjuəl] a. 智力的,显示智力的
retrieval [riˈtri:vəl] n. 信息检索,查找
crosshatch [ˈkrɔshætʃ] vt. 用交叉线画出阴影
interactive computer graphics (ICG) [图形学]交互计算机制图技术
peripheral device 外围设备

# NOTES

1) Computer-aided manufacturing involves the use of computers and computer technology to assist in all the phases of manufacturing a product, including process and production planning, machining, scheduling, management, and quality control.

计算机辅助制造的含义是:使用计算机和计算机技术来协助产品制造的所有环节,其中包括加工工艺和生产的辅助设计、加工、生产计划制定、管理和质量控制等。

2) The database developed during CAD is stored; then it is processed further, by CAM, into the necessary data and instructions for operating and controlling production machinery, material-handling equipment, and automated testing and inspection for product quality.

由CAD开发的数据库首先被存储,然后由CAM对其做进一步的处理,转化为对生产设备和材料处理设备进行操作和控制所必需的数据和指令,并对产品质量进行自动测试和检测。

第二句中的it指前句中的主语database。本句为被动语态,process和store为该句的并列谓语。短语for operating and controlling production machinery, material-handling equipment是对data and instructions的修饰。

3) The plane is constructed directly from the developed (an enhanced CATIA system) CAD/CAM software and no prototypes or mockups were built, which were required for previous models. The cost for this development was on the order of $6 billion.

这架飞机直接由CAD/CAM开发软件(功能强大的CATIA系统)构造,并且没有像以前的模型所要求的建造样机或实体模型。此开发过程的花费大约为60亿美元。

CATIA  computer-aided three dimensional interaction application system 计算机辅助三维互动应用系统

on the order of (1)相像,(在种类或样式上)与……相似

例:a house on the order of a mountain lodge 一所像山上小屋的房子

(2)大约,约略,近

例:equipment costing on the order of a million dollars 花费近百万美元的设备

4) These spin-off terms all refer to specific aspects of the CAD/CAM concept; CAD/CAM itself is a broader, more inclusive term. It is at the heart of automated and integrated manufacturing.

以上这些派生出来的术语都是针对CAD/CAM概念的某些专门领域而言的,因为CAD/CAM本身就是一个含义较广的、泛指的术语,它是自动化和集成制造的核心。

spin-off n. 副产品

inclusive a. 包括的,包含的,内容丰富的,范围广的

5) The graphic image can be presented in a two-dimensional (2-D), three-dimensional (3-D), or solids format.

图形图像可以以二维的、三维的或实体的形式表现出来。

6) A typical hardware configuration for an ICG system includes a computer, a display terminal, a disk drive unit for floppy diskettes, a hard disk, or both; and input/output devices, such as a keyboard, plotter, and printer.

交互计算机制图系统的典型硬件结构包括计算机、显示器、软盘驱动器、硬盘或两者兼备以及输入/输出设备,如键盘、绘图仪和打印机。

## EXERCISES

1. After reading the text above, summarize the main ideas in oral.

2. Fill in the blanks with proper words or phrases according to the text (note the proper tense).

(1) This combination of CAD and CAM allows the transfer of information from the d_____ into the stage of p_____ for the manufacture of a product, without the need to r_____ the data on part geometry.

(2) In machining operations, an important feature of CAD/CAM is its capability to d_____ for various operations, such as NC t_____, m_____, and d_____.

(3) The emergence of CAD/CAM has had a major impact on manufacturing, by s_____ and by reducing d_____, t_____, and p_____. It has made possible significantly reduced c_____ and improved p_____.

(4) The single development that has impacted manufacturing more quickly and significantly than any previous technology is the d_____.

(5) ICG images are constructed using such basic geometric characters as p_____, l_____, c_____, and c_____. Once created, these images can be easily edited and manipulated in a variety of ways including e_____, r_____, r_____, and m_____.

(6) The ICG systems could enhance the design process by allowing the h_____ to focus on the intellectual aspects of the design process, such as c_____ and m_____. The computer performs tasks for which it is better suited, such as m_____, s_____, and v_____ such as crosshatching.

3. Translate the following phrases into Chinese according to the text.

(1) material-handling equipment  (2) tool collision
(3) industrial robots  (4) dies and molds for casting
(5) computer-aided engineering (CAE)  (6) coordinate-measuring machine
(7) disk drive  (8) floppy diskette
(9) by reducing design effort, tryout, and prototype work
(10) computer-aided process planning (CAPP)

4. Translate the following phrases into English according to the text.
(1) 质量控制   (2) 工作站
(3) 材料处理设备   (4) 提高生产率
(5) 信息检索   (6) 计算机图形学
(7) 外围设备   (8) 实体模型

5. Write a 100-word summary according to the text.

# READING MATERIAL

## 1. CAD-to-CAM Interface

With CAD/CAM, the real interface between the design and manufacturing components is the common database they share. This is the essence of CAD/CAM. With manual design and manufacturing, engineers go through each step in the design process, drafters produce drawings and other documents to communicate the design, manufacturing personnel use the drawings to develop process plans, and shop personnel actually make the product.

With the old approach, until the design and drafting personnel completed their work, the manufacturing personnel did not see it. The design and drafting department did its job and "threw the plans over the wall" to manufacturing so it could do its job. This approach led to continual breakdowns in communication as well as poor relations between the design and manufacturing components. The result was a loss of productivity.

With CAD/CAM, manufacturing personnel have access to the data created during the design phase as soon as they are created. At any point in the design process, they can call up information from the design database and use it. Since the data are shared from start to finish, there are no surprises when the completed design is ready to be produced. While designers are creating the database and drafters are documenting the design, manufacturing personnel can be planning, setting up, ordering materials, and preparing parts programs.

Everything needed by manufacturing personnel to produce the product is contained in the common database. The mathematical models, graphic images, bills of material, parts lists, size, form, location dimensions, tolerance specifications and material specifications are all contained in the common database. (Figure 2.13)

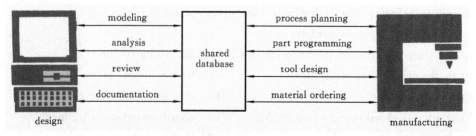

Figure 2.13 CAD-to-CAM Interface

## 2. Rationale for CAD/CAM

The rationale for CAD/CAM is similar to that used to justify any technology-based improvement in manufacturing. It grows out of a need to continually improve productivity, quality, and, in turn, competitiveness. There are also other reasons why a company might make a conversion from manual processes to CAD/CAM, such as high productivity, better quality, better communication, common database with manufacturing, low prototype construction costs, faster response to customers.

1) High Productivity

Productivity in the design process is increased by CAD/CAM. Time-consuming tasks such as mathematical calculations, data storage and retrieval, and design visualization are handled by the computer, which gives the designer more time to spend on conceptualizing and completing the design. In addition, the amount of time required to document a design can be reduced significantly with CAD/CAM. All of these taken together means a shorter design cycle, shorter overall project completion time, and a higher level of productivity.

2) Better Quality

Because CAD/CAM allows designers to focus more on actual design problems and less on time-consuming, nonproductive tasks, product quality improves with CAD/CAM. CAD/CAM allows designers to examine a wider range of design alternatives (e.g. product features) and to analyze each alternative more thoroughly before selecting on. In addition, because labor-intensive tasks are performed by the computer, fewer design errors occur. These all lead to better product quality.

3) Better Communication

Design documents, such as drawings, parts lists, bills of material, and specifications, are tools used to communicate the design to those who will manufacture it. The more uniform, standardized, and accurate these tools are, the better the communication will be. Because CAD/CAM leads to more uniform, standardized, and accurate documentation, it improves communication.

4) Common Database

This is one of the most important benefits of CAD/CAM. With CAD/CAM, the data generated during the design of a product can be used in producing the product. This sharing of a common database helps to eliminate the age-old "wall" separating the design and manufacturing functions.

5) Low Prototype Costs

With manual design, models and prototypes of a design must be made and tested, adding to the cost of the finished product. With CAD/CAM, 3-D computer models can reduce and, in some cases, eliminate the need for building expensive prototypes. Such CAD/CAM capabilities as solids modeling allow designers to substitute computer models for prototypes in many cases.

6) Faster Response to Customers

Response time is critical in manufacturing. How long does it take to fill a customer's order? The shorter the time, the better it is. A fast response time is one of the keys to being more competitive in an increasingly competitive marketplace. Today, the manufacturer with the fastest response time is as likely to win a contract as the one with the lowest bid. By shortening the overall design cycle and improving communication between the designs and manufacturing components, CAD/CAM can improve a company's response time.

# Lesson 15　CIMS

## TEXT

The various levels of automation in manufacturing operations have been extended further by including increasing information processing functions, utilizing an extensive network of interactive computers. The result is computer-integrated manufacturing, which is a broad term describing the computerized integration of all aspects of design, planning, manufacturing, distribution, and management.

Computer-integrated manufacturing is a methodology and a goal, rather than an assemblage of equipment and computers. The effectiveness of CIM critically depends on the use of a large-scale integrated communications system involving computers, machines, and their controls. Because CIM ideally should involve the total operation of a company, it must have an extensive database concerning technical and business aspects of the operation. Consequently, if implemented all at once, CIM can be prohibitively expensive, particularly for small-and medium-size companies.

Implementation of CIM in existing plants may begin with modules in various phases of the total operation. For new manufacturing plants, on the other hand, comprehensive and long-range strategic planning covering all phases of the operation is essential in order to fully benefit from CIM. Such plans must take into account the following considerations:

- Availability of financial, technical, and human resources;
- The mission, goals, and culture of the organization;
- Existing as well as emerging technologies in the areas of the products to be manufactured;
- The level of integration desired.

### 1. Subsystems of CIM

Computer-integrated manufacturing systems consist of subsystems that are integrated into a whole. These subsystems consist of the following (see Figure 2.14):

- Business planning and support;
- Product design;
- Manufacturing process planning;
- Process automation and control;
- Shop floor monitoring systems.

The subsystems are designed, developed, and implemented in such a manner that the output of one subsystem serves as the input of another subsystem. Organizationally, these subsystems usually are divided into two functions.

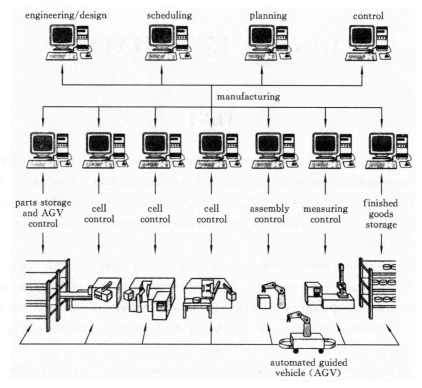

Figure 2.14　A schematic illustration of a computer-integrated manufacturing system

● Business planning functions: These include activities such as forecasting, scheduling, material-requirements planning, invoicing, and accounting.

● Business execution functions: include production and process control, material handling, testing, and inspection of the system.

The major benefits of CIM are as follows.

● Emphasis on product quality and uniformity, as implemented through better process control.

● Efficient use of materials, machinery, and personnel and major reduction of work-in-progress inventory, all of which improve productivity and lower product cost.

● Total control of the production, schedules, and management of the entire manufacturing operation.

● Responsiveness to shorter product life cycles, changing market demands, and global competition.

## 2. Database

An efficient computer-integrated manufacturing system requires a single database to be shared by the entire manufacturing organization. Database consist of up-to-date, detailed, and accurate information relating to products, designs, machines, processes, materials, production, finances, purchasing, sales, marketing, and inventory. This vast array of data is stored in computer memory and recalled or modified as necessary either by individuals in the organization or by the CIM system itself, while it is controlling various aspects of design and production.

A database generally consists of the following items, some of which are classified as technical and others as nontechnical.

- Product data: Part shape, dimensions, and specifications.
- Data management attributes: Revision level, and part number.
- Production data: Manufacturing processes used.
- Operational data: Scheduling, lot sizes, and assembly requirements.
- Resources data: Capital, machines, equipment, tooling, and personnel, and their capabilities.

Databases are built by individuals and by the use of various sensors in the production machinery and equipment. Data are collected automatically by a data-acquisition system (DAS), which can report the number of parts being produced per unit of time, their dimensional accuracy, surface finish, weight, and other characteristics at specified rates of sampling.

The components of DAS include microprocessors, transducers, and analog-to-digital converters (ADCs). Data-acquisition systems are also capable of analyzing the data and transferring them to other computers for purposes such as statistical analysis, data presentation, and the forecasting of product demand.

Several factors are important in the use and implementation of databases.

- They should be timely, accurate, easily accessible, easily shared, and user-friendly.
- Because it is used for various purposes and by many people, the database must be flexible and responsive to the needs of different uses.
- CIM systems can be accessed by designers, manufacturing engineers, process planners, financial officers, and the management of the company by using appropriate access codes. Of course, companies must protect data against tampering or unauthorized use.
- If there are problems with data accuracy, the correct data should be recovered and restored.

### 3. The CIM Wheel

The Computer and Automated Systems Association (CASA) of the Society of Manufacturing (SME) developed the CIM wheel (Figure 2.15) as a way to comprehensively but concisely illustrate the concept of CIM. The CASA/SME developed the CIM wheel to include several distinct components:

- Manufacturing management/ human resource management;
- Marketing;
- Strategic planning;
- Finance;
- Product/process design and planning;
- Manufacturing planning and control;
- Factory automation.

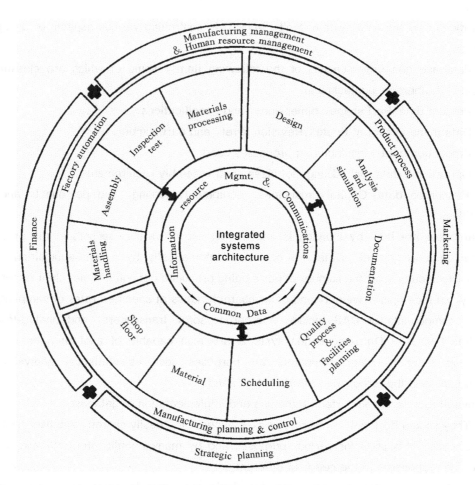

Figure 2.15 SME/CASA CIM wheel

# NEW WORDS AND EXPRESSIONS

methodology [meθə'dɔlədʒi] n. 操作法，方法学，工艺
assemblage [ə'semblidʒ] n. (机器的)安装，装配
comprehensive [ˌkɔmpri'hensiv] a. 全面的，广泛的
invoice ['invɔis] n. 发票，发货单，货物
uniformity [ˌjuːni'fɔːmiti] n. 均匀性，均匀度，一致性
inventory ['invəntri] n. 详细目录，存货
up-to-date ['ʌptə'deit] a. 最近的，最新状态的，文件内容更新的

specification [ˌspesifi'keiʃən] n. 说明书，技术要求
concisely [kən'saisli] ad. 简明扼要地
computer-integrated manufacturing 计算机集成制造
data-acquisition system (DAS) 数据采集系统
analog-to-digital converter (ADC) 模拟-数字转换器
CASA (Computer and Automated System Association) (美)计算机与自动化系统协会
SME (Society of Manufacturing Engineers) (美)制造工程师学会

# NOTES

1) The various levels of automation in manufacturing operations have been extended further by including increasing information processing functions, utilizing an extensive network of interactive computers.

在制造加工操作中各种自动化水平通过增加信息处理功能,使用交互式计算机的扩展网络功能,从而得以进一步扩展。

automation 为句中主语,have been extended 为谓语部分,由 by 引导的两个并列动名词短语 increasing information processing functions 和 utilizing an extensive network of interactive computers 作状语。

2) Because CIM ideally should involve the total operation of a company, it must have an extensive database concerning technical and business aspects of the operation.

理想的 CIM 应该包括一个公司所有的运转操作,因此它必须要有涉及操作过程的技术上和经营上的一个非常大的数据库。

concerning *prep.* 关于,涉及,就……来说

concerning the matter 提到那件事

3) For new manufacturing plants, on the other hand, comprehensive and long-range strategic planning covering all phases of the operation is essential in order to fully benefit from CIM.

另一方面,对于新的制造厂家,为了最大限度地获益于 CIM 技术,涵盖工厂运作的所有方面的广泛的、长期的策略计划是必须的。

4) The subsystems are designed, developed, and implemented in such a manner that the output of one subsystem serves as the input of another subsystem.

子系统的设计、开发和实现要按照一个子系统的输出作为另一个子系统的输入模式进行。

in a manner that *prep.* 以……的方式

5) This vast array of data is stored in computer memory and recalled or modified as necessary either by individuals in the organization or by the CIM system itself, while it is controlling various aspects of design and production.

这样大量的数据存储在计算机的存储器中,需要时由机构中的个人或 CIM 系统本身重新调用或改动,同时它也控制着设计和生产中的各个方面。

while 引导的从句中的 it 仍指 this vast array of data。

# EXERCISES

1. After reading the text above, summarize the main ideas in oral.

2. Fill in the blanks with proper words or phrases according to the text (note the proper tense).

(1) Computer-integrated manufacturing is a broad term describing the computerized integration of all aspects of d_____, p_____, m_____, d_____, and

m_____.

(2) Computer-integrated manufacturing systems consist of subsystems such as: b_____, p_____, m_____, p_____, and s_____.

(3) These subsystems usually are divided into two functions: b_____ and b_____.

(4) Databases are built by i_____ and by the use of v_____ in the production machinery and equipment. Data are collected automatically by a d_____.

(5) The components of DAS include m_____, t_____, and a_____.

3. Translate the following phrases into Chinese according to the text.

(1) statistical analysis    (2) access codes
(3) process planning    (4) shop floor
(5) ADC    (6) DAS
(7) dimensional accuracy    (8) rates of sampling
(9) material-requirements planning
(10) extensive network of interactive computers
(11) large-scale integrated communications system

4. Translate the following phrases into English according to the text.

(1) 信息处理功能    (2) 长期的策略计划
(3) 人力资源    (4) 存货清单
(5) 车间监控系统    (6) 单位时间内生产零件数
(7) 表面光洁度    (8) 统计分析
(9) 产品需求预测

5. Write a 100-word summary according to the text.

# READING MATERIAL

## 1. Introduction

Computer integrated manufacturing (CIM) is the term used to describe the modern approach to manufacturing. Although CIM encompasses many of the other advanced manufacturing technologies such as computer numerical control (CNC), computer-aided design/computer-aided manufacturing (CAD/CAM), robotics, and just-in-time delivery (JIT), it is more than a new technology or a new concept. Computer integrated manufacturing is an entirely new approach to manufacturing, a new way of doing business.

To understand CIM, it is necessary to begin with a comparison of modern and traditional manufacturing. Modern manufacturing encompasses all of the activities and processes necessary to convert raw materials into finished products, deliver them to the market, support them in the market, and support them in the field. These activities include the following:

● Identifying a need for a product;
● Designing a product to meet the needs;
● Obtaining the raw materials needed to produce the product;

- Applying appropriate processes to transform the raw materials into finished products;
- Transporting finished products to the market;
- Maintaining the product to ensure proper performance in the field.

This broad, modern view of manufacturing can be compared with the more limited traditional view that focused almost entirely on the conversion processed. The old approach excluded such critical pre-conversion elements as market analysis research, development, and design as well as after-conversion elements such as product delivery and product maintenance. In other words, in the old approach of manufacturing, only those processes that tool place on the shop floor were considered manufacturing. This traditional approach of separating the overall concept into numerous stand-alone specialized elements was not fundamentally changed with the advent of automation.

With CIM, not only are the various elements automated, but the islands of automation are all linked together or integrated. Integration means that a system can provide complete and instantaneous sharing of information. In modern manufacturing, integration is accomplished by computers. CIM, then, is the total integration of all components involved in converting raw materials into finished products and getting the products to the market, as shown in Figure 2.16.

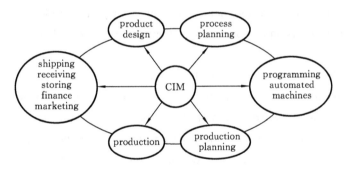

Figure 2.16  Major components of CIM

## 2. Historical Development of CIM

The term computer integrated manufacturing was developed in 1974 by Joseph Harrionton who wrote about tying islands of automation together through the use of computers as the title of a book. It has taken many years for CIM to develop as a concept, but integrated manufacturing is not really new. In fact, integration is where manufacturing actually began. Manufacturing has evolved through four distinct stages.

1) Manual manufacturing

Manual manufacturing using simple hand tools was actually integrated manufacturing. All information needed to design, produce, and deliver a product was readily available because it resided in the mind of the person who performed all of the necessary tasks. The tool of integration in the earliest years of manufacturing was the human mind of the craftsman who designed, produced, and delivered the product. An example of integrated manual manufacturing is the village blacksmith producing a special tool for a local farmer. The blacksmith would have in his mind all of the information needed to design, produce, and deliver the farmer's tools. In this example, all elements of manufacturing are integrated.

2) Mechanization/Specialization

With the advent of the industrial revolution, manufacturing processes became both specialized and mechanized. Instead of one person designing, producing, and delivering a product, workers and/or machines performed specialized tasks within each of these broad areas. Communication among these separate entities was achieved by using drawings, specifications, job orders, process plans, and a variety of other communication aids. To ensure that the finished product could match the planned product, the concept of quality control was introduced.

The advantage of the mechanization/specialization stage was that it permitted mass production interchangeability of parts, different levels of accuracy, and uniformity. The disadvantage is that the lack of integration led to a great deal of waste.

3) Automation

Automation improved the performance and enhanced the capabilities of both people and machines within specialized manufacturing components. For example, CAD enhanced the capability of designers and drafters. CNC enhanced the capabilities of machinists and computer-assisted planners. But the improvements brought on by automation were isolated within individual components or islands. Because of this, automation did not always live up to its potential.

To understand the limitations of automation with regard to overall productivity improvement, consider the following analogy. Suppose that various subsystems of an automobile (i.e., the engine, steering, brake) were automated to make the driver's job easier. Automatic acceleration, deceleration, steering, and braking would certainly be more efficient than the manual versions. However, consider what would happen if these various automated subsystems were not tied together in a way that allowed them to communicate and share accurate, up-to-date information instantly and continually. One system might attempt to accelerate the automobile while another system was attempting to apply the brakes. The same limitations apply in an automated manufacturing setting. These limitations are what led to the current stage in the development of manufacturing integration.

4) Integration

With the advent of the computer age, manufacturing has developed full circle. It began as a totally integrated concept and, with CIM, has once again become one. However, there are major differences in the manufacturing integration of today and that of the manual era of the past. First, the instrument of integration in the manual era was the human mind. The instrument of integration in modern manufacturing is the computer. Second, processes in the modern manufacturing setting are still specialized and automated.

Another way to view the historical development of CIM is by examining the ways in which some of the individual components of CIM have developed over the years. Such components as designing, planning, and production have evolved both in processes and in the tools and equipment used to accomplish the processes.

Design has evolved from a manual process using tools such as slide rules, triangles, pencils, scales, and erasers into an automated process known as CAD. Process planning has evolved from a manual process using planning tables, diagrams, and charts into an automated process known as CAPP. Production has evolved from a manual process involving manually controlled machines into an automated process known as computer-aided manufacturing (CAM).

These individual components of manufacturing evolved over the years onto separate islands of automation. However, communication among these islands was still handled manually. This limited the level of improvement in productivity that could be accomplished in the overall manufacturing process. When these islands and other automated components of manufacturing are linked together through computer networks, these limitations can be overcome.

# Lesson 16　Advanced Machining Processes

## TEXT

The traditional machining processes described in the preceding lessons remove material by chip formation, abrasion, or microchipping. There are situations, however, where these processes are not satisfactory, economical, or even possible.

- The hardness and strength of the material is very high (typically above 400 HB) or the material is too brittle.
- The workpiece is too flexible, slender, or delicate to withstand the cutting or grinding forces, or the parts are difficult to fixture—that is, to clamp in workholding devices.
- The shape of the part is complex, including such features as internal and external profiles or small-diameter holes in fuel-injection nozzles.
- Surface finish and dimensional tolerance requirements are more rigorous than those obtained by other processes.
- Temperature rise and residual stresses in workpiece are not desirable or acceptable.

The requirements led to the development of chemical, electrical, laser, and other means of material removal. Beginning in the 1940s, these advanced methods, which in the past have been called nontraditional or unconventional machining, are outlined in Table 2.1.

Table 2.1　Advanced machining processes

| Process | Characteristics | Process parameters and typical material removal rate or cutting speed |
|---|---|---|
| Chemical machining (CM) | Shallow removal (up to 12 mm) on large flat or curved surfaces; blanking of thin sheets; low tooling and equipment cost; suitable for low production runs. | 0.0025—0.1 mm/min |
| Electrochemical machining (ECM) | Complex shapes with deep cavities; highest rate of material removal among nontraditional processes; expensive tooling and equipment; high power consumption; medium to high production quantity. | V: 5—25dc; A:1.5—8A/mm$^2$; 2.5—12 mm/min, depending on current density |
| Electrochemical grinding (ECG) | Cutting off and sharpening hard materials, such as tungsten-carbide tools; also used as a honing process; higher removal rate than grinding. | A: 1—3 A/mm$^2$; Typically 25 mm$^3$/s per 1000A |
| Electrical-discharge machining (EDM) | Shaping and cutting complex parts made of hard materials; some surface damage may result; also used as a grinding and cutting process; expensive tooling and equipment. | V:50—380;A:0.1—500;Typically 300 mm$^3$/min |

续表

| Process | Characteristics | Process parameters and typical material removal rate or cutting speed |
|---|---|---|
| Wire EDM | Contour cutting of flat or curved surfaces; expensive equipment. | Varies with material and thickness |
| Laser-beam machining(LBM) | Cutting and holemaking on thin materials; heat-affected zone; does not require a vacuum; expensive equipment; consumes much energy. | 0.50—7.5 m/min |
| Electron-beam machining (EBM) | Cutting and holemaking on thin materials; very small holes and slots; heat-affected zone; requires a vacuum; expensive equipment. | 1—2 mm³/min |
| Water-jet machining (WJM) | Cutting all types of nonmetallic materials to 25 mm and greater in thickness; suitable for contour cutting of flexible materials; no thermal damage; noisy. | Varies considerably with material |
| Abrasive water-jet machining (AWJM) | Single or multilayer cutting of metallic and nonmetallic materials. | Up to 7.5 m/min |
| Abrasive-jet machining (AJM) | Cutting, slotting, deburring, etching, and cleaning of metallic and nonmetallic materials; manually controlled; tends to round off sharp edges; hazardous. | Varies considerably with material |

Advanced machining processes have unique capabilities, and involve chemical, electrochemical, electrical, laser, and high-energy-beam sources of energy. The mechanical properties of the workpiece material are not significant because these processes rely on mechanisms that do not involve the strength, hardness, ductility, or toughness of the material. Rather, they involve physical, chemical, and electrical properties.

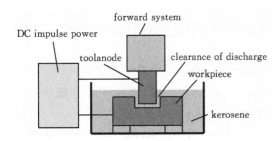

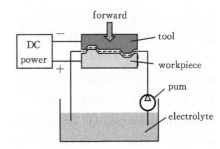

Figure 2.17  Schematic diagram of EDM       Figure 2.18  Schematic diagram of ECM

Chemical and electrical methods of machining are particularly suitable for hard materials and complex shapes. They do not produce forces (and can therefore be used for thin, slender, and flexible workpiece), significant temperatures, or residual stresses. However, the effects of these processes on surface integrity must be investigated, as they can damage surfaces considerably, reducing the fatigue life of the product.

High-energy-beam machining processes basically utilize laser beams, electron beams, and plasma arc. They have important industrial applications, possess high flexibility of operation, and are economically competitive with various other processes.

Water-jet, abrasive water-jet and abrasive-jet machining processes can be used for cutting as well as deburring operations. Because they do not utilize hard tooling, they have inherent flexibility of operation.

The need for economical methods of material removal will increase further because of the development of new materials, ceramics, and composites as well as complex shapes that are difficult to machine with traditional processes.

Electrochemical machining is becoming increasingly important because of the demanding requirements of computer-chip and microelectromechanical systems (MEMS) manufacture.

In spite of their advantages, the effects of advanced machining processes on the properties and service life of workpieces are important considerations, particularly for critical applications.

The trend in the machinery for advanced machining processes is for computer controls, using multiple-axis robots, as well as exploring possibilities of combining different processes for flexibility and improved productivity.

Laser-beam and electrical-discharge machining of automotive and various other components are being implemented at an increasing rate.

## NEW WORDS AND EXPRESSIONS

abrasion [əˈbreiʒən] n. 磨蚀，剥蚀
profile [ˈprəufail] n. 外形，轮廓
rigorous [ˈrigərəs] a. 严格的
nonmetallic [ˌnɔnmiˈtælik] a. 非金属的
hazardous [ˈhæzədəs] a. 凭运气的
toughness [ˈtʌfnis] n. 韧性
plasma [ˈplæzmə] n. 等离子体，等离子区
inherent [inˈhiərənt] a. 固有的，内在的
fuel-injection nozzle 喷油嘴
chemical machining (CM) 化学加工
electrochemical machining (ECM) 电化学加工
electrochemical grinding (ECG) 电化学磨削
tungsten carbide 硬质合金碳化钨
electrical-discharge machining (EDM) 电火花加工
wire EDM 线切割加工
laser-beam machining (LBM) 激光束加工
electron-beam machining (EBM) 电子束加工
water-jet machining (WJM) 水射流加工
abrasive-jet machining (AJM) 磨料射流加工
abrasive water-jet machining (AWJM) 磨料水射流加工
round off 倒圆，使完美完成
plasma arc 等离子弧，等离子体电弧
computer-chip 计算机芯片
microelectromechanical systems (MEMS) 微机电系统

## NOTES

1) The traditional machining processes described in the preceding lessons remove material by chip formation, abrasion, or microchipping. There are situations, however, where these processes are not satisfactory, economical, or even possible.

在前面课程中介绍的传统加工方法是通过形成切屑,磨料加工,或者微细切屑等方式切除材料。然而,在有些切削条件下,这些加工方法要么不能满足加工要求,要么不经济,甚至于难以实现。

2) The requirements led to the development of chemical, electrical, laser, and other means of material removal.

这些要求促使了如化学去除法、电去除、激光去除以及用其他材料去除的方法的发展。

3) Advanced machining processes have unique capabilities, and involve chemical, electrochemical, electrical, laser, and high-energy-beam sources of energy. The mechanical properties of the workpiece material are not significant because these processes rely on mechanisms that do not involve the strength, hardness, ductility, or toughness of the material. Rather, they involve physical, chemical, and electrical properties.

先进制造工艺具有其独特的加工能力,其加工原理涉及化学、电化学、电、激光和高能束等能源的应用。由于这类加工方法的原理与材料的强度、刚度、延展性和韧性无关,而只与其物理、化学和电特性有关,因此在加工时工件材料的力学性能并不重要。

4) The trend in the machinery for advanced machining processes is for computer controls, using multiple-axis robots, as well as exploring possibilities of combining different processes for flexibility and improved productivity.

采用计算机控制是先进制造工艺设备的发展趋势。通过应用多轴机器人和寻求不同工艺方法的组合,达到增加设备柔性和提高生产率的目的。

## EXERCISES

1. After reading the text above, summarize the main ideas in oral.
2. Fill in the blanks with proper words or phrases according to the text (note the proper tense).

(1) The workpieces is too f_____, s_____, or delicate to withstand the cutting or grinding forces.

(2) Temperature rise and r_____ stresses in workpiece are not desirable or acceptable.

(3) In _____ of their advantages, the effects of advanced machining processes on the properties and service life of workpieces are important considerations, particularly for c_____ applications.

(4) Advanced machining processes have u_____ capabilities.

(5) Surface finish and dimensional tolerance requirements are more r_____ than those obtained by other processes.

(6) They have important industrial applications, possess h_____ of operation, and are economically c_____ with various other processes.

3. Translate the following phrases into Chinese according to the text.

(1) at an increasing rate

(2) in spite of their advantages

(3) high-energy-beam sources of energy
(4) reducing the fatigue life of the product
(5) inherent flexibility of operation
(6) complex shapes with deep cavities
(7) small-diameter holes in fuel-injection nozzle
(8) surface finish and dimensional tolerance

4. Translate the following phrases into English according to the text.
(1) 激光束加工          (2) 电火花切割
(3) 电化学火花磨削      (4) 计算机控制
(5) 材料的力学性能      (6) 微机电系统
(7) 硬质合金刀具

5. Write a 100-word summary according to the text.

# READING MATERIAL

## Nanofabrication

Nanofabrication involves the generation and manipulation of structures with characteristic lengths less than 1 μm (40 μin.), nano meaning $10^{-9}$. While devices with scales on the order of micrometers have been produced for decades, nanoscale processes promise to provide major improvements and revolutionize small-scale devices. Potential applications of these materials and devices include electronics applications, drug delivery, revolutionary mechanical devices, sensors, and medical diagnostic systems.

A distinction should be made between (a) the production of nanoscale materials or particles (nanosynthesis) and (b) those processes which manipulate particles or geometries on a nanoscale (nanofabrication). Each of these has very different approaches and limitations.

Many of the nanofabrication processes are more accurate and precise versions of the processes used in integrated-circuit manufacture, such as photolithography, lithography, and related processes. Some limited lithography can be performed on an atomic force microscope (AFM) which can even allow the manipulation of individual atoms.

With the extremely small length scales and associated close dimensional tolerances that must be maintained in the fabrication of nanoscale structures, chemical etching or wet etching cannot be applied because of the tendency to undercut below a protective mask. For this reason, extremely fine structures are produced with reactive ion etching (RIE) or dry etching. In this process, ionized gas plasma is driven by radio frequency power applied to the workpiece electrode and strikes (usually) the metallic workpiece. This causes the metal to sputter, and can generate very high-quality etches with very high depth-to-width ratios.

Reactive ion etching shows great promise as a nanofabrication approach, but it will undercut a vertical wall. Recent developments include coating side walls with a one or two molecular layer thick. Polymer to eliminate undercut. Special care must be taken to eliminate residual stresses in the workpiece, since as material is removed; warpage is likely if such stresses are present.

Atomic force microscopes have been used in nanoscale lithography and have great potential for small-scale surface etching. These microscopes are mainly used as surface visualization tools. However, when used with the proper cantilever, AFMs can perform lithography with atomic resolution, and have even been used to manipulate single molecules and atoms on surfaces.

Nanofabrication has the potential to revolutionize many industries, including information storage, integrated circuit manufacture, and medical drug delivery systems. For example, it has been estimated that if a bit of information could be stored in 100 atoms, then all of the books ever written could be stored in a 0.5 mm cube. Scientists have envisioned the days when microscopic robots will be injected into the body and deliver drugs exactly where needed.

The greatest hindrance to nanofabrication thus far has been the limited capability of nanofabrication processes. For example, an atomic force microscope can only process a section of a surface approximately $0.01 \text{ mm}^2$ at a time, and typical lithography speeds are on the order of 10 μm per second. These are orders of magnitude too low for industrial uses other than for fundamental research, although new methods of increasing capacity are constantly being investigated.

# Lesson 17  Material Handling and Movement

## TEXT

During a typical manufacturing operation, raw materials and parts are moved from storage to machines, from machine to machine, from inspection to assembly and inventory, and finally to shipment. Workpieces are loaded on machines (for example, a forging is mounted on a milling machine bed for further processing, or sheet metal is fed into a press for stamping), parts are removed from one machine and loaded on another (for example, a machined forging is subsequently ground for better surface finish and dimensional accuracy), and finished parts are inspected prior to being assembled into a finished product.

Similarly, tools, molds, dies and various other equipment and fixtures are also moved in manufacturing plants. Cutting tools are mounted on lathes, dies are placed in presses or hammers, grinding wheels are mounted on spindles, and parts are mounted on special fixtures for dimensional measurement and inspection.

These materials must be moved either manually or by some mechanical means, and time is required to transport them from one location to another. Material handling maybe defined as the functions and systems associated with the transportation, storage, and control of materials and parts in the total manufacturing cycle of a product. The total time required for manufacturing depends on part size and shape and on the set of operations required. Idle time and the time required for transporting materials can constitute the majority of the time consumed.

Plant layout is an important aspect of the orderly flow of materials and components throughout the manufacturing cycle. The time and distances required for moving raw materials and parts should be minimized, and storage areas and service centers should be organized accordingly. For parts requiring multiple operations, equipment should be grouped around the operator or the industrial robot.

Material handling should, therefore, be an integral part of the planning, the implementing, and the controlling of manufacturing operations. Further more, material handling should be repeatable and predictable. Consider, for example, what happens if a part or workpiece is loaded improperly into a forging die, a chuck, or the collet on a lathe. The consequences of such action may well be broken dies and tools, improperly made parts, or parts that are out of dimensional tolerance. This action can also present safety hazards and possibly cause injury to the operator and nearby personnel.

### 1. Methods of Material Handling

Several factors have to be considered in selecting a suitable material-handling method for a particular manufacturing operation.

- the shape, weight, and characteristics of the parts;
- the types and distances of movements, and the position and orientation of the parts during movement and at their final destination;
- the conditions of the path along which the parts are to be transported;
- the degree of automation, the level of control desired, and integration with other systems and equipment;
- the operator skill required;
- and economic considerations.

For small-batch manufacturing operations, raw materials and parts can be handled and transported by hand, but this method is generally costly. Moreover, because it involves human beings, this practice can be unpredictable and unreliable. It can even be unsafe to the operator, because of the weight and shape of the parts to be moved and because of environmental factors (such as heat and smoke in foundries and forging plants). In automated manufacturing plants, computer-controlled material and parts flow are rapidly being implemented. These changes have resulted in improved repeatability and in lower labor costs.

## 2. Equipments

Various types of equipment can be used to move materials, such as conveyors, rollers, self powered monorails, carts, forklift trucks, and various mechanical, electrical, magnetic, pneumatic, and hydraulic devices and manipulators. Manipulators can be designed to be controlled directly by the operator, or they can be automated for repeated operations ( such as the loading and unloading of parts from machine tools, presses, and furnaces).

Manipulators are capable of gripping and moving heavy parts and of orienting them as required between the manufacturing and assembly operations. Machines are often used in a sequence, so that workpieces are transferred directly from machine to machine. Machinery combinations having the capability of conveying parts without the use of additional material-handling apparatus are called integral transfer devices.

Flexible material handling and movement, with real-time control, has become an integral part of modern manufacturing. Industrial robots, specially designed pallets, and automated guided vehicles (AGVs) are used extensively in flexible manufacturing systems to move parts and to orient them as required (Figure 2.19).

Automated guided vehicles, which are the latest development in material movement in plants, operate automatically along pathways with in-floor wiring (or tapes for optical scanning) and without operator intervention. This transport system has high flexibility and is capable of random delivery to different workstations. It optimizes the movement of materials and parts in case of congestion around workstations, machine break down (downtime), or the failure of one section of the system. The movements of AGVs are planned so that they interface with automated storage / retrieval systems (AS / RS), to utilize warehouse space efficiently and to reduce labor costs. Nowadays, however, these systems are considered undesirable, because of the current focus on minimal inventory and on just-in-time production methods.

Figure 2.19 Automated Guided Vehicles (AGVs)

## NEW WORDS AND EXPRESSIONS

subsequently [ˈsʌbsikwəntli] ad. 后来，随后
die [dai] n. 冲模
unpredictable [ˌʌnpriˈdiktəbl] n. 不可预测的事
unreliable [ˌʌnriˈlaiəbl] a. 不可靠的
unsafe [ˌʌnˈseif] a. 不安全的，危险的
foundry [ˈfaundri] n. 铸造，翻砂，铸造工厂
repeatability [riˌpiːtəˈbiliti] n. 可重复性，重合性，再现性
cart [kɑːt] n. 手推车
pneumatic [njuː(ː)ˈmætik] a. 气动的
hydraulic [haiˈdrɔːlik] a. 液压的
manipulator [məˈnipjuleitə] n. 操作者，操纵者，操纵器
pathway [ˈpɑːθwei] n. 路，径
intervention [ˌintə(ː)ˈvenʃən] n. 干涉

delivery [diˈlivəri] n. 发送，传输
congestion [kənˈdʒestʃən] n. 拥塞，[医]充血
warehouse [ˈwɛəhaus] 仓库
raw materials 毛坯，原材料
special fixture 专用夹具
industrial robot 工业机器人
self powered monorail 自引轨道
forklift truck 叉车
in-floor wiring 埋线方式
optical scanning 光学扫描
in case of 如果发生，万一
break down 中止，停机
downtime 停机时间
automated storage system 自动储存系统
retrieval system (RS) 自动检索系统
interface with 同……接口

## NOTES

1) Material handling maybe defined as the functions and systems associated with the transportation, storage, and control of materials and parts in the total manufacturing cycle of a product. The total time required for manufacturing depends on part size and shape and on the set of operations required. Idle time and the time required for transporting materials can constitute the majority of the time consumed.

物料传输可以定义为在产品的整个制造周期中原材料和工件的输送、储存及其控制的功能模块和系统。制造所需要的总时间取决于工件尺寸、形状复杂程度以及相关的工艺过程，其中空载时间和传送物料的时间可能占据总消耗时间的大部分。

2) Material handling should, therefore, be an integral part of the planning, the

implementing, and the controlling of manufacturing operations. Further more, material handling should be repeatable and predictable. Consider, for example, what happens if a part or workpiece is loaded improperly into a forging die, a chuck, or the collet on a lathe. The consequences of such action may well be broken dies and tools, improperly made parts, or parts that are out of dimensional tolerance. This action can also present safety hazards and possibly cause injury to the operator and nearby personnel.

因此，物料传输应该是制造活动的计划、实施和控制环节中不可或缺的组成部分。此外，物料传输应该是可重复的和可预报的。想想看，当零件在锻模中安装不恰当，或在车床的卡盘、弹簧夹具中安装不正确，这会引起什么样的后果？其结果要么是损坏模具、夹具，要么是加工出尺寸超差的不合格零件，甚至还可能引起安全事故，伤及操作者和附近人员。

3) Manipulators are capable of gripping and moving heavy parts and of orienting them as required between the manufacturing and assembly operations. Machines are often used in a sequence, so that workpieces are transferred directly from machine to machine. Machinery combinations having the capability of conveying parts without the use of additional material-handling apparatus are called integral transfer devices.

根据指令要求，机械手能够根据要求在加工和装配工作位置之间抓取并移动工件，还可以使工件定向。通常机床是按顺序摆放的，这使得工件可以直接从一台机床传送到另一台机床。不用额外的物料传输设备就可以完成传输零件任务的机械装置的组合称为集成传输装置。

4) Flexible material handling and movement, with real-time control, has become an integral part of modern manufacturing. Industrial robots, specially designed pallets, and automated guided vehicles (AGVs) are used extensively in flexible manufacturing systems to move parts and to orient them as required.

具备实时控制功能的柔性物料传输装置已经是现代制造系统的核心组成部分。为了按照指令要求移动和定向零件，在柔性制造系统中广泛地采用了工业机器人、专用工件托盘和自动导向运输小车系统（AGVs）。

# EXERCISES

1. After reading the text above, summarize the main ideas in oral.
2. Fill in the blanks with proper words or phrases according to the text (note the proper tense).

(1) Finished parts are inspected p_____ being assembled into a finished product.

(2) These materials must be moved e_____ manually _____ by some mechanical means, and time is required to transport them f_____ one location _____ another.

(3) The total time required for manufacturing d_____ on part size and shape and on the set of operations required.

(4) This action can also p_____ safety hazards and possibly c_____ injury to the operator and nearby personnel.

(5) It optimizes the movement of materials and parts i_____ congestion around workstations, machine b_____ (downtime), or the failure of one section of

the system.

3. Translate the following phrases into Chinese according to the text.

(1) to ground for better surface finish and dimensional accuracy

(2) the functions and systems associated with the transportation, storage, and control of materials

(3) the total manufacturing cycle of a product

(4) out of dimensional tolerance

(5) to present safety hazards

(6) an integral part of modern manufacturing

(7) constitute the majority of the time consumed

4. Translate the following phrases into English according to the text.

(1) 毛坯和零件　　　　　　(2) 物料传输装置

(3) 自动导向运输小车系统　　(4) 工业机器人

(5) 专用工件托盘　　　　　　(6) 集成传输装置

(7) 条码译码系统　　　　　　(8) 磁条编码

(9) 无线射频系统　　　　　　(10) 机器视觉识别

5. Write a 100-word summary according to the text.

# READING MATERIAL

## 1. Flexible Manufacturing Systems (FMS)

A flexible manufacturing system integrates all major elements of manufacturing into a highly automated system. FMS consists of a number of manufacturing cells, each containing an industrial robot (serving several CNC machines) and an automated material-handling system, all interfaced with a central computer. Different computer instructions for the manufacturing process can be downloaded for each successive part passing through the workstation.

This system is highly automated and is capable of optimizing each step of the total manufacturing operation. These steps may involve one or more processes and operations (such as machining, grinding, cutting, forming, powder metallurgy, heat treating, and finishing), as well as handling of raw materials, inspection, and assembly. The most common applications of FMS to date have been in machining and assembly operations. A variety of FMS technologies are available from machine-tool manufacturers.

Flexible manufacturing systems represent the highest level of efficiency, sophistication, and productivity that has been achieved in manufacturing plants (Figure 2.20). The flexibility of FMS is that it can handle a variety of part configurations and produce them in any order.

FMS can be regarded as a system which combines the benefits of two other systems:(a) the highly productive but inflexible transfer lines, and (b) job-shop production, which can produce large product variety on stand-alone machines but is inefficient. The relative characteristics of transfer lines and FMS are shown in Table 2.2. Note that in FMS, the time

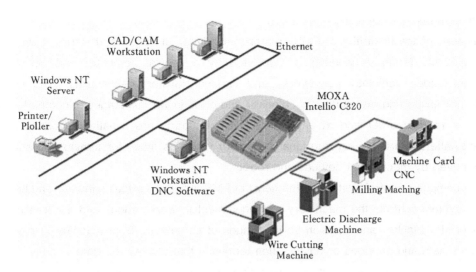

Figure 2.20 Flexible Manufacturing Systems (FMS)

required for changeover to a different part is very short. The quick response to product and market-demand variations is a major attribute of FMS.

Table 2.2 Comparison of the characteristics of transfer lines and flexible manufacturing systems

| Characteristic | Transfer Line | FMS |
| --- | --- | --- |
| Types of part made | Generally few | Infinite |
| Lot size | >100 | 1—50 |
| Part changing time | 0.5 hr to 8 hr | 1 min |
| Tool change | Manual | Automatic |
| Adaptive control | Difficult | Available |
| Inventory | High | Low |
| Production during break down | None | Partial |
| Efficiency | 60%—70% | 85% |
| Justification for capital expenditure | Simple | Difficult |

## 2. Elements of FMS

The basic elements of a flexible manufacturing system are (a) workstations, (b) automated handling and transport of materials and parts, and (c) control systems. The workstations are arranged to yield the greatest efficiency in production, with an orderly flow of materials, parts, and products through the system.

The types of machines in workstations depend on the type of production. For machining operations, they usually consist of a variety of three-to five-axis machining centers, CNC lathes, milling machines, drill presses, and grinders, also included various other equipments, such as that for automated inspection (including coordinate-measuring machines), assembly, and cleaning.

Other types of operations suitable for FMS include sheet metal forming, punching and shearing, and forging. They incorporate furnaces, forging machines, trimming presses, heat-treating facilities, and cleaning equipment.

Because of the flexibility of FMS, material-handling, storage, and retrieval systems are very important. Material handling is controlled by a central computer and performed by automated guided vehicles, conveyors, and various transfer mechanisms. The system is capable of transporting raw materials, blanks, and parts in various stages of completion to any machine in random order and at any time. Prismatic parts are usually moved on specially designed pallets. Parts having rotational symmetry (such as those for turning operations) are usually moved by mechanical devices and robots.

The computer control system as the heart of FMS includes various software and hardware. This sub-system controls the machinery and equipment in workstations and the transporting of raw materials, blanks, and parts in varies stages of completion from machine to machine. It also stores data and provides communication terminals that display the data visually.

Integrated manufacturing systems are being implemented to various degrees to optimize operations, reduce costs, and improve product quality.

Computer-integrated manufacturing has become the most important means of improving productivity, responding to changing market demands, and better controlling manufacturing and management functions. With extensive use of computers and of the rapid developments in sophisticated software, product designs (and their analysis and simulation) are now more detailed and thorough.

New developments in manufacturing operations, such as group technology, cellular manufacturing, and flexible manufacturing systems, are contributing significantly to improved productivity.

Artificial intelligence is likely to create new opportunities in all aspects of manufacturing science, engineering, and technology.

The trend in manufacturing is toward greater product variety, shorter product life cycles, and increased and continuing emphasis on high product quality at low cost.

Utilization of computers in all phases of manufacturing will continue to grow. An increasing trend is the use of networking tools (hardware, software, and protocols) within a company to link all departments and functions into a self-contained, fully compatible network.

Material-requirements planning activities are incorporating marketing and business issues directly into the database, in an activity referred to as Enterprise Resource Planning (ERP).

# Part III

# Mechatronics

# Lesson 18  Mechatronics

## TEXT

Mechatronics is an engineering field which, together with intelligent structures, robotics, micro-, and nanoelectromechanical systems, etc., appears as part of "high-tech" fields of mechanical and electrical engineering. Mechatronics systems represent integrated mixed systems. Besides a mechanical structure and mechanisms for motion transmission, such systems contain electrical and electronic components, as well as sensors and actuators, under computer monitoring and control.

Mechatronics is the engineering field of the design of mixed computer integrated electromechanical systems. Modeling mixed systems, virtual prototyping, and hardware in the loop experimentation are some of the methods used in mechatronic system design.

Traditional mechanical systems (mechanisms or machines) can be built with mechanical components only. In the case of James Watt's steam engine, steam energy is converted into kinetic energy of the rotational motion of a shaft. The incoming flow rate of steam is controlled by a fly ball governor. This is an example of a mechanical feedback controller for velocity.

Electric energy and electric signals were made available for industrial applications in the twentieth century and proved to be more efficient for the conversion into mechanical energy and easier to process as signals for measurement and control. In the last few decades, digital computers (for example personal computers and embedded microcontrollers) replaced most of the analog devices used previously for signal processing. As a result, most systems that provide motion and force (for example vehicles, manipulators, etc.) to contain a mixture of mechanical, electrical, electronic, and digital components. In fact, today most systems are mixed systems. The design of these mixed systems requires knowledge from all these fields. To be able to communicate, engineers specialized in any of these fields need working knowledge from other fields. The purpose of mechatronics is to provide knowledge about the mechanical, electrical, electronics, and digital components needed for choosing the components of the systems, for analyzing the interface requirements for signals, power transmission, and conversion, and for investigating the performance of the integrated system. Mechanical engineers have to deal with issues regarding to electrical and computer engineering design, whereas electrical and computer engineers have to understand mechanical structure as well as mechanism machine design issues. Mixed systems design requires a mechatronics specialization.

Electrical, mechanical, structural, and electronic components of a mechatronic system operate as an integrated system under real-time computer monitoring and control with interface for operator supervision and direction. Mixed system integration requires energy transmission and conversion (for example electrical in mechanical energy) such that power output is modulated to be in agreement with operator direction and computer control algorithms. Using a terminology in fashion today, this is the case of "intelligent" energy that uses a raw energy source and modulates its output rate for end-use requirements. In the example of a car, the raw energy of the gas stored in the tank is modulated in the carburetor to follow the driver's control of the acceleration pedal. Car velocity is modified by changing the gas flow rate. Given the constant specific energy content of the gas, the change of the flow rate changes the rate of energy transfer from the gas, after combustion in the engine, to the motor shaft. Because it follows the driver's commands, this can be seen as an "intelligent" power output (or, less than intelligent in the case of careless driving).

In mechatronic systems, not only the energy is subject to conversion, but also the signals. The integration of the system required sensors to convert physical variables in analog to digital signals that carry information. The energy consumption for sensing is irrelevant to the information content transmitted. Analog-to-digital and digital-to-analog conversion of signals is needed for interfacing digital devices (often, computers) with sensors and actuators. Monitoring and control algorithms are executed mostly by digital computers. The commands to actuators, in the form of pulses or analog signals, require a conversion from signal to power form. In the case of a car, the velocity commands of the driver are converted from mental form into a position signal of the acceleration pedal, then in the flow rate command for the gas flow rate, and finally in the modulated power output of the engine. The conversion from signal command to modulated power form uses the control of the flow rate of gas. The specific energy content of the gas being constant, its multiplication with the time-varying flow rate of the gas gives the desired modulated power output.

In mechatronic systems, power transmission, conversion and modulation, signal transmission, digital-to-analog and analog-to-digital conversions as well as signal conditioning and processing are aspects of mixed system integration. Mechatronics issues appear in system design, fabrication, and operation. In the design stage, system modeling, virtual prototyping, and hardware-in-the-loop experimentation are used to achieve system integration. Similarly, modeling and simulation tools might be used in parallel with actual testing for justifying production changes and operations planning. Development of operating strategies involves modeling and simulation as well as testing.

The integration of signal and power transmission issues in mechatronic systems appear also in hardware-in-the-loop experimentation. In particular, signal conversion in power form is a common issue and, in fact, mechatronics provides a theoretical background and practical solutions to hardware-in-the-loop experimentation.

Figure 3.1 shows the schematic diagram of computer-based monitoring and control of a process. In Figure 3.1, the process variables, measured by transducers, are signal conditioned and converted from analog to digital form and then transmitted to the computer. Transducers with digital output (for example, optical encoders) can be directly compatible with computer digital input. The computer performs real-time monitoring and control as well as signal analysis and has two types of outputs. One type of output is for actuator commands and the other type of output goes only to the display for system monitoring.

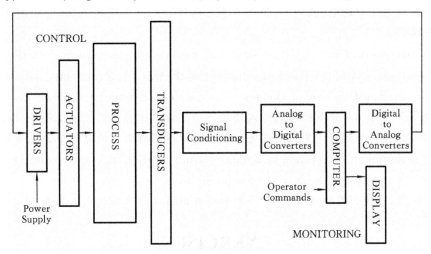

Figure 3.1　A schematic diagram of computer-based monitoring and control of a process

Computer output for control sends commands to actuators. The signals are first converted from digital to analog form. The commands are either operator commands, which can be applied in open loop control configuration, or computered commands (based on processed signals from transducers), which are applied in a closed loop control configuration.

Both open-loop and closed-loop control commands are signals sent to drivers that modulate the power from an external power supply for supplying the actuators.

# NEW WORDS AND EXPRESSIONS

mechatronics [ˌmekənə'trɔniks] n. 机电一体化
algorithm ['ælgəriðm] n. 算法
terminology [ˌtəːmi'nɔlədʒi] n. 术语
combustion [kəm'bʌstʃən] n. 燃烧
fabrication [ˌfæbri'keiʃən] n. 制作，构成

nanoelectromechanical a. 微机电工程的
integrated mixed system 集成混合系统
embedded microcontroller 嵌入式微处理器
acceleration pedal 加速度踏板
optical-encoder 光学编码器

# NOTES

1) Mechatronics is an engineering field which, together with intelligent structures, robotics, micro-, and nanoelectromechanical systems, etc., appears as part of "high-tech" fields of mechanical and electrical engineering.

机电一体化是一个工程领域，它和智能结构、机器人技术、微机电系统等一样都是机电工程高科技领域的一部分。

2) Electrical, mechanical, structural, and electronic components of a mechatronic system operate as an integrated system under real-time computer monitoring and control with interface for operator supervision and direction.

机电一体化系统中的电、机械、结构和电子元件作为一个集成的系统,它们利用实时计算机进行监控操作。

3) The conversion from signal command to modulated power form uses the control of the flow rate of gas. The specific energy content of the gas being constant, its multiplication with the time-varying flow rate of the gas gives the desired modulated power output.

从信号命令到可调节能量的转换形式使用了对气体流速的控制。由于气体的特定能量系数是常数,所以,从它和随时间变化的流速的乘积可以得到所需要的可调节的能量输出。

4) In the design stage, system modeling, virtual prototyping, and hardware-in-the-loop experimentation are used to achieve system integration.

在设计阶段,常使用系统建模、虚拟原型和硬件回路试验来实现系统集成。

## EXERCISES

1. After reading the text above, summarize the main ideas in oral.
2. Fill in the blanks with proper words or phrases according to the text (note the proper tense).

(1) Modeling mixed systems, virtual prototyping, and hardware in the loop experimentation are some of the methods used in m_____ system design.

(2) Analog-to-digital and digital-to-analog conversion of s_____ is needed for interfacing digital devices (often, computers) with sensors and actuators.

(3) Transducers with digital output (for example, optical encoders) can be directly compatible with c_____ digital input.

(4) The computer performs real-time monitoring and control as well as signal analysis and has two types of outputs. One type of output is for a_____ commands and the other type of output goes only to the d_____ for system monitoring.

(5) The commands are either o_____ commands, which can be applied in open loop control configuration, or computered commands (based on processed signals from transducers), which are applied in a closed loop control configuration.

3. Translate the following phrases into Chinese according to the text.

  (1) quality function deployment　　　(2) product realization process
  (3) materials processing　　　　　　(4) closed-loop control
  (5) virtual prototyping　　　　　　　(6) transducers with digital output
  (7) hardware-in-the-loop experimentation

4. Translate the following phrases into English according to the text.

  (1) 信号调理　　　　　　　　　　　(2) 原理图
  (3) 高科技领域　　　　　　　　　　(4) 电子元件
  (5) 实时监控　　　　　　　　　　　(6) 信号转换

5. Write a 100-word summary according to the text.

# READING MATERIAL

**Mechanical Structure, Sensors and Actuators, Computer Monitoring and Control**

## 1. Components

An obvious mechanical part of a mixed system is represented by the mechanical structure, which has to be able to sustain static and slow-varying forces and show an acceptable vibration response. Dynamical parts of the systems refer to transmission and conversion of signals and energy. Actuators transform chemical energy of fuels (e.g. combustion engines) into rotational or translational kinetic energy or, more often today, transform electric energy into rotational kinetic energy (direct current motors, stepping motor, etc.). In most cases, sensors convert (transform) measurement signals into electric signals, which are easy to transmit and process. For example, motion sensors transform velocity and acceleration into voltages, whereas force and torque sensors convert these variables also into voltages.

Electrical part refers to analog signal transmission (wiring) and can be modeled by electric circuits containing resistances, capacitances, and inductances. The electric part of sensors, which give their voltage output, is also modeled by electric circuit components.

Electronic part refers to thyristors, triacs, power transistors, and operational amplifiers, used in analog signal conditioning devices and power amplifiers.

Digital part refers to analog-to-digital converters (denoted ADC or A/D), digital-to-analog converters (denoted DAC or D/A), microprocessors, and other devices associated with computer monitoring and control. Hardware and software used in mixed systems permit computer integration of system monitoring and control and are the main reasons for the development of mechatronics engineering. The level of system integration with digital computers is much higher than the one with mechanical, electrical, and electronic components only. Until 1970, cars did not require the level of mechatronic system integration needed today. Today, however, the performance of the engine and the maneuverability of the car are highly dependent on the use of digital control.

## 2. Computers for system integration

Products and production systems share most of the concepts of computer integration, but often differ in actural implementation. Most production systems (plants or factories) are fixed and do not have significant weight and volume constraints. This distinguishes production systems from products for which weight and volume constraints are common due to mobility requirements. For production systems, mainframe and minicomputers can be used, but lately more and more powerful PC networks have replaced them. For products, in most cases the integration is achieved with single chip embedded computers.

PC Configuration   Since the 1970s, arithmetic logic units (ALUs), registers, and other digital components were combined in a single-chip microprocessor which, over years, changed the word length from 8-bit to 32-bit. In a PC, besides the microprocessor chip, there are volatile read-only memory (ROM), nonvolatile hard drive memory, and input-output (I/O) devices (keyboard, monitor, disk drives, mouse, etc.).

A PC can be used for computer system integration (system monitoring and/or control) when it equipped with devices to transmit measurement signals from sensors to the computer and command signals from the computer to the actuators. This requires analog-to-digital converters (ADCs) and digital-to-analog converters (DACs).

Some real-time control applications require very fast operation that can not be guaranteed, given the interrupt priorities in a PC. This problem can be alleviated by introducing a digital signal processor (DSP) between the PC and the system. The DSP would be dedicated to real-time control computations and permit fast and uninterrupted operation.

Embedded computers include the microprocessor, memory (ROM, random-access memory (RAM), and I/O devices parallel port, serial port, digital-to-analog converter, analog-to-digital converter, pulse-width modulation (PWM), etc.) on the same chip. Embedded computers do not normally connect to a keyboard, monitor, or mouse, but to sensors and actuators using a limited number of chip pins. For the same number of word bits, embedded computers tend to appear on the market a few years after the microprocessors.

Given the absence of operator I/O interface, an embedded computer is programmed differently from a PC (for example, using a specialized development system).

### 3. Virtual Instrumentation

PC-based integration of systems benefits from various software package that often use graphical programming for creating virtual instrumentation. In this case, displays, controls, and wire connections of the physical instrument are replaced by a monitor-based instrument display and controls. Graphical programming for instrument design is based on click-and-drag method on the monitor using readily available components. LabVIEW, a product of National Instrument (NI), HP VEE, a product of Hewlett Packard, and DASYLABTM, a product of OmegaTM are examples of such software.

NI Hardware, a basic National Instruments data acquisition hardware is the plug-in DAQ board.

Portable data acquisition NI hardware for PC integration of measurement and control using LabVIEW is DAQPad-MIO-16XE-50, available as an external box that communicates with a desktop or laptop PC through the parallel port. For connections to sensors and actuators, the DAQPad has:

● 16 single-ended (in case of one wire with common ground return for each sensor) or 8 differential (two wires for each sensor) analog inputs that go to a multiplexor, a 16-bit ADC, a buffer, and a central DAQ-STC, which is a system timing controller.

● Eight bi-directional digit I/O lines connected to DAQ-STC.

● Two analog outputs from two ADC receiving digital outputs from DAQ-STC.

Actual connections to sensors and actuators are made in a detachable Terminal Block DAQPad-TB-52, with screw terminals.

LabVIEW software is a program development application using the graphical programming language G. LabVIEW programs are not textual programs (like C or Fortran programs), but block diagram programs. Programming with LabVIEW consists in graphically clicking and dragging given icons of components and wiring them together with a mouse.

# Lesson 19  Automation

## TEXT

Although there can be variations in definition, automation generally is defined as the process of enabling machines to follow a predetermined sequence of operations with little or no human labor and using specialized equipment and devices that perform and control manufacturing processes. Full automation is achieved through various devices, sensors, actuators, techniques, and equipment that are capable of (a) monitoring all aspects of the manufacturing operation, (b) making decisions concerning the changes that should be made in the operation, and (c) controlling all aspects of it.

In manufacturing plants, automation has been implemented especially in the following basic areas of activity.

● Manufacturing process: Forging, cold extrusion, casting, powder metallurgy, and grinding operations are major examples of processes that have been automated extensively.

● Material handling and movement: Materials and parts in various stages of completion are moved throughout a plant by computer-controlled equipment with little or no human guidance.

● Inspection: Parts are inspected automatically for dimensional accuracy, surface finish, quality, and various specific characteristics while being made (in-process inspection).

● Assembly: Individually manufactured parts and components are assembled automatically into subassemblies and assemblies to form a product.

● Packaging: Products are packaged automatically for shipment.

### 1. Evolution of Automation

It was not until the beginning of the industrial revolution in the 1750s (also referred to as the First Industrial Revolution) that automation began to be introduced in the production of goods. Machine tools (such as turret lathes, automatic screw machines, and automatic bottle-making equipment) began to be developed in the late 1890s. Mass-production techniques and transfer machines were developed in the 1920s. These machines had fixed automatic mechanisms and were designed to produce specific products best represented by the automobile industry which produced passenger cars at a high production rate and low cost.

The major breakthrough in automation began with numerical control (NC) of machine tools. Since this historic development, rapid progress has been made in automating most aspects of manufacturing. These developments involve the introduction of computers into automation, computerized numerical control (CNC), adaptive control (AC), industrial robots, computer-aided design, computer-aided engineering, and computer-aided manufacturing (CAD/CAE/CAM), and computer-integrated manufacturing (CIM) systems.

## 2. Implementation of Automation

Automation has the following primary goals:

- To integrate various aspects of manufacturing operations so as to improve product quality and uniformity, minimize cycle times and effort, and reduce labor costs.
- To improve productivity by reducing manufacturing costs through better control of production. Parts loaded, fed, and unloaded on machines are used more effectively, and production is organized more efficiently.
- To improve product quality by using more repeatable processes.
- To reduce human involvement, boredom, and thus the possibility of human error.
- To reduce workpiece damage caused by the manual handling of parts.
- To raise the level of safety for personnel, especially under hazardous working conditions.
- To economize on floor space in the plant by arranging machines, material handling and movement, and auxiliary equipment more efficiently.

## 3. Automation and Production Quantity

Production quantity is crucial in determining the type of machinery and the level of automation required to produce parts economically. Total production quantity is defined as the total number of parts to be made. This volume can be produced in individual batches of various lot sizes. Lot size greatly influences the economics of production. Production rate is defined as the number of parts produced per unit time, such as per day, per month, or per year.

The approximate and generally accepted ranges of production volume are shown in Table 3.1 for some typical applications. As expected, experimental or prototype products represent the lowest volume.

Table 3.1 Approximate annual production quantity

| Type of production | Number produced | Typical products |
| --- | --- | --- |
| Experimental or prototype products | 1—10 | All |
| Piece or small-batch | 10—5 000 | Aircraft, missiles, special machinery, dies, jewelry and orthopedic implants |
| Batch or high-volume | 5 000—100 000 | Trucks, agricultural machinery, jet engines, diesel engines, computer components, and sporting goods |
| Mass production | 100 000 and over | Automobiles, appliances, fasteners, and food and beverage containers |

Job shops typically produce small quantities per year using various standard general-purpose machine tools (stand-alone machines) or machining centers. The operations performed typically have high part variety—meaning that different parts can be produced in a short time without extensive changes in tooling and in operations. On the other hand, machinery in job shops generally requires skilled labor to operate and production quantities and rates are low. As a result, production cost per part is high. When parts involve a large labor component, the production is called intensive.

Piece-part production usually involves very small quantities and is suitable for job shops. The majority of piece-part production involves lot sizes of 50 or less.

Small-batch production quantities typically range from 10 to 100, and the equipment used consists of general-purpose machines and machining centers with various computer controls.

Batch production usually involves lot sizes between 100 to 5 000. It utilizes machinery similar to that used for small-batch production but with specially designed fixtures for higher productivity.

Mass production involves quantities often over 100 000. It requires special-purpose machinery (called dedicated machines) and automated equipment for transferring materials and parts in progress. Although the machinery, equipment, and specialized tooling are expensive, both the labor skills required and the labor costs are relatively low. These production systems are organized for a specific type of product; hence, they lack flexibility.

### 4. Applications of Automation

Automation can be applied to the manufacturing of all types of goods, from raw materials to finished products, from job shops to large manufacturing facilities. The decision to automate a new or existing production facility requires taking into account the following additional considerations:

- Type of product manufactured;
- Production quantity and rate of production required;
- Particular phase of the manufacturing operation to be automated;
- Level of skill in the available workforce;
- Any reliability and maintenance problems that may be associated with automated systems.

### 5. Economics of the Process

Because automation generally involves high initial equipment cost and requires knowledge of operation and maintenance principles, a decision about the implementation of even low levels of automation must involve a careful study of the true needs of an organization. In some situation, selective automation rather than total automation of a facility is desirable.

## NEW WORDS AND EXPRESSIONS

grind [graind] v. 磨(碎),碾(碎)
automation [ɔːtəˈmeiʃən] n. 自动控制
assembly [əˈsembli] n. 装配
integrate [ˈintigreit] v. 集成,结合

breakthrough [ˈbreikθruː] n. 突破
productivity [ˌprɔdʌkˈtiviti] n. 生产力
powder metallurgy 粉末冶金
surface finish 表面加工,表面抛光

turret lathe 塔式车床　　　　　　　　　　adaptive control 可适应控制
screw machine 攻丝机，螺纹切削机

# NOTES

1) Full automation is achieved through various devices, sensors, actuators, techniques, and equipment that are capable of (a) monitoring all aspects of the manufacturing operation, (b) making decisions concerning the changes that should be made in the operation, and (c) controlling all aspects of it.

全自动化是通过多种设备、传感器、作动器、技术和能执行下述功能的装置完成的：(a) 监视制造操作的所有方面，(b) 对操作变化做出决策，(c) 控制制造过程的所有方面。

2) Individually manufactured parts and components are assembled automatically into subassemblies and assemblies to form a product.

单个制造的零部件自动进行局部装配，然后再装配成产品。

3) These developments involve the introduction of computers into automation, computerized numerical control (CNC), adaptive control (AC), industrial robots, computer-aided design, engineering, and manufacturing (CAD/CAE/CAM), and computer-integrated manufacturing (CIM) systems.

这些发展包括把计算机引入自动化、计算机数字控制(CNC)、可适应控制(AC)、工业机器人、计算机辅助设计、计算机辅助工程、计算机辅助制造和计算机集成制造系统(CIMS)。

4) Piece-part production usually involves very small quantities and is suitable for job shops. The majority of piece-part production involves lot sizes of 50 or less.

计件产品生产的数量通常非常小，适合手工作坊。大多数计件产品的生产规模在 50 件或者更少。

# EXERCISES

1. After reading the text above, summarize the main ideas in oral.

2. Fill in the blanks with proper words or phrases according to the text (note the proper tense).

(1) Improve product q_____ by using more repeatable processes.

(2) Raise the level of s_____ for personnel, especially under hazardous working conditions.

(3) Production q_____ is crucial in determining the type of machinery and the level of automation required to produce parts economically.

(4) J_____ shops typically produce small quantities per year using various standard general-purpose machine tools (stand-alone machines) or machining centers.

(5) M_____ production involves quantities often over 100 000. It requires special-purpose machinery (called dedicated machines) and automated equipment for transferring materials and parts in progress.

(6) A decision about the implementation of even low levels of a＿＿＿＿ must involve a careful study of the true needs of an organization. In some situation, selective automation rather than total automation of a facility is desirable.

3. Translate the following phrases into Chinese according to the text.
(1) full automation                     (2) mass-production techniques
(3) cold extrusion                      (4) raw materials
(5) dimensional accuracy                (6) piece-part production

4. Translate the following phrases into English according to the text.
(1) 作坊                                (2) 计算机数字控制
(3) 计算机集成制造系统                  (4) 产品数量
(5) 攻丝机                              (6) 冷挤压

5. Write a 100-word summary according to the text.

# READING MATERIAL

## An Introduction of Control System Technology

Control systems are everywhere around us and within us. Many complex control systems are included among the functions of the human body. An elaborate control system centered in the hypothalamus of the brain maintains body temperature at 37 degrees Celsius despite changes in physical activity and external ambience. In one control system—the eye—the diameter of the pupil automatically adjusts to control the amount of light that reaches the retina. Another control system maintains the level of sodium ion concentration in the fluid that surrounds the individual cells.

Threading a needle and driving an automobile are two ways in which the human body functions as a complex controller. The eyes are the sensor that detects the position of the needle and thread or of the automobile and the center of the road. A complex controller, the brain, compares the two positions and determines which actions must be performed to accomplish the desired result. The body implements the control action by moving the thread or turning the steering wheel. An experienced driver will anticipate all types of disturbances to the system, such as a rough section of pavement or a slow-moving vehicle ahead. It would be very difficult to reproduce in an automatic controller the many judgments that an average person makes daily and unconsciously.

Control systems regulate temperature in homes, schools, and buildings of all types. They also affect the production of goods and services by ensuring the purity and uniformity of the food we eat and by maintaining the quality of products from paper mills, steel mills, chemical plants, refineries, and other types of manufacturing plants. Control systems help protect our environment by minimizing waste material that must be discarded, thus reducing manufacturing costs and minimizing the waste disposal problem. Sewage and waste treatment also require the use of automatic control systems.

## Lesson 19  Automation

A control system is a group of components that maintain a desired result or value. From the previous examples it is clear that a great variety of components may be a part of a single control system. Whether they are electrical, electronic, mechanical, hydraulic, pneumatic, human or any combination of these. The desired result is a value of some variable in the system, for example, the direction of an automobile, the temperature of a room, the level of liquid in a tank, or the pressure in a pipe. The variable whose value is controlled is called the controlled variable.

To achieve control, there must be another variable in the system that can influence the controlled variable. Most systems have several such variables. The control system maintains the desired result by manipulating the value of one of this influential variable. The steering wheel of an automobile is an example of a manipulated variable.

Control systems are becoming steadily more important in our society. We depend on them to such an extent that life would be unimaginable without them. Automation control has increased the productivity of each worker by releasing skilled operators from routine tasks and by increasing the amount of work done by each worker. Control systems improve the quality and uniformity of manufactured goods and services; many of the products we enjoy would be impossible to produce without automatic controls. Servo systems place tremendous power at our disposal, enabling us to control large equipment such as jet airplanes and ocean ships.

Control systems increase efficiency by reducing waste of materials and energy, an increasing advantage as we seek ways to preserve our environment. Safety is yet another benefit of automatic control. Finally, control systems such as the household heating system and the automatic transmission provide us with increased comfort and convenience.

In summary, the benefits of automatic control fall into the following six broad categories:
- Increased productivity
- Improved quality and uniformity
- Increased efficiency
- Power assistance
- Safety
- Comfort and convenience

The objective of a control system seems quite simple—to maintain the controlled variable exactly equal to the setpoint at all times, regardless of load changes or setpoint changes. To do this, the control system must respond to a change before the error occurs; unfortunately, feedback is never perfect because it does not act until an error occurs. First, a load change must change the controlled variable; this produces an error. Then the controller acts on the error to produce a change in the manipulated variable. Finally, the change in the manipulated variable drives the controlled variable back toward the setpoint.

It is more realistic for us to expect a control system to obtain as nearly perfect operation as possible. Because the errors in a control system occur after load changes and setpoint changes, it seems natural to define the objectives in terms of the response to such changes.

One obvious objective is to minimize the maximum value of the error signal. Some control systems (with an integral mode) will eventually reduce the error to zero, whereas others require a residual error to compensate for a load change. In either case, the control system should eventually return the error to a steady, nonchanging value. The time required to achieve is called the settling time. A second objective of a control system is to minimize the settling time. A third objective is to minimize the residual error after settling out.

Unfortunately, above three objectives tend to be incompatible. For instance, the problem of reducing the residual error can be solved by increasing the gain of the controller so that a smaller residual error is required to produce the necessary corrective control action. However, an increase in gain tends to increase the settling time and may increase the maximum value of the error as well. The optimum response is always achieved through some sort of compromise.

# Lesson 20 | Industrial Robots

## TEXT

An industrial robot has been described by the International Organization for Standardization (ISO) as "a machine formed by a mechanism including several degrees of freedom, often having the appearance of one or several arms ending in a wrist capable of holding a tool, a workpiece, or an inspection device". In particular, its control unit must use a memorizing device, and it sometimes may use sensing or adaptation appliances to take into account environment and circumstances. These multipurpose machines generally are designed to carry out a repetitive function and can be adapted to other operations.

The first industrial robots were introduced in the early 1960s. Industrial robots first were used in hazardous operations (such as for the handling of toxic and radioactive materials) and the loading and unloading of hot workpieces from furnaces and in foundries. Simple, rule-of-thumb applications for robots are the "three D's" (dull, dirty, and dangerous, including demeaning but necessary tasks) and the "three H's" (hot, heavy, and hazardous).

### 1. Components of Robots

To appreciate the functions of robot components and their capabilities, we simultaneously might observe the flexibility and capability of diverse movements of our own arm, wrist, hand, and fingers in reaching for and grabbing an object from a shelf, in using a hand tool, or in operating a car or a machine. Described next are the basic components of an industrial robot.

1) Manipulator

Manipulator is also called arm and wrist. The manipulator is a mechanical unit that provides motions similar to those of a human arm and hand. The end of the wrist can reach a point in space having a specific set of coordinates and in a specific orientation.

2) End effector

The end of the wrist in a robot is equipped with an end effector. Depending on the type of operation, conventional end effectors may be equipped with any of the following (Figure 3.2):

- Grippers, hooks, scoops, electromagnets, vacuum cups, and adhesive fingers for material handling
  - Spray guns for painting
  - Attachments for spot and arc welding and for arc cutting
  - Power tools (such as drills)
  - Measuring instruments

3) Power supply

Each motion of the manipulator is controlled and regulated by independent actuators that

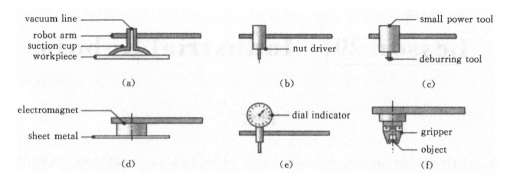

Figure 3.2 Types of devices and tools attached to end effectors to perform a variety of operations

use an electrical, a pneumatic, or a hydraulic power supply. Each source of energy or each type of motor has its own characteristics, advantages, and limitations.

4) Control system

Also known as the controller, the control system is the communications and information-processing system that gives commands for the movements of the robot. It is the brain of the robot and stores data to initiate and terminate movements of the manipulator. The control system is also the nerves of the robots; it interfaces with computers and other equipment, such as manufacturing cells or assembly systems.

Feedback device is an important part of the control system. Robots with a fixed set of motions have open-loop control. In this system, commands are given and the robot arm goes through its motions. Unlike feedback in closed-loop systems, accuracy of the movements is not monitored. Consequently, this system does not have a self-correcting capability.

As in numerical control machines, the type of control in industrial robots are point-to-point and continuous-path. Depending on the particular task, the positioning repeatability required may be as small as 0.050 mm, as in assembly operations for electronic printed circuitry. Specialized robots can reach such accuracy. Accuracy and repeatability varing greatly with payload and with position within the work envelope are difficult to quantify for most robots.

## 2. Classification of Robots

Robots may be classified by basic type as follows:
- Cartesian or rectilinear
- Cylindrical
- Spherical or polar
- Articulated, revolute, jointed, or anthropomorphic

Robots may be attached permanently to the floor of a manufacturing plant, they may move along overhead rails (gantry robots), or they may be equipped with wheels to move along the factory floor (mobile robots). However, a broader classification of robots currently in use is most helpful for our purposes here, as described next.

1) Fixed and variable sequence robots. The fixed-sequence robot (also called a pick-and-place robot) is programmed for a specific sequence of operations. Its movements are from

point to point, and the cycle is repeated continuously. These robots are simple and relatively inexpensive. The variable-sequence robot can be programmed for a specific sequence of operations but can be reprogrammed to perform another sequence of operations.

2) Playback robot. An operator leads or walks the playback robot and its end effector through the desired path; in other words, the operator teaches the robot by showing it what to do. The robot records the path and sequence of motions and can repeat them continually without any further action or guidance by the operator. Another type is the teach pendant, which utilizes hand-held button boxes that are connected to the control panel; they are used to control and guide the robot and its tooling through the work to be performed. These movements then are registered in the memory of the controller and reenacted automatically by the robot whenever needed.

3) Numerically controlled robot. The numerically controlled robot is programmed and operated much like a numerically controlled machine. The robot is servocontrolled by digital data, and its sequence of movements can be changed with relative ease. As in NC machines, there are two basic types of controls: point-to-point and continuous-path.

Point-to-point robots are easy to program and have a higher load-carrying capacity and a large work envelop, which is the maximum extent or reach of the robot hand or working tool in all directions. Continuous-path robots have greater accuracy than point-to-point robots, but they have lower load-carrying capacity. Advanced robots have a complex system of path control, enabling high-speed movements with great accuracy.

4) Intelligent (sensory) robot. The intelligent robot is capable of performing some of the functions and tasks carried out by humans. It is equipped with a variety of sensors with visual (computer vision) and tactile capabilities. Much like humans, the robot observes and evaluates the immediate environment and its proximity to other objects, especially machinery, by perception and pattern recognition. It then makes appropriate decisions for the next movement and proceeds accordingly. Because its operation is very complex, powerful computers are required to control this type of robot.

Developments in intelligent robots include:
● Behaving more like humans, performing tasks such as moving among a variety of machines and equipment on the shop floor and avoiding collisions.
● Recognizing, selecting and properly gripping the correct raw material or workpiece.
● Transporting the part to a machine for further processing or inspection.
● Assembling the components into subassemblies or a final product.

## NEW WORDS AND EXPRESSIONS

appliance [ə'plaiəns] n. 用具,器具
robot ['rəubɔt] n. 机器人
toxic ['tɔksik] a. 有毒的
anthropomorphic [ˌænθrəpəu'mɔːfik] a. 被赋予人形的,拟人的

articulated [ɑː'tikjulitid] a. 连接的,有关节的
servocontrol ['səːvəkən'trəul] n. 伺服控制
end effector 末端执行器
work envelop 工作区域

# NOTES

1) An industrial robot has been described by the International Organization for Standardization (ISO) as "a machine formed by a mechanism including several degrees of freedom, often having the appearance of one or several arms ending in a wrist capable of holding a tool, a workpiece, or an inspection device".

国际标准化组织(ISO)对"工业机器人"的定义是:"一种由包括多个自由度的机构组成的机器,这种机器通常有一个或者几个手臂,这些手臂由腕关节连接,能够抓取工具、工件或者监控设备"。

2) Specialized robots can reach such accuracy. Accuracy and repeatability vary greatly with payload and with position within the work envelope and, as such, are difficult to quantity for most robots.

专用机器人能达到这样的精度。精度和重复定位精度随负载和工作区域的变化有很大的变化,上述能力对于大多数种类的机器人来说是很困难的。

3) The fixed-sequence robot (also called a pick-and-place robot) is programmed for a specific sequence of operations. Its movements are from point to point, and the cycle is repeated continuously.

固定顺序机器人(也叫点位机器人)是按照一定的操作顺序来编程的,它的运动是从点到点,不断重复这个周期。

4) An operator leads or walks the playback robot and its end effector through the desired path; in other words, the operator teaches the robot by showing it what to do.

操作者指导示教再现机器人和它的末端执行器按照指定的路径操作,换句话说,操作者示教机器人如何进行操作。

# EXERCISES

1. After reading the text above, summarize the main ideas in oral.

2. Fill in the blanks with proper words or phrases according to the text (note the proper tense).

(1) The m_____ is a mechanical unit that provides motions similar to those of a human arm and hand.

(2) The end of the wrist in a robot is equipped with an e_____ effector.

(3) The c_____ system is the communications and information-processing system that gives commands for the movements of the robot.

(4) As in numerical control machines, the type of control in industrial robots are p_____ and continuous-path.

(5) The numerically controlled r_____ is programmed and operated much like a numerically controlled machine.

(6) The i_____ robot is capable of performing some of the functions and tasks carried

out by humans.

3. Translate the following phrases into Chinese according to the text.
(1) "three D's" (dull, dirty, and dangerous)
(2) "three H's" (hot, heavy, and hazardous)
(3) vacuum cup
(4) closed-loop system
(5) gantry robot
(6) playback robot

4. Translate the following phrases into English according to the text.
(1) 移动机器人
(2) 开环控制
(3) 辐射材料
(4) 熔炉
(5) 控制面板
(6) 伺服控制
(7) 点到点机器人

5. Write a 100-word summary according to the text.

# READING MATERIAL

## Background of Industrial Robots

The history of industrial automation is characterized by periods of rapid change in popular methods. Either as a cause or, perhaps, an effect, such periods of change in automation techniques seem closely tied to world economics. Use of the industrial robot, which became identifiable as a unique device in the 1960s, along with computer-aided design (CAD) systems and computer-aided manufacturing (CAM) systems, characterizes the latest trends in the automation of the manufacturing process. These technologies are leading industrial automation through another transition, the scope of which is still unknown.

In north America, there was much adoption of robotic equipment in the early 1980s, followed by a brief pull-back in the late 1980s. Since that time, the market has been growing, although it is subject to economic swings, as are all markets.

A major reason for the growth in the use of industrial robots is their declining cost. Through the decade of the 1990s, robot prices dropped while human labor costs increased. Also, robots are not just getting cheaper, they are becoming more effective—faster, more accurate, more flexible. If we factor these quality adjustments into the numbers, the cost of using robots is dropping even faster than their price tag is. As robots become more cost effective at their jobs, and as human labor continues to become more expensive, more and more industrial jobs become candidates for robotic automation. This is the single most important trend propelling growth of the industrial robot market. A secondary trend is that, as robots become more capable they become able to do more and more tasks that might be dangerous or impossible for human workers to perform.

The applications that industrial robots perform are gradually getting more sophisticated, but it is still the case that, in the year 2000, approximately 78% of the robots installed in the US were welding or material-handling robots. A more challenging domain, assembly by industrial robot, accounted for 10% of installations.

Major applications of industrial robots include the following:

● Material handling consists of the loading, unloading, and transferring of workpieces in manufacturing facilities. These operations can be performed reliably and repeatedly with robots, thereby improving quality and reducing scrap losses. Some examples are: (a) casting and molding operations in which molten metal, raw materials, lubricants, and parts in various stages of completion are handled without operator interference; (b) heat-treating operations in which parts are loaded and unloaded from furnaces and quench baths; (c) forming operations in which parts are loaded and unloaded from presses and various other types of metalworking machinery.

● Spot welding unitizes automobile and truck bodies, producing welds of good quality. Robots also perform other similar operations, such as arc welding, arc cutting, and riveting.

● Operations such as deburring, grinding, and polishing can be done by using appropriate tools attached to the end effectors.

● Applying adhesives and sealants, such as in the automobile frame.

● Spray painting (particularly of complex shapes) and cleaning operations are frequent applications because the motions for one piece are repeated accurately for the next piece.

● Automated assembly.

● Inspection and gaging at speeds much higher than those that can be achieved by humans.

Factors that influence the selection of robots in manufacturing are as follows:

● Load-carrying capacity

● Speed of movement

● Reliability

● Repeatability

● Arm configuration

● Degrees of freedom

● Program memory

● Work envelop

In addition to the technical factors, cost and benefit considerations also are significant aspects of robot selection and their use. The increasing availability and reliability and the reduced costs of sophisticated, intelligent robots are having a major economic impact on manufacturing operations. Such robots gradually are displacing human labor.

Depending on the size of the robot's work envelop, speed, and proximity to humans, safety considerations in a robot environment are important, particularly for programmers and maintenance personnel who are in direct physical interaction with robots, in addition, the movement of the robot with respect to other machinery required a high level of reliability in order to avoid collisions and damage to equipment. Its material-handling activities require the proper securing of raw materials and parts in the robot gripper at various stages in the production line.

# Lesson 21  Open-Loop Control and Closed-Loop Control

## TEXT

Control systems are everywhere around us. However, not any type of control system has the automatic feature. Usually, the automatic feature is achieved by feeding the output variable back and comparing it with the command signal. When a system does not have the feedback structure, it is called an open-loop system, which is the simplest and most economical type of control system. Unfortunately, open-loop control system lack accuracy and versatility and can be used in none but the simplest type of applications. A system with one or more feedback paths is called a closed-loop system. Human being are probably the most complex and sophisticated feedback control system in existence. A human being may be considered to be a control system with many inputs and outputs, capable of carrying out highly complex operations.

### 1. Open-Loop Control

An open-loop control system does not compare the actual results with the desired results to determine the control action. Instead, a calibrated setting—previously determined by some sort of calibration procedure or calculation—is used to obtain the desired results.

The firing of a rifle bullet is an example of an open-loop control system. The desired result is to direct the bullet to the bull's-eye. The actual result is the direction of the bullet after the gun has been fired. The open-loop control occurs when the rifle is aimed at the bull's eye and the trigger is pulled. Once the bullet leaves the barrel, it is on its own: If a sudden gust of wind comes up, the direction will be changed and no correction will be possible.

An electric washing machine is another typical example of an open-loop system, because the amount of wash time is entirely determined by the judgment and estimation of the human operator. A true automatic electric washing machine should have the means of checking the cleanliness of the clothes continuously and turn itself off when the desired degree of cleanliness has been reached.

The primary advantage of open-loop control is that it is less expensive than closed-loop control; it is not necessary to measure the actual result. In addition, the controller is much simpler because corrective action based on the error is not required. The disadvantage of open-loop control is that errors caused by unexpected disturbances can not be corrected. Often the human operator must correct slowly changing disturbances by manual adjustment. In this case, the operator is actually closing the loop by providing the feedback signal.

What is missing in the open-loop control system for more accurate and more adaptive control is a link or feedback from the output to the input of the system. To obtain more accurate control, the controlled signal proportional to the difference of the input and the output must be sent back to the system to correct the error. A system with one or more CS such as that just described is called a closed-loop system.

## 2. Closed-Loop Control: Feedback

Feedback is the action of measuring the difference between the actual result and the desired result, and using that difference to drive the actual result toward the desired result. The term feedback comes from the direction in which the measured value signal travels in the block diagram. The signal begins at the output of the controlled system and ends at the input of the controller. The output of the controller is the input to the controlled system. Thus the measured value signal is fed back from the output of the controlled system to the input. The term closed-loop refers to the loop created by the feedback path.

A closed-loop idle-speed control system is shown in Figure 3.3. The reference input $\omega_r$ sets the desired idling speed. The engine speed at idle should agree with the reference value $\omega_r$, and any difference such as the load torque $T_L$ is sensed by the speed transducer and the error detector. The controller will operate on the difference and provide a signal to adjust the throttle angle to correct the error.

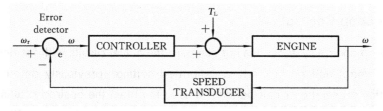

Figure 3.3  Block diagram of a closed-loop idle-speed control system

The objective of the idle-speed control system illustrated, also known as a regulator system, is to maintain the system output at a prescribed level.

To illustrate the human being as a feedback control system, let us consider that the objective is to reach for an object on a desk. As one is reaching for the object, the brain sends back out a signal to the arm to perform the task. The eyes serve as sensing devices which feed back continuously the position of the hand. The distance between the hand and the object is the error, which is eventually brought to zero as the hand reaches the object. This is a typical example of closed-loop control. However, if one is told to reach for the object and then is blindfoldly, one can only reach toward the object by estimating its exact position. It is quite possible that the object may be missed by a wide margin. With the eyes blindfoldly, the feedback path is broken, and the human is operating as an open-loop system.

To understand the effects of feedback on a control system, it is essential to examine this phenomenon in a broad sense. When feedback is deliberately introduced for the purpose of control, its existence is easily identified. However, there are numerous situations wherein a physical system that we recognize as an inherently nonfeedback system turns out to have feedback when it is observed in a certain manner. In general, we can state that whenever a closed sequence of cause-and-effect relationships exists among the variables of a system, feedback is said to be existent. This viewpoint will inevitably admit the existence of feedback in a large number of systems that ordinarily would be identified as nonfeedback systems. However, control-system theory allows numerous systems, with or without physical feedback, to be studied in a systematic way once the existence of feedback in the sense mentioned previously is established.

## NEW WORDS AND EXPRESSIONS

sophistication [sə,fisti'keiʃən] *n.* 复杂性,完善(化),采用先进技术
feedback ['fi:dbæk] *n.* 反馈
error ['erə] *n.* 误差,偏差
blindfoldly ['blaindfəuldli] *ad.* 蒙上眼睛地
wherein [(h)wɛərin] *ad.* 在何处,在哪方面
desired value 预期值
calibration procedure 校准过程
the error detector 偏差探测器
the block diagram 波特图

## NOTES

1) An open-loop control system does not compare the actual result with the desired result to determine the control action.
开环控制系统不对实际输出结果和理想输出结果进行比较来决定控制行为。

2) Often a human operator must correct slowly changing disturbances by manual adjustment. In this case, the operator is actually closing the loop by providing the feedback signal.
操作工经常必须通过手动调整慢慢修正偏差。在这种情况下,操作工通过提供反馈信号实际上实现了闭环。

3) The reference input $\omega_r$ sets the desired idling speed. The engine speed at idle should agree with the reference value $\omega_r$, and any difference such as the load torque $T_L$ is sensed by the speed transducer and the error detector. The controller will operate on the difference and provide a signal to adjust the throttle angle to correct the error.
参考输入信号$\omega_r$设定了需要的空转速度。发动机在空转时,速度应该和参考值$\omega_r$一致,任何变化如负载转矩$T_L$都会被速度传感器和偏差探测器检测到。控制器根据这个变化提供一个信号来调整阀门开度以达到修正偏差的目的。

4) The eyes serve as sensing devices which feed back continuously the position of the hand. The distance between the hand and the object is the error, which is eventually brought to zero as the hand reaches the object.
眼睛作为传感设备不断地反馈手的位置。手和物体的距离就是偏差,这个偏差随着手接触到物体最终变为0。

## EXERCISES

1. After reading the text above, summarize the main ideas in oral.

2. Fill in the blanks with proper words or phrases according to the text (note the proper tense).

(1) An o_____ control system does not compare the actual result with the desired result to determine the control action.

(2) The primary advantage of open-loop control is that it is less e_____ than closed-loop control.

(3) A system with one or more feedback paths such as that just described is called a c_____ system.

(4) F_____ is the action of measuring the difference between the actual result and the desired result, and using that difference to drive the actual result towards the desired result.

(5) We can state that whenever a closed sequence of cause-and-effect relationships exists among the variables of a system, f_____ is said to be existent.

(6) What is missing in the open-loop control system for more a_____ and more adaptive control is a link or feedback from the output to the input of the system.

3. Translate the following phrases into Chinese according to the text.

(1) idle-speed control system   (2) speed transducer

(3) output variable   (4) reference input

(5) manual adjustment   (6) throttle angle

(7) electric washing machine

4. Translate the following phrases into English according to the text.

(1) 开环控制   (2) 闭环控制

(3) 波特图   (4) 校准过程

(5) 负载扭矩   (6) 误差监测器

(7) 预期值

5. Write a 100-word summary according to the text.

# READING MATERIAL

## Hard Automation and Soft Automation

In hard automation or fixed-position automation, the machines are designed to produce a standard products, such as a gear, a shaft, or an engine block. Although product size and processing parameters (such as speed, feed, and depth of cut) can be changed, these machines are specialized and lack of flexibility. They cannot be modified to accommodate products that have different shapes and dimensions. Because these machines are expensive to design and build, their economical use requires the production of parts in very large quantities. The machines used in hard-automation applications usually are built on the modular (building-block) principle. They generally are called transfer machines and consist of two major components: powerhead production units and transfer mechanisms.

## Lesson 21  Open-Loop Control and Closed-Loop Control

1) Powerhead production units

Consisting of a frame or bed, electric drive motors, gearboxes, and tool spindles, these units are self-contained. Their components are available commercially in various standard sizes and capacities. Because of this inherent modularity, they easily can be regrouped for producing a different part and thus have some adaptability and flexibility.

2) Transfer machines

Typically consisting of two or more powerhead units, these machines can be arranged on the shop floor in linear, circular, or U-shaped patterns. The weight and shape of the workpieces influence the arrangement selected, which is important for continuity of operation in the event of tool failure or machine breakdown in one or more of the units. Buffer storage features are incorporated in these machines to permit continued operation in such an event.

Transfer mechanisms and transfer lines. Transfer mechanisms are used to move the workpiece from one station to another in the machine or from one machine to another to enable various operations to be performed on the part.

The transfer of parts from station to station usually is controlled by sensors and other devices. Tools on transfer machines easily can be changed using toolholders with quick-change features, and the machines can be equipped with various automatic gaging and inspection system. These systems are utilized between operations to ensure that the dimensions of a part produced in one station are within acceptable tolerances before that part is transferred to the next station. Transfer machines also are used extensively in automated assembly.

We have seen that hard automation generally involves mass-production machines that lack flexibility. In soft automation (also called flexible or programmable automation), greater flexibility is achieved through the use of computer control of the machine and of its functions; thus, it can produce parts with complex shapes. Soft automation is an important development, because the machine can be reprogrammed easily and readily to produce a part that has a shape or dimensions different from the one produced just prior to it. Further advances in flexible automation include the extensive use of modern computers leading to the development of flexible manufacturing systems with high levels of efficiency and productivity.

A flexible manufacturing system (FMS) integrates all of the major elements of manufacturing into a highly automated system. First utilized in the late 1960s, an FMS consists of a number of manufacturing cells, each containing an industrial robot (serving several CNC machines) and an automated material-handling system, and all interfaced with a central computer. Different computer instruction can be downloaded for each successive part passing through a particular workstation. The system can handle a variety of part configurations and produce them in any order.

This highly automated system is capable of optimizing each step of the whole operation. These steps may involve (a) one or more processes and operations, such as machining, grinding, cutting, forming, powder metallurgy, heat treating, and finishing, (b) handling of raw materials, (c) measurement and inspection, and (d) assembly. The most common applications of FMS to data have been in machining and assembly operation.

FMS can be regarded as a system that combines the benefits of two other systems: (1) the highly productive but inflexible transfer lines and (2) job-shop production, which can produce large product variety on stand-alone machines but is inefficient. Note that in FMS, the time required for changeover to a different part is very short. The quick response to product and market-demand variations is a major attribute of FMS.

Compared to conventional manufacturing systems, the major benefits of FMS are the following:

Parts can be produced randomly, in batch sizes as small as one, and at a lower unit cost.

Direct labor and inventories are reduced or eliminited.

The lead times required for product changes are shorter.

Because the system is self-correcting, the production is more reliable and product quality is uniform.

# Lesson 22  Sensor Technology

## TEXT

A sensor is a device which produces a signal in response to its detecting or measuring a property, such as position, force, torque, pressure, temperature, humidity, speed, acceleration, or vibration. Traditionally, sensors (such as actuators and switches) have been used to set limits on the performance of machines. Common examples are (a) stops on machine tools to restrict work table movements, (b) pressure and temperature gages with automatics shut-off features, and (c) governors on engines to prevent excessive speed of operation. Sensor technology has become an important aspect of manufacturing processes and systems. It is essential for proper data acquisition and for the monitoring, communication, and computer control of machines and systems.

Because they convert one quantity to another, sensors often are referred to as transducers. Analog sensors produce a signal, such as voltage, which is proportional to the measured quantity. Digital sensors have numeric or digital outputs that can be transferred to computers directly. Analog-to-digital converter (ADC) is available for interfacing analog sensors with computers.

### 1. Classifications of Sensor

Sensors that are of interest in manufacturing may be classified generally as follows:

Mechanical sensors measure such quantities as position, shape, velocity, force, torque, pressure, vibration, strain, and mass.

Electrical sensors measure voltage, current, charge, and conductivity.

Magnetic sensors measure magnetic field, flux, and permeability.

Thermal sensors measure temperature, flux, conductivity, and special heat.

Other types are acoustic, ultrasonic, chemical, optical, radiation, laser, and fiber-optic.

Depending on its application, a sensor may consist of metallic, nonmetallic, organic, or inorganic materials, as well as fluids, gases, plasmas, or semiconductors. Using the special characteristics of these materials, sensors convert the quantity or property measured to analog or digital output. The operation of an ordinary mercury thermometer, for example, is based on the difference between the thermal expansion of mercury and that of glass.

Similarly, a machine part, a physical obstruction, or barrier in a space can be detected by breaking the beam of light when sensed by a photoelectric cell. A proximity sensor (which senses and measures the distance between it and an object or a moving member of a machine) can be based on acoustics, magnetism, capacitance, or optics. Other actuators contact the object and take appropriate action (usually by electromechanical means). Sensors are essential to the control of intelligent robots, and are being developed with capabilities that resemble those of humans (smart sensors, see the following).

Tactile sensing is the continuous sensing of variable contact forces, commonly by an array of sensors. Such a system is capable of performing within an arbitrary three-dimensional space.

In visual sensing (machine vision, computer vision), cameral optically sense the presence and shape of the object. A microprocessor then processes the image (usually in less than one second), the image is measured, and the measurements are digitized (image recognition). Machine vision is suitable particularly for inaccessible parts, in hostile manufacturing environments, for measuring a large number of small features, and in situations where physics contact with the part may cause damage.

Smart sensors have the capability to perform a logic function, to conduct two-way communication, and to make decisions and take appropriate actions. The necessary input and the knowledge required to make a decision can be built into a smart sensor. For example, a computer chip with sensors can be programmed to turn a machine tool off when a cutting tool fails. Likewise, a smart sensor can stop a mobile robot or a robot arm from accidentally coming in contact with an object or people by sensing quantities such as distance, heat, and noise.

Sensor fusion. Sensor fusion basically involves the integration of multiple sensors in such a manner where the individual data from each of the sensors (such as force, vibration, temperature, and dimensions) are combined to provide a higher level of information and reliability. A common application of sensor fusion occurs when someone drinks a cup of hot coffee. Although we take such a quotidian event for granted, it readily can be seen that this process involves data input from the person's eyes, lips, tongue, and hands. Through our basic senses of sight, hearing, smell, taste, and touch, there is real-time monitoring of relative movements, positions, and temperatures. Thus if the coffee is too hot, the hand movement of the cup toward the lip is controlled and adjusted accordingly.

The earliest applications of sensor fusion were in robot movement control, missile flight tracking, and similar military applications, primarily because these activities involve movements that mimic human behavior. Another example of sensor fusion is a machine operation in which a set of different but integrated sensors monitors (a) the dimensions and surface finish of the workpiece, (b) tool forces, vibrations, and wear, (c) the temperatures in various regions of the tool-workpiece system, and (d) the spindle power.

An important aspect in sensor fusion is sensor validation: the failure of one particular sensor is detected so that the control system maintains high reliability. For this application, the receiving of redundant data from different sensors is essential. It can be seen that the receiving, integrating, and processing of all data form various sensors can be a complex problem.

With advances in sensor size, quality, and technology and continued developments in computer-control systems, artificial intelligence, expert systems, and artificial neural networks, sensor fusion has become practical and available at relatively low cost.

Fiber-optic sensors are being developed for gas-turbine engines. These sensors will be installed in critical locations and will monitor the conditions inside the engine, such as temperature, pressure, and flow of gases. Continuous monitoring of the signals from these sensors will help detect possible engine problems and also provide the necessary data for improving the efficiency of the engines.

# NEW WORDS AND EXPRESSIONS

actuator ['æktjueitə] n. 作动器
switch [switʃ] n. 开关,转换器
strain [strein] n. 应变
flux [flʌks] n. 通量
permeability [ˌpəːmiəˈbiliti] n. 渗透性
conductivity [ˌkɔndʌkˈtiviti] n. 传导率
acoustic [əˈkuːstik] a. 声学的

ultrasonic [ˈʌltrəˈsɔnik] a. 超声的,超音速的
 n. 超声波
shut-off 关断
data acquisition 数据拾取
mercury thermometer 水银温度计
smart sensor 智能传感器

# NOTES

1) Depending on its application, a sensor may consist of metallic, nonmetallic, organic or inorganic materials, as well as fluids, gases, plasmas, or semiconductors.
根据应用的不同,传感器可以由金属、非金属、有机或者无机材料、流体、气体、乳浆体或者半导体构成。

2) A machine part, a physical obstruction, or barrier in a space can be detected by breaking the beam of light when sensed by a photoelectric cell.
光电传感单元根据被阻挡的光束能检测到一个机器部件、一个物理障碍物或者是一个空间中的障碍物的存在。

3) Tactile sensing is the continuous sensing of variable contact forces, commonly by an array of sensors. Such a system is capable of performing within an arbitrary three-dimensional space.
触觉传感技术通常是利用多个触觉传感器组成的阵列不间断的采样变化的接触压力。这样的传感系统能够监控任意的三维空间。

4) The earliest applications of sensor fusion were in robot movement control, missile flight tracking, and similar military applications, primarily because these activities involve movements that mimic human behavior.
传感器融合技术最早应用于机器人移动控制、导弹飞行追踪和类似的军事运用上,主要是因为这些检测活动是在模仿人的行为。

# EXERCISES

1. After reading the text above, summarize the main ideas in oral.
2. Fill in the blanks with proper words or phrases according to the text (note the proper

tense).

(1) Sensors (such as actuators and switches) have been used to set l_____ on the performance of machines.

(2) A_____ sensors produce a signal, such as voltage, which is proportional to the measured quantity. D_____ sensors have numeric or digital outputs that can be transferred to computers directly.

(3) M_____ sensors measure such quantities as position, shape, velocity, force, torque, pressure, vibration, strain, and mass.

(4) T_____ sensors measure temperature, flux, conductivity, and special heat.

(5) In v_____ sensing, cameral optically sense the presence and shape of the object. A microprocessor then processes the image (usually in less than one second), the image is measured, and the measurements are digitized (image recognition).

(6) An important aspect in sensor f_____ is sensor validation: the failure of one particular sensor is detected so that the control system maintains high reliability.

3. Translate the following phrases into Chinese according to the text.
(1) analog-to-digital converter        (2) data acquisition
(3) sensor fusion                      (4) gas-turbine engines
(5) smart sensors                      (6) tactile sensing
(7) fiber-optic sensors

4. Translate the following phrases into English according to the text.
(1) 模拟传感器                         (2) 水银温度计
(3) 表面处理                           (4) 人工智能
(5) 专家系统                           (6) 智能机器人

5. Write a 100-word summary according to the text.

# READING MATERIAL

## Signal Conditioning

A signal conditioner prepares a signal for use by another component. The input to a signal conditioner is usually the output from a sensor (or primary element). The operations performed by a signal conditioner include isolation, impedance conversion, noise reduction, amplification, linearization, and conversion.

A measuring transmitter consists of two parts: a primary element (or sensor) and a signal conditioner. The primary element uses some characteristic of its material and construction to convert the value of a measured variable into an electrical, mechanical, or fluidic signal. The output of the primary element may be a small voltage or an electrical resistance. It may be a force, a displacement, a pressure, or some other phenomenon. No matter what form it takes, the primary element output depends on the value of the measured variable.

The output of the primary element is a measure of the variable where it is sensing, but it is seldom in a form suitable for transmission and use by other components in a system. Usually, a signal conditioner is required to convert the primary element output into an electrical (or pneumatic) signal suitable for use by a controller or display device. The standard transmission signals are a 4 to 20 mA electric current or a 3 to 15 psi pneumatic pressure. For example, a thermocouple (T/C) is a primary element that converts temperature into a small voltage. A signal conditioner converts the millivolt output of the thermocouple into a 4 to 20 mA electric current. A T/C temperature transmitter includes both the thermocouple and the signal conditioner. The following are some of the tasks performed by a signal conditioner:

- Isolation and impedance conversion;
- Amplification and analog-to-analog conversion;
- Noise reduction (filtering);
- Linearization;
- Data sampling;
- Digital-to-analog conversion;
- Analog-to-digital conversion.

The operational amplifier is the heart of many modern signal conditioners. An operational amplifier is a high-gain DC amplifier with two inputs and one output. The output is equal to the difference between the voltages on the two inputs multiplied by the gain of the amplifier. The operating characteristics of an operational amplifier circuit depend almost entirely on components external to the amplifier. The gain, input impedance, output impedance, and frequency response depend on the external resistors and capacitors in the circuit, not on the gain, input impedance, or output impedance of the amplifier. This means that the behavior of an op-amp circuit can be made to fit a particular application by proper selection and placement of a few resistors and capacitors. Also, the stability of these components can be selected to meet the requirements of the application. With this versatility and ease of design, so it is not hard to understand why the op amp has become such a popular component in control systems.

One of the objectives of a measuring transmitter is to minimize the effect of the measurement on the measured variable. In some situations, this means electrical isolation of the primary element with an isolation amplifier. In other situations, it means providing a high impedance at the input to the signal conditioner.

Another objective of a measuring transmitter is to convert the output from the primary element into a signal suitable for use by a controller or display device. Some primary elements convert changes in the measured variable into small changes in resistance. Strain gages and resistance temperature detectors (RTDs) are two examples. A bridge circuit is often used to convert the change in resistance into a small change in voltage. This small voltage is then amplified and converted to an electric current signal suitable for use by the controller.

Industry presents a harsh environment for making precise measurements. There are many sources of electrical interference, and noise is always a concern when electrical signals are transmitted.

The ideal measuring transmitter output is a linear signal that goes from 0 to 100% as the measured variable goes from the lower range limit to the upper range limit. Sometimes the signal is close to the ideal. At other times, the signal is nonlinear. An orifice flow element, for example, produces a pressure drop that is proportional to the square of the flow rate. Linearization of this type of signal is a very desirable goal. Thermocouples also produce a nonlinear signal, although not nearly as nonlinear as the flow orifice. Linearization of thermocouple signals is also desirable.

Data sampling is a process in which a switch momentarily closes to connect an analog signal to a sample-and-hold circuit. The sample-and-hold circuit maintains the analog signal until the next momentary switch closure. While the analog signal is held, an analog-to-digital converts the analog signal into an equivalent digital signal. Once the signal is converted to digital, a microprocessor can use the digital samples to perform digital signal conditioning such as filtering, linearization, calibration, and conversion to engineering units. A digital controller receives the digital samples and produces a digital output signal. A digital-to-analog converter converts the digital output of the controller into an analog signal suitable for use by the final control element.

# Lesson 23 | An Introduction to Hydraulics

## TEXT

History shows that devices such as pumps and water wheels were known in very ancient times. However it was not until the 17th century that the branch of hydraulics with which we are to be concerned first came into use. Based upon a principle discovered by the French scientist Blaise Pascal, hydraulics related to the use of confined fluids in transmitting power, multiplying force and modifying motions.

### 1. Components of a Hydraulic System

1) Power supply section

The most important component in the power supply unit is the hydraulic pump. This draws in the hydraulic fluid from a reservoir (tank) and delivers it via a system of lines in the hydraulic installation against the opposing resistances. Pressure does not build up until the flowing liquids encounter a resistance. The oil filtration unit is also often contained in the power supply section. Filters are installed in the hydraulic circuit to remove dirt particles from the hydraulic fluid. Water and gases in the oil are also disruptive factors so special measures must be taken to remove them. Heaters and coolers are also installed for conditioning the hydraulic fluid. The extent to which this is necessary depends on the requirements of the particular exercise for which the hydraulic system is being used.

2) Valves

Valves are devices for controlling energy flow. They can control and regulate the flow direction of the hydraulic fluid, the pressure, the flow rate and, consequently, the flow velocity.

There are four valve types selected in accordance with the problem in question.

i) Directional control valves

These valves control the direction of flow of the hydraulic fluid and, thus, the direction of motion and the positioning of the working components. Directional control valves may be actuated manually, mechanically, electrically, pneumatically or hydraulically. They convert and amplify signals (manual, electric or pneumatic) forming an interface between the power control section and the signal control section.

ii) Pressure valves

These valves have the job of influencing the pressure in a complete hydraulic system or in a part of the system. The method of operation of these valves is based on the fact that the effective pressure from the system acts on a surface in the valves. The resultant force is balanced out by a counteracting spring.

iii) Flow control valves

These valves interact with pressure valves to affect flow rate. They make it possible to control or regulate the speed of motion of the power components, where the flow rate is constant, division of flow must take place. This is generally effected through the interaction of the flow control valve with a pressure valve.

iv) Non-return valves

In the case of this type of valves, a distinction is made between ordinary non-return valves and piloted non-return valves. In the case of the piloted non-return valves, flow in the blocked direction can be released by a signal.

3) Cylinders (linear actuators)

Cylinders are drive components which convert hydraulic power into mechanical power. They generate linear movements through the pressure on the surface of the movable piston. Distinction is made between the following types of cylinder.

i) Single-acting cylinders

The fluid pressure can be applied to only one side of the piston with the result that the drive movement is only produced in one direction. The return stroke of the piston is effected by an external force or by a return spring.

ii) Double-acting cylinders

The fluid pressure can be applied to either side of the piston meaning that drive movements are produced in two directions.

4) Hydraulic motors

Hydraulic motors are drive components controlled by valves. They also convert hydraulic power into mechanical power with the difference that they generate rotary or swivel movements instead of linear movements.

## 2. Advantages of Hydraulics

1) Variable speed

Most electric motors run at a constant speed. It is also desirable to operate an engine at a constant speed. The actuator (linear or rotary) of a hydraulic system, however, can be driven from maximum speeds to reduced speeds by varying the pump delivery using a flow control valve.

2) Reversible

Few prime movers are reversible. Those that are reversible usually must be slowed to a complete stop before reversing them. A hydraulic actuator can be reversed instantly while in full motion without damage. A four-way directional valve (Figure 3.4) provides the reversing control, while a pressure relief valve protects the system components from excess pressure.

3) Overload protection

Pressure relief valves in a hydraulic system protect it from overload damage. When the load exceeds the valve setting, pump delivery is directed to the tank. The result is definite limit to torque or force output. Pressure relief valves also provide a means of setting a machine for a

## Lesson 23  An Introduction to Hydraulics

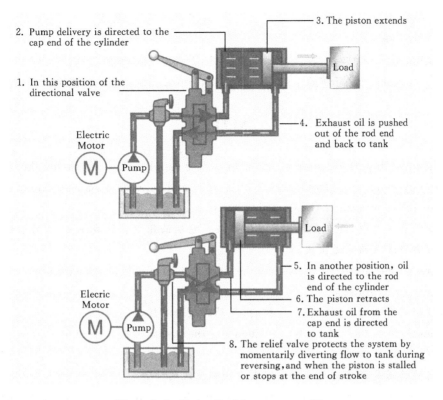

Figure 3.4  Hydraulic drives are reversible

specified amount of torque or force, as in a chucking or a clamping operation.

4) Small packages

Hydraulic components, because of their high speed and pressure capabilities, can provide high power output with very small weight and size.

5) Can be stalled

Stalling an electric motor will cause damage or blow a fuse. Likewise, engines cannot be stalled without the need for restarting. A hydraulic actuator, though, can be stalled without damage when overloaded, and will start up immediately when the load is reduced. During stall, the relief valve simply diverts delivery from the pump to the tank. The only loss encountered is in wasted horsepower.

6) Nocompressible hydraulic oil

Any liquid is essentially nocompressible and therefore will transmit power. The most common liquid used in hydraulic systems is petroleum oil. Oil transmits power readily because it is minimally compressible. The most desirable property of oil is its lubricating ability. The hydraulic fluid must lubricate most moving parts of the components.

# NEW WORDS AND EXPRESSIONS

hydraulic [hai'drɔːlik] *a.* 液压的  
hydraulics [hai'drɔːliks] *n.* 液压  
filtration [fil'treiʃən] *n.* 过滤  
pump [pʌmp] *n.* 泵

reservoir ['rezəvwɑ:] n. 油箱
valve [vælv] n. 阀
cylinder ['silində] n. 汽缸
reversible [ri'və:səbl] a. 可逆的
stall [stɔ:l] n. 熄火
horsepower ['hɔ:s,pauə] n. 马力
hydraulic motor 液压马达
overload protection 过载保护

# NOTES

1) The most important component in the power supply unit is the hydraulic pump. This draws in the hydraulic fluid from a reservoir (tank) and delivers it via a system of lines in the hydraulic installation against the opposing resistances.

在能源供应单元中,最重要的构件是液压泵。它从油箱中抽取液压油,然后通过液压管线系统克服阻力将液压油输送出去。

2) Directional control valves may be actuated manually, mechanically, electrically, pneumatically or hydraulically.

方向控制阀有手动的、机械的、电控的、气动的或者液压控制的。

3) These valves have the job of influencing the pressure in a complete hydraulic system or in a part of the system.

压力阀的作用是调整整个液压系统或者局部系统的压力。

4) The actuator (linear or rotary) of a hydraulic system, however, can be driven from maximum speeds to reduced speeds by varying the pump delivery using a flow control valve.

通过使用流量控制阀改变液压泵传送的油量,液压系统的作动器(直线的或者旋转的)能从最高速开始减速。

# EXERCISES

1. After reading the text above, summarize the main ideas in oral.

2. Fill in the blanks with proper words or phrases according to the text (note the proper tense).

(1) V_____ are devices for controlling energy flow. They can control and regulate the flow direction of the hydraulic fluid, the pressure, the flow rate and, consequently, the flow velocity.

(2) C_____ are drive components which convert hydraulic power into mechanical power.

(3) H_____ motors are drive components controlled by valves.

(4) The most common liquid used in hydraulic systems is p_____ oil. Oil transmits power readily because it is minimally compressible. The most desirable property of oil is its l_____ ability.

(5) A hydraulic actuator can be reversed instantly while in full motion without d_____.

(6) Pressure relief valves in a hydraulic system protect it from overload damage. When the load exceeds the valve setting, p_____ delivery is directed to the tank.

3. Translate the following phrases into Chinese according to the text.
(1) oil filtration unit  (2) directional control valve
(3) double-acting cylinder  (4) flow control valve
4. Translate the following phrases into English according to the text.
(1) 水轮机  (2) 液压泵
(3) 减压阀  (4) 液压马达
(5) 过载保护  (6) 润滑能力
5. Write a 100-word summary according to the text.

# READING MATERIAL

## Reservoir

### 1. Function of Reservoir

The main function of the reservoir in a hydraulic system is to store and supply hydraulic fluid for use by the system, in addition to holding the system fluid supply, a reservoir can also serve several secondary functions, some system designers feel that the reservoir is the key to effective hydraulic system operation.

By transferring waste heat through its wall, the reservoir acts as a heat exchanger that cools the fluid within. As a de-aerator, the reservoir allows entrained air to rise and escape while solid contaminants settle to the bottom of the tank, making it a fluid conditioner.

In some instances, the reservoir may be used as a platform to support the pump, motor, and other system components. This saves floor space and is a simple way to keep the pumps and valves at a good height for servicing.

### 2. Reservoir Components

A typical industrial reservoir is constructed of welded steel plate with end-plate extensions that support the unit. To reduce the change of condensed moisture within the tank causing rust, the inside of the reservoir is painted with a sealer which is compatible to the fluid being used. Because the reservoir is designed for easy fluid maintenance, a plug is placed at a low point on the tank to allow complete drainage.

1) Oil Level Gage

To check the fluid level in the reservoir, either a sight glass or two small portholes are installed in the clean-out plates. This allows the upper and lower fluid limits to be checked without exposing the reservoir to the contamination that can occur when using a dipstick.

2) Breather Assembly

A vented breather cap is installed to accommodate with the air exchange that results from the constant change of pressure and temperature within the tank. As the hydraulic cylinders extend and retract, air is taken in and expelled through this filter. Generally, the breather must be large enough to handle the airflow required to maintain atmospheric pressure, whether the tank is empty or full (the higher the flow rate, the larger the breather).

On a pressurized reservoir, the breather is replaced by an air valve that regulates the tank pressure between preset limits. As oil bath filter is sometimes used in atmospheres that are exceptionally dirty.

3) Filler Opening

The filler opening is often a part of the breather assembly. The opening has a removable screen that keeps contaminants out of the tank when fluid is being added to the reservoir. A cap that will provide a tight seal should be chained to the reservoir.

Another type of filler opening is a quick-disconnect fitting, screwed into a pipe that extends to within a few inches of the bottom of the tank. A portable oil cart, equipped with a small pump and filter, supplies fluid to the tank. This keeps the new fluid clean and prevents contamination of the reservoir.

4) Clean-out Plates

Clean-out plates are usually installed on both ends of the tank. This is especially true on reservoirs sized above ten gallons. The plates are easily removed and large enough to provide complete access when the interior of the reservoir is being cleaned or painted.

5) Baffle Plate

Because fluid returning to the reservoir is usually warmer than the supply fluid and probably contains air bubbles, baffles are used to prevent the returning fluid from directly entering the pump inlet. A baffle plate is installed lengthwise through the center of the tank, forcing the fluid to move along the reservoir walls, where much of the heat is dissipated to the outer surfaces of the reservoir. This long, low-velocity travel also allows the contaminants to settle at the bottom of the tank and provides an opportunity for the fluid to be cleared of any entrained air. The end result is less turbulence in the tank.

6) Line Connections and Fittings

Most lines leading to the reservoir terminate below the oil level. The line connections at the tank cover are often packed (sealed), slip-joint type flanges. This design prevents contaminants from entering through these openings and makes it easy to remove inlet line strainers for cleaning.

Connections made on the top of the reservoir are often set on risers to keep them above dirt and other contaminants that may collect on the reservoir.

To prevent the hydraulic fluid from foaming and becoming aerated, pump return lines must terminate below the fluid level, usually two inches from the bottom of the tank.

Valve drain lines may terminate above the fluid level, but it is generally better to extend them approximately two inches below the fluid level. In all cases, pump and motor drain lines must terminate below the lowest possible fluid level.

Lines that terminate near the tank bottom and are not equipped with strainers should be cut at a 45 degree angle. This prevents the line opening from bottoming in the tank and cutting off flow. On a return line, the angled opening is often positioned so that flow is directed at the tank walls and away from the pump inlet line.

# Lesson 24 | AC Motors[①]

## TEXT

Electric motors are by far the most ubiquitous of the actuators, occurring in virtually all electromechanical systems. Electric motors can be classified either by function or by electrical configuration. In the functional classification, motors are given names suggesting how the motor is to be used. Examples of functional classifications include torque, gear, servo, instrument servo, and stepping. However, it is usually necessary to know something about the electrical design of the motor to make judgments about its application for delivering the power and controlling the position. Figure 3.5 provides a configuration classification of electrical motors found in mechatronics applications. The differences are due to motor winding and rotor designs, resulting in a large variety of operating characteristics. The price-performance ratio of electric motors continues to improve, making them important additions to all sorts of mechatronic systems from appliances to automobiles.

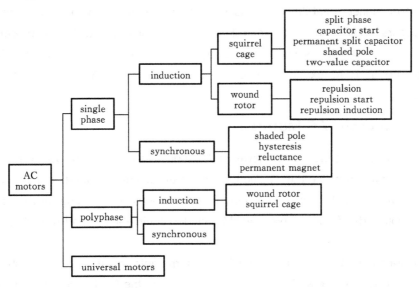

**Figure 3.5　Configuration classification of AC motors**

Invented in the same era as the brush DC motor, the AC motor itself is divided into two major categories: asynchronous (induction) and synchronous. When driven by a fixed-frequency AC source with a constant load, the induction motor operates near the frequency of the input source (or multiple thereof), while the synchronous motor will operate at the input source

---

① The ELECTRIC MOTOR: Here and Now, http://www.freescale.com/

frequency (or multiple thereof). As the frequency of the source is varied, both motor classes will change rotational speed accordingly. However, as the load changes, the difference between the input line frequency and the rotational speed of the rotor for the induction machine will be greater than that of the synchronous machine because of magnetic slip (the difference in rotor speed versus stator speed in a motor) caused by induction.

AC motors rotate by producing a rotating magnetic field pattern in the stator that causes the rotor to follow the rotation of this field pattern. While induction machines produce rotor movement by inducing a magnetic field in the rotor, the rotation tends to lag and be asynchronous to the movement of the stator magnetic field. However, synchronous AC motors produce magnetic fields that cause the rotor to synchronize to the rotation of the stator magnetic field and tend to be more efficient than induction motors in applications requiring more than several hundred horsepower. In addition, synchronous motors are often employed with asynchronous motors in large industrial applications to stabilize voltage and to improve overall power factor performance due to the synchronous motor's ability to provide leading power factor.

Single-phase AC motors are extremely low-cost and usually operate at a multiple of line speed for single speed operation. Poly-phase AC machines are the choice for higher-performance drives requiring more torque in smaller motor frames, a reduction in phase current demands and/or higher reliability (or "no stop") operation. With the emergence of digital signal processors (DSP) and microcontrollers (MCU) combined with new power electronic devices, closed-loop control systems employing vector, direct torque and adaptive controls methods can be used to expand the low-cost capabilities of AC motors into many new applications.

## 1. Asynchronous AC Motors

Asynchronous AC motors, also known as AC induction motors (ACIM), are probably the most widely used motor of the day. Induction motors are simple, rugged, reliable and easy-to-manufacture. They include single-and poly-phase designs developing power levels from fractional to thousands of horsepower. ACIM includes squirrel-cage and wound-rotor induction designs.

In squirrel-cage motors, the rotor consists of permeable metal containing embedded strips of magnetic material. As the stator magnetic field rotates, the field interacts with the magnetic field established by the magnetic poles of the rotor, causing the rotor to turn at nearly the speed of the rotating stator magnetic field.

In wound-rotor designs, the permanent magnets used in the squirrel-cage motor are replaced by a rotor having windings. In this motor, when the stator magnetic field rotates and the rotor windings are shorted, the stator magnetic field motion induces a field into the wound-rotor, once again causing the rotor to turn at nearly the speed of the rotating stator magnetic field. However, if the rotor windings are connected externally through slip rings on the shaft, the winding current can be controlled to increase or decrease the slip speed of the rotor.

## 2. Synchronous AC Motors

Synchronous AC motors are not as widely used as ACIM because of having a more complex and expensive rotor design. Synchronous AC motor types include: permanent magnet, field wound, stepper and reluctance. Of these, both permanent magnet and field wound synchronous motors are used in "brushless" DC motor implementations.

# NEW WORDS AND EXPRESSIONS

ubiquitous [juːˈbikwitəs] a. 普遍存在的,无处不在的
electromechanical [iˌlektrəumiˈkænikəl] a. 机电的
functional [ˈfʌŋkʃənl] a. 功能的
rotor [ˈrəutə] n. 转子
polyphase [ˈpɔlifeiz] a. 多相的
induction [inˈdʌkʃən] n. (电磁)感应
synchronous [ˈsiŋkrənəs] a. 同时的,[物]同步的
repulsion [riˈpʌlʃən] n. (电动机)推斥,排斥,推斥式
hysteresis [ˌhistəˈriːsis] n. 滞后作用,[物]磁滞现象,(电动机)磁滞式
reluctance [riˈlʌktəns] n. (电动机)磁阻
asynchronous [eiˈsiŋkrənəs] a. 不同时的,[电]异步的
single phase 单相的
motor winding 电机绕组
universal motor 交直流两用电动机
squirrel cage (电动机)鼠笼式
wound rotor (电动机)绕线转子
split phase (电动机)分相式
capacitor start (电动机)电容(器)启动
permanent split capacitor (电动机)固定分相的电容式
shaded pole (电动机)屏蔽极式
two-value capacitor start (电动机)两价电容(器)启动
repulsion start (电动机)推斥式启动
repulsion induction (电动机)推斥式感应
permanent magnet (电动机)永磁

# NOTES

1) As the frequency of the source is varied, both motor classes will change rotational speed accordingly. However, as the load changes, the difference between the input line frequency and the rotational speed of the rotor for the induction machine will be greater than that of the synchronous machine because of magnetic slip (the difference in rotor speed versus stator speed in a motor) caused by induction.
由于电源频率的变化,这两类电机的转速也将相应改变。然而,随着负载的变化,输入线频率与发动机转子的转速之间的差别,感应式发动机会较同步式发动机的增大,这是由于感应引起的电磁转差率(即电动机中转子的速度与定子的速度差)的原因。

2) While induction machines produce rotor movement by inducing a magnetic field in the rotor, the rotation tends to lag and be asynchronous to the movement of the stator magnetic field. However, synchronous AC motors produce magnetic fields that cause the rotor to synchronize to the rotation of the stator magnetic field and tend to be more efficient than

induction motors in applications requiring more than several hundred horsepower.

当感应式电动机由转子中的磁场而使得转子转动时,其转动是滞后且异步于定子磁场的转动的。然而,同步交流电动机产生的磁场使得转子与定子的磁场同步旋转。在功率要求达到几百马力的情况下,同步交流电动机将比感应式电动机效率更高。

3) With the emergence of digital signal processors (DSP) and microcontrollers (MCU) combined with new power electronic devices, closed-loop control systems employing vector, direct torque and adaptive controls methods can be used to expand the low cost capabilities of AC motors into many new applications.

随着数字信号处理器和微控制器的出现,将新的电源电子装置、应用矢量方程的闭环控制系统、直接转矩技术和自适应控制系统方法结合起来,用于改造低成本性能的交流发动机,从而开发出许多新的应用。

4) As the stator magnetic field rotates, the field interacts with the magnetic field established by the magnetic poles of the rotor, causing the rotor to turn at nearly the speed of the rotating stator magnetic field.

随着定子磁场的旋转,在转子磁极产生的磁场的共同作用下,转子将转动,其转动的速度与定子磁场旋转的速度相近。

5) However, if the rotor windings are connected externally through slip rings on the shaft, the winding current can be controlled to increase or decrease the slip speed of the rotor.

然而,通过轴上的滑环从外部将转子绕组连接起来,就可以控制绕组电流,达到增加或减少转子滑动速度的目的。

# EXERCISES

1. After reading the text above, summarize the main ideas in oral.

2. Fill in the blanks with proper words or phrases according to the text (note the proper tense).

(1) Electric motors are by f_____ the most u_____ of the actuators, occurring in virtually all electromechanical systems.

(2) The p_____-p_____ ratio of electric motors continues to improve, making them important additions to all sorts of m_____ systems from appliances to automobiles.

(3) Invented in the same era as the brush DC motor, the AC motor itself is divided into two major categories: a_____ (induction) and s_____.

(4) I_____ motors are simple, rugged, r_____ and easy-to-manufacture.

(5) In s_____-cage motors, the rotor c_____ of permeable metal containing embedded strips of magnetic material.

(6) Other identification systems are b_____ on acoustic waves, optical character recognition, and machine vision.

3. Translate the following phrases into Chinese according to the text.

(1) electromechanical system

(2) be divided into two major categories: asynchronous (induction) and synchronous

(3) the induction motor operates near the frequency of the input source

(4) more than several hundred horsepower

(5) asynchronous AC motors

(6) synchronous AC motors

4. Translate the following phrases into English according to the text.

(1) 简单的、粗糙的、可靠的和易于制造的

(2) 随着数字信号处理器和微控制器的出现

(3) 多相交流电动机　　　　　(4) 增减转子的滑动速率

(5) 转子磁场运动　　　　　　(6) 磁滞式电动机

(7) 鼠笼式电动机　　　　　　(8) 电机绕组

(9) 绕线转子电动机

(10) 定子的设计更复杂和价格更贵

5. Write a 100-word summary according to the text.

# READING MATERIAL

Generally, AC servo motors have no parts that wear off or that must be replaced periodically, unlike DC servo motors, which have brushes that must be replaced periodically.

However, you should perform periodic maintenance for servo motors so as to keep their initial performance as long as possible and to prevent breakdowns. AC servo motors have precision detectors. Their incorrect use or damage caused during transportation or assembling can result in breakdowns or accidents. We recommend that you inspect the servo motors periodically according to the descriptions given below.

## 1. Receiving and Keeping AC Servo Motors

When you receive an AC servo motor, make sure that:

● The motor is exactly the one you ordered, in term of model, shaft, and detector specifications.

● No damage has been caused on the motor.

● The hand can rotate the shaft normally.

● The brake works normally.

● There is no loose bolt or play.

Because FANUC inspects servo motors strictly before shipment, you do not in principle, have to inspect them when you receive them. However, you should check the specifications (wiring, current, and voltage) of the motor and detector carefully as required.

The servo motors should be kept indoors as a rule. Do not place or install AC servo motors in the place where:

a) It is extremely humid and dew is prone to form;

b) There is a steep change in temperature;

c) There is constant vibration, which may cause damage to the shaft bearings;
d) There is lots of dust and trash.

## 2. Daily Inspection of AC Servo Motors

Before starting operation, or periodically (once a week or month), you should inspect the AC servo motors in terms of the following:

1) Vibration and noise

Check the motor for abnormal vibration (by the hand) and noise (by the ear) when the motor is: a) not rotating; b) rotating at low speed; c) accelerating or decelerating.

If you find anything unusual, contact your FANUC service staff.

2) Damage on the outside

Check the motor cover (red plastic) for crevices and the motor surface (black coating) for scratches and cracks.

If you find a crevice in the motor cover, you should replace it as quick as possible. If there is a scratch or crack on the motor surface, the user should repair it by himself as required. if coating has come off, dry the portions of interest (or the entire surface) and coats it with paint for machines such as urethane paint.

3) Stains and smudges

Check the motor surface and bolt holes for oil or cutting fluid. Wipe off oil and cutting fluid on the motor surface periodically. Oil or cutting fluid can damage the coating by chemical reaction, possibly leading to a failure. Also check how such a liquid leaks onto the motor, and repair it if needed.

4) Overheating

Check to see if the motor is too hot during normal operation. Attach a thermolator on the motor surface and check it visually to see if the motor becomes too hot during normal operation.

**Note**: Temperature on the motor surface can exceed 80℃ under some conditions. Never touch it by the hand.

## 3. Periodic Inspection of AC Servo Motor

You'd better inspect the AC servo motor for the following items at least once a year.

1) Observation of torque command (TCMD) and speed command (VCMD) waveforms

Observe normal voltage waveforms with an oscilloscope, and keep notes of them. During periodic inspection, check the current waveforms with the records.

The waveforms vary according to the operating conditions such as load and cutting speed. Note that you should make comparisons under the same condition.

2) Diagnosis by waveforms

Check the measured waveforms to see whether:

A. The peak current is within the limit to the current in the amplifier. The limit to the amplifier current is listed below.

The motor used to accelerate/decelerate with the amplifier current within the limit (the acceleration/ deceleration torque used to be sufficient), but something is wrong now. If this is the case, the probable causes are:

—The load conditions in the machine have changed because of changed friction or reduced machine efficiency after long period of use.

—Motor failure.

B. The waveform has ripple during constant-speed feeding.

C. The current waveform has ripple or jumps when the motor is not rotating.

# Lesson 25  DC Motors

## TEXT

Direct current (DC) motors are used in a large number of mechatronic designs because of the torque-speed characteristics achievable with different electrical configurations. DC motor speeds can be smoothly controlled and in most cases are reversible. Since DC motors have a high ratio of torque to rotor-inertia, they can respond quickly. Also, dynamic braking, where motor-generated energy is fed to a resistor dissipater, and regenerative braking, where motor-generated energy is fed back to the DC power supply, can be implemented in applications where quick stops and high efficiency are desired.

Based on how the stator magnetic fields are created, DC motors are classified into four categories: permanent magnet, shunt wound, series wound, and compound wound. The electrical schematics, torque-speed curves, and current-torque curves for each configuration are illustrated in Figure 3.6 through Figure 3.10. Figure 3.6 illustrates a typical torque-speed curve that displays the torques a motor can provide at different speeds at rated voltage. For a given torque provided by the motor, the current-torque curve can be used to determine the amount of current required when rated voltage is applied. As a general rule of thumb, motors deliver large torques at low speeds, and large torques implies large motor currents. The starting torque or stall torque $T_s$ is the maximum torque the motor can produce, at zero speed, associated with starting or overloading the motor. The no-load speed $\omega_{max}$ is the maximum sustained speed the motor can attain. This speed can be reached only when no load or torque is applied to the motor (i.e., only when it is free running).

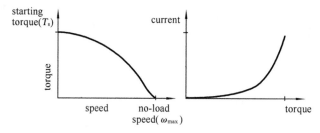

Figure 3.6  Motor torque-speed curve

In Figure 3.6 through Figure 3.10, V is the DC voltage supply, $I_A$ is the current in the rotor (armature) windings, $I_F$ is the current in the stator (field) windings, and $I_L$ is the total load current delivered by the DC supply.

The stator fields in permanent magnet (PM) motors (see Figure 3.7) are provided by permanent magnets, which require no external power source and therefore produce no $I^2R$ heating. A PM motor is lighter and smaller than other equivalent DC motors because the field strength of permanent magnets is high. The radial width of a typical permanent magnet is roughly one-fourth that of an equivalent field winding. PM motors are easily reversed by switching the direction of the applied voltage, because the current and field change direction only in the rotor. The PM motor is ideal in computer control applications because of the linearity of its torque-speed relation. The design of a controller is always easier when the actuator is linear since the system analysis is greatly simplified. When a motor is used in a position or speed control application with sensor feedback to a controller, it is referred to as a servomotor. PM motors are used only in low-power applications since their rated power is usually limited to 5 hp (3 728 W) or less, with fractional horsepower ratings being more common. PM DC motors can be brushed, brushless, or stepper motors.

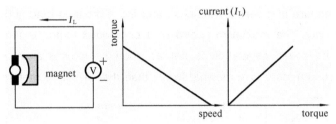

Figure 3.7　DC permanent motor schematic and torque-speed curve

Shunt motors (see Figure 3.8) have armature and field windings connected in parallel, which are powered by the same supply. The total load current is the sum of the armature and field currents. Shunt motors exhibit nearly constant speed over a large range of loading, have starting torques about 1.5 times the rated operating torque, have the lowest starting torque of any of the DC motors, and can be economically converted to allow adjustable speed by placing a potentiometer in series with the field windings.

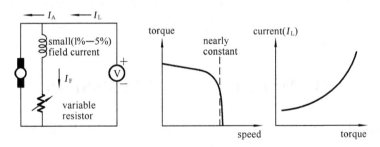

Figure 3.8　DC shunt motor schematic and torque-speed curves

Series motors (see Figure 3.9) have armature and field windings connected in series so the armature and field currents are equal. Series motors exhibit very high starting torques, highly variable speed depending on load, and very high speed when the load is small. In fact, large series motors can fail catastrophically when they are suddenly unloaded (e.g., in a belt drive application when the belt fails) due to dynamic forces at high speeds. This is called runaway. As long as the motor remains loaded, this poses no problem. The torque-speed curve for a series motor is hyperbolic in shape, implying an inverse relationship between torque and speed and nearly constant power over a wide range.

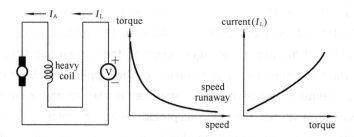

Figure 3.9 DC series motor schematic and torque-speed curves

Compound motors (see Figure 3.10) include both shunt and series field windings, resulting in combined characteristics of both shunt and series motors. Part of the load current passes through both the armature and series windings, and the remaining load current passes through the shunt windings only. The maximum speed of a compound motor is limited, unlike with a series motor, but its speed regulation is not as good as with a shunt motor. The torque produced by compound motors is somewhat lower than that of series motors of similar size.

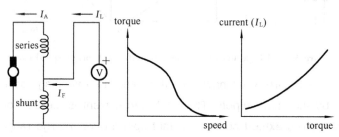

Figure 3.10 DC compound motor schematic and torque-speed curves

Note that, unlike the permanent magnet motor, when voltage polarity for a shunt, series, or compound DC motor is changed, the direction of rotation does not change. The reason is that the polarity of both the stator and rotor changes, because the field and armature windings are excited by the same source.

# NEW WORDS AND EXPRESSIONS

reversible [ri'və:səbl] a. 可逆的
equivalent [i'kwivələnt] a. 相等的，相当的，同意义的
dissipater ['disipeitə] v. 耗尽，用完
regenerative [ri'dʒenərətiv] a. 再生的，反馈的
fractional ['frækʃənl] a. 部分的，碎片的，分数的，小数的
armature ['ɑ:mətjuə] n. 转子，电枢
catastrophically [,kætə'strɔfikli] ad. 毁灭性地，彻底失败地

hyperbolic [,haipə'bɔlik] a. 双曲线的
somewhat ['sʌm(h)wɔt] ad. 稍微，有点，有些
dynamic braking 动态制动(装置)
regenerative braking 再生制动，反馈制动
shunt wound (电动机)并激[励]
series wound (电动机)串激[励]
compound wound (电动机)复激[励]
fractional horsepower (rating) 小功率电动机(小于1马力)
runaway 失控

## NOTES

1) Since DC motors have a high ratio of torque to rotor-inertia, they can respond quickly. Also, dynamic braking, where motor-generated energy is fed to a resistor dissipater, and regenerative braking, where motor-generated energy is fed back to the DC power supply, can be implemented in applications where quick stops and high efficiency are desired.

由于直流电机的扭矩-转动惯量之比较高,因此直流电机响应灵敏。比如,在动态制动装置中,电动机产生的能量供电阻器消耗;在再生制动装置中,电动机产生的能量作为直流电动机的电源供给。将直流电动机应用于以上两种装置中,可以期望获得快速停止和高效率的性能。

2) As a general rule of thumb, motors deliver large torques at low speeds, and large torques implies large motor currents. The starting torque or stall torque $T_s$ is the maximum torque the motor can produce, at zero speed, associated with starting or overloading the motor.

按常规来说,电动机在低速时提供的扭矩大,而扭矩大电动机电流就大。启动扭矩或停止扭矩 $T_s$ 是电动机能提供的最大扭矩,当速度为零时,电动机启动会出现过载。

3) PM motors are used only in low-power applications since their rated power is usually limited to 5 hp or less, with fractional horsepower ratings being more common.

由于永磁电动机的额定功率总是被限制在 5 马力(1 马力=735.499 瓦)或 5 马力以下,且小马力更常用,故它们只能用在动力要求低的场合。

4) Compound motors include both shunt and series field windings, resulting in combined characteristics of both shunt and series motors.

复激电动机包含并激和串激两种磁场绕组电路,从而也就具有并激和串激电动机的双重特性。

5) The reason is that the polarity of both the stator and rotor changes, because the field and armature windings are excited by the same source.

其原因是改变了转子和定子的极性,而磁场和电枢绕组的激励源不变。

6) Shunt motors exhibit nearly constant speed over a large range of loading, have starting torques about 1.5 times the rated operating torque, have the lowest starting torque of any of the DC motors, and can be economically converted to allow adjustable speed by placing a potentiometer in series with the field windings.

并激电动机表现出如下特性:当负载在一个大范围内变化时,速度恒定不变;启动扭矩大约是工作扭矩的 1.5 倍;所有的直流电机的启动扭矩都是最低的;通过在磁场绕组电路中串联一个电压表,就可以经济地做到速度调节。

## EXERCISES

1. After reading the text above, summarize the main ideas in oral.

2. Fill in the blanks with proper words or phrases according to the text.

(1) Direct current (DC) motors are used in a large number of m_____ designs because of the torque-speed characteristics a_____ with different electrical configurations.

(2) B_____ on how the stator magnetic fields are created, DC motors are classified into four c_____: permanent magnet, shunt wound, series wound, and compound wound.

(3) A PM motor is lighter and s_____ than other e_____ DC motors because the field strength of permanent magnets is high.

(4) In fact, large series motors can fail c_____ when they are suddenly unloaded (e. g., in a belt drive application when the belt fails) due to dynamic forces at high speeds. This is called r_____.

(5) The torque-speed curve for a series motor is h_____ in shape, implying an inverse relationship between torque and speed and n_____ constant power over a wide range.

3. Translate the following phrases into Chinese according to the text.

(1) the torque-speed characteristics

(2) have a high ratio of torque to rotor-inertia

(3) large torques at low speeds

(4) the no-load speed

(5) the linearity of its torque-speed relation

(6) the field strength of permanent magnet

4. Translate the following phrases into English according to the text.

(1) 并激直流电动机  (2) 永磁直流电动机
(3) 串激直流电动机  (4) 复激直流电动机
(5) 反馈制动装置    (6) 称为失控状态
(7) 小马力直流电机  (8) 按惯例

5. Write a 100-word summary according to the text.

# READING MATERIAL

## Stepper Motor

A special type of DC motor, known as a stepper motor, is a permanent magnet or variable reluctance DC motor that has the following performance characteristics:

It can rotate in both directions, move in precise angular increments, sustain a holding torque at zero speed, and be controlled by digital circuits. It moves in accurate angular increments, known as steps, in response to the application of digital pulses to an electric drive circuit. The number and rate of the pulses control the position and the speed of the motor shaft. Generally, stepper motors are manufactured with steps per revolution of 12, 24, 72, 144, 180, and 200, resulting in shaft increments of 30°, 15°, 5°, 2.5°, 2°, and 1.8° per step. Special micro-stepping circuitry can be designed to allow much more steps per revolution, often 10 000 steps/rev or more.

Stepper motors are either bipolar, requiring two power sources or a switchable polarity power source, or unipolar, requiring only one power source. They are powered by DC sources and require digital circuitry to produce coil energizing sequences for rotation of the motor. Feedback is not always required for control, but the use of an encoder or other position sensor can ensure accuracy when exact position control is critical. The advantage of operating without feedback (i.e., in open loop mode) is that a closed loop control system is not required. Generally, stepper motors produce less than 1 hp (746 W) and are therefore used only in low-power position control applications.

A commercial stepper motor has a large number of poles that define a large number of equilibrium positions of the rotor. In the case of a permanent magnet stepper motor, the stator consists of wound poles, and the rotor poles are permanent magnets. Exciting different stator winding combinations moves and holds the rotor in different positions. The variable reluctance stepper motor has a ferromagnetic rotor rather than a permanent magnet rotor. Motion and holding result from the attraction of stator and rotor poles to positions with minimum magnetic reluctance that allow for maximum magnetic flux. A variable reluctance motor has the advantage of lower rotor inertia and therefore a faster dynamic response. The permanent magnet stepper motor has the advantage of a small residual holding torque, called the detent torque, even when the stator is not energized.

To understand how the rotor moves in an incremental fashion, consider a simple design consisting of four stator poles and a permanent magnet rotor as illustrated in Figure 3.11. In step 0, the rotor is in equilibrium, because opposite poles on the stator and rotor are adjacent to and attract each other. Unless the magnet polarities of the stator poles are changed, the rotor remains in this position and can withstand an opposing torque up to a value called the holding torque. When the stator polarities are changed as shown (step 0 to step 1), a torque is applied to the rotor, causing it to move 90° in the clockwise direction to a new equilibrium position shown as step 1. When the stator polarities are again changed as shown (step 1 to step 2), the rotor experiences a torque driving it to step 2. By successively changing the stator polarities in this manner, the rotor can move to successive equilibrium positions in the clockwise direction. The sequencing of the pole excitations is the means by which the direction of rotation occurs. Counterclockwise motion can be achieved by applying the polarity sequence in the opposite direction. The motor torque is directly related to the magnetic field strength of the poles and the rotor.

The dynamic response of the rotor and attached load must be carefully considered in applications that involve starting or stopping quickly, changing or ramping speeds quickly, or driving large or changing loads. Due to the inertia of the rotor and attached load, rotation can exceed the desired number of steps. Also, as illustrated in Figure 3.12, a stepper motor driving a typical mechanical system through one step will exhibit an underdamped response. If damping is increased in the system, for example, with mechanical, frictional, or viscous damping, the response can be modified to reduce oscillation, as shown in the figure. Note,

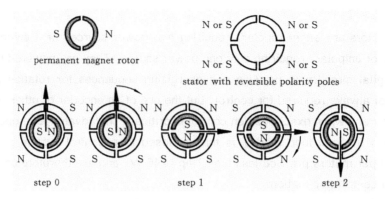

Figure 3.11  Stepper motor step sequence

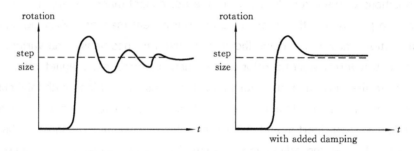

Figure 3.12  Dynamic response of a single step

however, that even with an ideal choice for damping, the motor requires time to totally settle into a given position, and this settling time varies with the step size and the amount of damping. It is also important to note that the torque required from the motor increases with added damping.

The torque-speed characteristics for a stepper motor are usually divided into two regions as illustrated in Figure 3.13. In the locked step mode, the rotor decelerates and may even come to rest between each step. Within this region, the motor can be instantaneously started, stopped, or reversed without losing step integrity. In the slewing mode, the speed is too fast to allow instantaneous starting, stopping, or reversing. The rotor must be gradually accelerated to enter this mode and gradually decelerated to leave the mode. While in slewing mode, the rotor is in synch with the stator field rotation and does not settle between steps. The curve between the two regions in the figure indicates the maximum torques that the stepper can provide at different speeds without slewing. The curve bordering the outside of the slewing mode region represents the absolute maximum torques the stepper can provide at different speeds.

Figure 3.14 illustrates a unipolar stepper motor field coil schematic with external power transistors that must be switched on and off to produce the controlled sequence of stator polarities to cause rotation. The wire colors indicated in the figure are standard for most manufacturers.

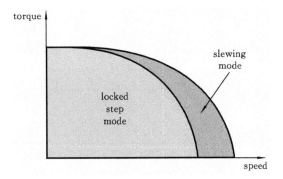

Figure 3.13  Stepper motor torque-speed curves

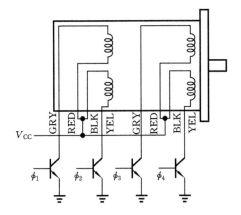

Figure 3.14  Standard unipolar stepper motor field

# Part IV

# Automobile

# Part 1

## Automobile

# Lesson 26 | The Layout and Main Components of Automobile

## TEXT

### 1. Automobile Layout

In automobile design layout is the place where both the engine and driven wheels are.

1) FF layout

In automobile design, an FF, or front-engine, front-wheel drive layout places both the engine and driven wheels at the front of the vehicle. This layout is typically chosen for its compact packaging, that is, it takes up very little space, allowing the rest of the vehicle to be designed more flexibly.

2) FR layout

In automobile design, an FR, or front-engine, rear wheel drive means a layout where the engine is in the front of the vehicle and drive wheels at the rear. This was the traditional automobile layout for most of the 20th century.

3) RMR layout

In automobile design, an RMR or rear mid-engine, rear-wheel drive layout is one in which the rear wheels are driven by an engine placed just in front of them, behind the passenger compartment. In contrast to the rear-engine RR layout, the center of mass of the engine is in front of the rear axle. This layout is typically chosen for its low polar inertia and relatively favorable weight distribution (the heaviest component is near the center of the car, making the main component of its moment of inertia relatively low). The layout does suffer from a tendency toward being heavier in the rear than the front, which is not ideal for handling. However, it is generally felt that the lower polar inertia more than makes up for this. The mid-engine layout also takes up central space, making it impractical for any but two-seater sports cars.

4) MF layout

In automobile design, an MF or mid-engine, front wheel drive layout is one in which the front wheels are driven by an engine placed just behind them, in front of the passenger compartment. In contrast to the front-engine FF layout the center of gravity of the engine is behind the front axle. This layout is typically chosen for its better weight distribution (the heaviest component is near the center of the car, lowering its moment of inertia).

5) RR layout

In automobile design, an RR, or rear-engine, rear-wheel drive layout places both the engine and drive wheels at the rear of the vehicle. In contrast to the RMR layout, however, the center of gravity of the engine itself is actually past the rear axle. This is not to be confused with the center of gravity of the whole vehicle, as an imbalance of such proportions would make it impossible to keep the front wheels on the ground.

## 2. Principal Components

Today's average car contains more than 15 000 separate, individual parts that must work together. These parts can be grouped into four major categories: engine, body, chassis and electrical equipment (Figure 4.1).

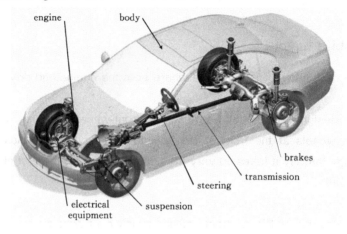

Figure 4.1  Layout of a car

1) Engine

The engine acts as the power unit. The internal combustion engine is the most common: this obtains its power by burning liquid fuel inside the engine cylinder. There are two types of engine: gasoline (also called a spark-ignition engine) and diesel (also called a compression-ignition engine). Both are called heat engines; the burning fuel generates heat which causes the gas inside the cylinder to increase its pressure and supply power to rotate a shaft connected to the transmission.

2) Body

An automobile body is a sheet metal shell with windows, doors, a hood, and a trunk deck built into it. It provides a protective covering for the engine, passengers, and the cargo. The body is designed to keep passengers safe and comfortable. The body style provides art attractive, colorful, modern appearance for the vehicle.

3) Chassis

The chassis is an assembly of those systems that are the major operating parts of a vehicle. The chassis includes the transmission, suspension, steering, and brake systems.

The power train system conveys the drive to the wheels.

The steering controls the direction of the movement of the car.

The suspension and wheels absorb the road shocks.

The brake slows down the vehicle.

4) Electrical Equipment

The electrical system supplies electricity for the ignition, horn, lights, heater, and starter. The electricity level is maintained by a charging circuit. The charging system provides electrical energy for all of the electrical components on the vehicles. The main parts of the charging system include: the battery, the alternator, the voltage regulator which is usually integral to alternator, a charging warning or indicator light and wiring that complete the circuit. The starting system consists of battery, cables, starter motor, flywheel ring gear and the ignition switch. A basic ignition system consists of the battery, low-tension cables, the ignition coil, distributor, coil high-tension cables, spark plug cables and spark plugs.

## NEW WORDS AND EXPRESSIONS

compartment [kəmˈpɑːtmənt] n. 间隔间，车厢
imbalance [imˈbæləns] n. 不平衡，不均衡
hood [hud] n. （发动机）罩
chassis [ˈtʃæsi] n. 车身底盘
brake [breik] n. 制动器
suspension [səsˈpenʃən] n. 悬架
transmission [trænzˈmiʒən] n. 变速器，传动系，传动装置
differential [ˌdifəˈrenʃəl] n. 差速器

steering [ˈstiəriŋ] n. 转向系
alternator [ˈɔːltə(ː)neitə] n. 交流发动机
ignition [igˈniʃən] n. 点火
high-tension [ˈhaiˈtenʃən] a. 高压的
low-tension [ˈləuˈtenʃən] a. 低压的
flywheel [ˈflaiwiːl] n. 飞轮，调速轮
distributor [diˈstribjutə] n. 分电器
trunk deck 行李箱盖
electrical equipment 电气装置
spark plug 火花塞

## NOTES

1) In automobile design, an RMR or rear mid-engine, rear-wheel drive layout is one in which the rear wheels are driven by an engine placed just in front of them, behind the passenger compartment. In contrast to the rear-engine RR layout, the center of mass of the engine is in front of the rear axle.

在汽车设计中，RMR 方式，也称为后中置发动机、后轮驱动布局方式，驱动后轮的发动机安装在后轮前、车厢后。和后置发动机的 RR 布局方式相比，这种布局的发动机的重心在后轴的前面。

2) The body is designed to keep passengers safe and comfortable. The body styling provides art attractive, colorful, modern appearance for the vehicle.

车身的设计应考虑乘客的安全和舒适度。其造型讲究艺术美、色彩美和时尚美。

3) The chassis is an assembly of those systems that are the major operating parts of a vehicle. The chassis includes the transmission, suspension, steering, and brake systems.

车身底盘系统由汽车的主要操纵部件装配而成，它包括传输系统、悬挂系统、方向系统和制动系统。

4) The charging system provides electrical energy for all of the electrical components on the vehicles. The main parts of the charging system include the battery, the alternator, the voltage regulator which is usually integral to the alternator, a charging warning or indicator

light and wiring that complete the circus.

充电系统为车上所有的电气元件提供电源。该部分主要由蓄电池、交流发电机、电压调节器(通常被整合到交流发电机中)、一个电池电量警示或指示灯以及连接的导线组成。

5) A basic ignition system consists of the battery, low-tension cables, the ignition coil, distributor, coil high-tension cables, spark plug cables and spark plugs.

点火系统的基本组成部分包括蓄电池、低压电缆、点火线圈、分电器、线圈高压电缆、火花塞电缆以及火花塞。

# EXERCISES

1. After reading the text above, summarize the main ideas in oral.

2. Fill in the blanks with proper words or phrases according to the text (note the proper tense).

(1) In c_____ to the rear-engine RR layout, the center of mass of the engine is in f_____ of the rear axle.

(2) The mid-engine layout also t_____ up central space, making it i_____ for any but two-seater sports cars.

(3) This is not to be c_____ with the center of gravity of the whole vehicle, as an imbalance of such p_____ would make it impossible to keep the front wheels on the ground.

(4) An automobile body is a s_____ metal shell with windows, doors, a hood, and a trunk d_____ built into it.

(5) The internal c_____ engine is the most common; this obtains its power by burning liquid fuel inside the engine c_____.

3. Translate the following phrases into Chinese according to the text.

(1) to be chosen for its compact packaging

(2) the center of gravity of the engine

(3) the internal combustion engine

(4) a spark-ignition engine

(5) a compression-ignition engine

(6) to keep passengers safe and comfortable

4. Translate the following phrases into English according to the text.

(1) 电气系统            (2) 点火系统
(3) 启动系统            (4) 悬挂系统
(5) 方向系统            (6) 制动系统
(7) 供电系统            (8) 金属外壳
(9) 行李箱盖            (10) 动力装置

5. Write a 100-word summary according to the text.

*Lesson 26   The Layout and Main Components of Automobile*

# READING MATERIAL

## The Basic Components of Automobile

The three basic components of the automobile are the engine, chassis and body (see Figure 4 2)

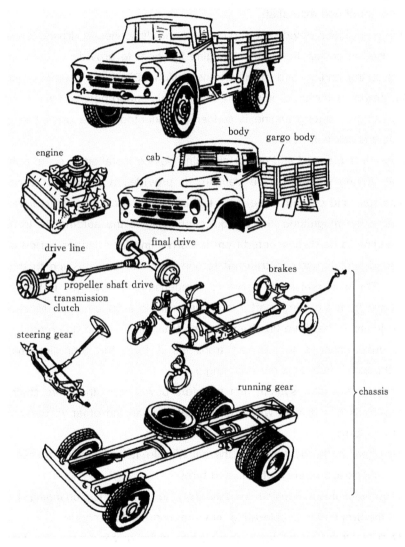

Figure 4.2   Basic components of the automobile

The engine converts the fuel energy into mechanical power. An internal combustion engine powers our modern automobile. The engine burns its fuel within the engine proper, as compared to a steam engine where the fuel is burned externally. The gasoline and air mixture of the internal combustion engine is compressed by a piston inside an airtight cylinder and ignited by a spark. The trapped air-fuel mixture burns fiercely, causing tremendous heat which expands the trapped gases and pushes the piston down. This is the motive power of the automobile. The automobile engine is essentially a heat engine. It requires fuel to burn, a spark to ignite, lubrication to minimize friction, and a cooling system to dissipate unwanted heat.

The chassis comprises the drive line, running gear (undercarriage) and control mechanisms.

The drive line consists of mechanisms and units which transmit torque from the engine to the drive wheels and change torque and rpm in magnitude and direction. Among these mechanisms and units are the clutch, transmission (gearbox), propeller shaft, and final drive comprising differential and axle shaft.

The clutch is a friction device used to connect and disconnect a driving force from a driven member. It is used in conjunction with an engine flywheel to provide smooth engagement and disengagement of the engine and manual transmission. Since an internal combustion engine develops little power or torque at low rpm, it must gain speed before it will move the vehicle. However, if a rapidly rotating engine is suddenly connected to the drive line of a stationary vehicle, a violent shock will result.

A transmission is a speed and power changing device installed at some point between the engine and the driving wheels of the vehicle. It provides a means for changing the ratio between engine rpm and driving wheel rpm to best meet each particular driving situation. It converts torque in the magnitude and the direction, allows the automobile to move forth and back and the engine to be disconnected from the drive line for a longer period of time.

The universal joint is used to transmit torque from the transmission to the final drive at varying angles. The universal joints serve to compensate for changes in the line of drive by transmitting power from a driving shaft through an angle to a driven shaft. Most cars use two or three universal joints in the drive line between the transmission and differential.

The final drive changes torque and transmits it from the propeller shaft through the differential to the axle shafts at a constant angle.

The differential is a gear system that transfers power from the drive shaft to the driving axles. It also permits one driving wheel to turn faster than the other to prevent skidding and scuffing of tires on turns.

The running gear is the backbone of the automobile; it includes the frame, front and rear axles, springs, shock absorbers, wheels and tyres.

The control mechanism consists of the steering system for changing the direction of movement and the brakes for decelerating and stopping the automobile.

The body of the truck comprises a cargo body and a driver's cab. The fenders, radiator grille, hood, and mudguards also belong to the body.

# Lesson 27 | Engine Classification and Overall Mechanics

## TEXT

### 1. Engine Classification

The automobile engine can be classified according to: (1) the number of cylinders; (2) the arrangement of cylinders; (3) the arrangement of valves; (4) the type of the cooling system; (5) the number of cycles (two or four); (6) the type of the fuel burned; (7) the type of the ignition (see Figure 4.3—Figure 4.5).

| gasoline    diesel | single    multiple | vertical    V configuration |

Figure 4.3 Classification by the burning liquid fuel inside the engine

Figure 4.4 Classification by the number of cylinders

Figure 4.5 Classification by the arrangement of cylinders

The way engine cylinders are arranged is called the engine configuration. In-line engines have the cylinders in a line. This design creates a simply cast engine block. In vehicle applications, the number of cylinders is normally from 2 up to 6 (see Figure 4.4). Usually, the cylinders are vertical. As the number of the cylinders increases, the length of the block and crankshaft would become a problem. One way to avoid this is with a V configuration (see Figure 4.5). This design makes the engine block and crankshaft shorter and more rigid.

The engine is the source of power that makes the wheels rolling and the car move. The automobile engine is an internal combustion engine because the fuel (gasoline) is burned inside it. The burning of gasoline inside the engine generates high pressure in the engine combustion chamber. This high pressure forces piston to move, the movement is carried by connecting rods to the engine crankshaft. The crankshaft is thus made to rotate, the rotary motion is carried through the power train to the car wheels so that they rotate and the car moves.

### 2. Engine Overall Mechanics

The engine has hundreds of other parts (see Figure 4.6). The major parts of engine are engine block, engine heads, pistons, connecting rods, crankshafts and valves. The other parts

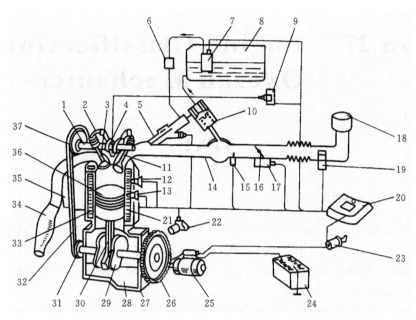

**Figure 4.6 Overall mechanics of a engine**

1. camshaft; 2. rocker arm; 3. exhaust valve; 4. plug; 5. electric-control injector; 6. fuel filter; 7. electric fuel pump; 8. fuel tank; 9. ignition coil module; 10. fuel pressure regulator; 11. intake valve; 12. cooling fluid temperature sensor; 13. detonation sensor; 14. intake manifold; 15. intake temperature sensor; 16. throttle valve; 17. throttle valve sensor; 18. air filter; 19. air quality sensor; 20. electric control unit (ECU); 21. cooling fluid sleeve ;22. engine speed sensor; 23. igniter; 24. battery; 25. starting motor; 26. flywheel; 27. oil pan; 28. oil; 29. crankshaft; 30. connecting rod; 31. tensioning pulley; 32. belt; 33. cylinder; 34. exhaust three-way converter; 35. oxygen sensor; 36. piston; 37. camshaft pulley

are joined to make systems. These systems are the fuel system, intake system, ignition system, cooling system, lubrication system and exhaust system. Each of these systems has a definite function.

## 3. Engine Block and Cylinder Head

1) Engine Block

The engine block is the basic frame of the engine. All other engine parts either fit inside it or fasten to it. It holds the cylinders, water jackets and oil galleries (see Figure 4.7). The engine block also holds the crankshaft, which fastens to the bottom of the block. The camshaft also fits inside the block, except on overhead-cam engines (OHC). In most cars, this block is made of gray iron, or an alloy (mixture) of gray iron and other metals, such as nickel or chromium. Engine blocks are castings.

2) Cylinder Head

The cylinder head fastens to the top of the block, just as a roof fits over a house (see Figure 4.8). The underside forms the combustion chamber with the top of the piston. The most common cylinder head types are the hemi, wedge, and semi-hemi (see Figure 4.9). The whole three of these terms refer to the shape of the engine's combustion chamber. The cylinder head carries the valves , valve springs and the rockers on the rocker shaft , this part of the valve

*Lesson 27   Engine Classification and Overall Mechanics*

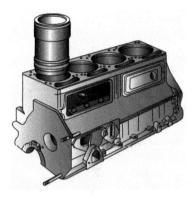

Figure 4.7   Engine block

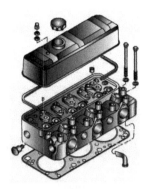

Figure 4.8   Engine cylinder head

gears being worked by the push-rods. Sometimes the camshaft is fitted directly into the cylinder head and operates on the valves without rockers. This is called an overhead camshaft arrangement. Like the cylinder block, the head is made from either cast iron or aluminum alloy.

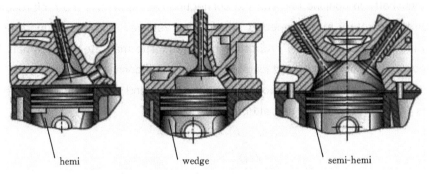

Figure 4.9   The three most common cylinder head types

## 4. Piston, Connecting Rod, and Crankshaft

1) Piston

The piston (Figure 4.10) is an important part of a four-stroke cycle engine. Most pistons are made from cast aluminum. The piston, through the connecting rod, transfers the force created by the burning fuel mixture to the crankshaft. This force turns the crankshaft. Thin, circular, steel bands fit into grooves around the piston to seal the bottom of the combustion chamber. These bands are called piston rings. The grooves into which they fit are called ring grooves.

A piston pin fits into a round hole in the piston. The piston pin joins the piston to the connecting rod. The thick part of the piston that holds the piston pin is the pin boss.

2) Connecting Rod

The connecting rods (Figure 4.11) little end is connected to the piston pin. A bush made from a soft metal, such as bronze, is used for this joint. The lower end of the connecting rod fits the crankshaft journal. This is called the big end. For this big-end bearing, steel-backed lead or tin shell bearings are used. These are the same as those used for the main bearings. The

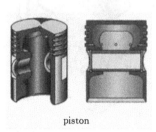

Figure 4.10 Piston of the engine

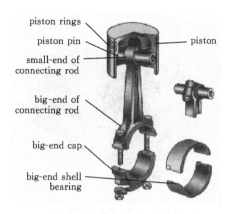

Figure 4.11 Connecting rod of the engine

split of the big end is sometimes at an angle, so that it is small enough to be withdrawn through the cylinder bore. The connecting rod is made from forged alloy steel.

3) Crankshaft

The crankshaft, in conjunction with the connecting rod, converts the reciprocating motion of the piston to the rotary motion needed to drive the vehicle. It is usually made from carbon steel which is alloyed with a small proportion of nickel. The main bearing journals fit into the cylinder block and the connecting rod journals align with the connecting rods. At the rear end of the crankshaft is attached the flywheel, and at the front end are the driving wheels for the timing gears, fan, cooling water and alternator.

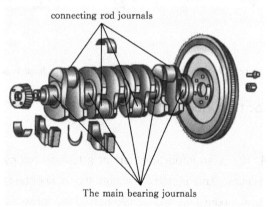

Figure 4.12 Crankshaft and flywheel of the engine

## NEW WORDS AND EXPRESSIONS

rocker ['rɔkə] n. 摇臂
camshaft ['kæmʃɑːft] n. 凸轮轴
semi-hemi ['semi'hemi] n. 准半球形
gasket ['gæskit] n. 衬垫
steel-backed [stiːl'bækt] a. 钢背的

reciprocate [ri'siprəkeit] v. 互换,往复
journal ['dʒəːnl] n. 轴颈
exhaust valve 排气阀,排气门
electric-control injector 电子控制喷油器
fuel filter 燃油滤清器

## Lesson 27  Engine Classification and Overall Mechanics

electric fuel pump 电动燃油泵
ignition coil module 点火线圈模块
fuel pressure regulator 燃油调压阀
cooling fluid temperature sensor 冷却液温度传感器
detonation sensor 爆震(爆燃)传感器
intake manifold 进气歧管
throttle valve 节气阀
air filter 空气滤清器
air quality sensor 空气质量传感器
electric control unit（ECU）电控装置
cooling fluid sleeve 冷却液套筒
oil pan 油底壳
tensioning pulley 张紧带轮
exhaust three-way converter 排气三通转化器
oxygen sensor 氧传感器
camshaft pulley 凸轮轴张紧轮
water jacket 水套
oil gallery 油道
overhead-cam（OHC）顶置凸轮
cylinder sleeve 汽缸套
piston ring 活塞环
push-rod 推杆
steel band 钢圈
piston pin 活塞销
pin boss 活塞销凸台
cylinder bore 缸筒
crankshaft journal 曲柄轴颈
align with 与……匹配
timing gear 正时齿轮

## NOTES

1) The piston is an important part of a four-stroke cycle engine. Most pistons are made from cast aluminum. The piston, through the connecting rod, transfers to the crankshaft the force created by the burning fuel mixture.

活塞是一个四冲程发动机的重要零部件。大部分活塞都是铸铝的。活塞通过连杆把燃油混合燃烧后产生的力传递给曲轴。

2) The crankshaft, in conjunction with the connecting rod, converts the reciprocating motion of the piston to the rotary motion needed to drive the vehicle.

与连杆连接在一起的曲轴将活塞的往复运动转换为驱动汽车所的旋转运动。

3) The cylinder head fastens to the top of the block, just as a roof fits over a house. The underside forms the combustion chamber with the top of the piston. The most common cylinder head types are the hemi, wedge, and semi-hemi. All three of these terms refer to the shape of the engine's combustion chamber.

汽缸盖固定在发动机机体的顶面，就好像屋顶套在房子上面一样。内腔和活塞顶部一起构成燃烧室。最常见的汽缸盖类型有半球形、楔形和准半球形。以上所说的形状指的是发动机燃烧室的形状。

4) The main bearing journals fit into the cylinder block and the connecting rod journals align with the connecting rods.

（曲轴的）主轴承轴颈安装在缸体（轴承孔）中，连杆轴颈与连杆（孔）相配合。

5) At the rear end of the crankshaft is attached the flywheel, and at the front end are the driving wheels for the timing gears, fan, cooling water and alternator.

曲轴的末端安装有飞轮，而其前端安装有驱动轮。驱动轮是用来驱动正时齿轮、风扇、冷却水系统和发动机的。

6) The split of the big end is sometimes at an angle, so that it is small enough to be withdrawn through the cylinder bore.

(连杆)大头的剖分有时要有一定的角度,以便使大头小得足够能从缸筒内部穿过。

## EXERCISES

1. After reading the text above, summarize the main ideas in oral.

2. Fill in the blanks with proper words or phrases according to the text (note the proper tense).

(1) The major parts of engine are engine b_____, engine heads, pistons, c_____ rods, crankshafts and valves.

(2) Sometimes the c_____ is fitted directly into the cylinder head and operates on the valves without r_____.

(3) The thick part of the piston that holds the piston p_____ is the pin b_____.

(4) The lower end of the connecting rod fits the crankshaft j_____. This is called the big end.

(5) These are the same _____ those used for the main bearings.

(6) Most pistons are made from cast a_____.

3. Translate the following phrase into Chinese according to the text.

(1) in conjunction with the connecting rod

(2) to convert the reciprocating motion of the piston to the rotary motion

(3) to be made from forged alloy steel

(4) to seal the bottom of the combustion chamber

(5) to be withdrawn through the cylinder bore

(6) to fasten to the top of the block

(7) to align with the connecting rods

4. Translate the following phrases into English according to the text.

(1) 发动机构造          (2) 铸铝合金
(3) 像屋顶套在一所房子上面一样    (4) 四冲程发动机
(5) 加了少量镍的碳钢合金
(6) 正时齿轮、风扇、冷却水系统和发动机的驱动轮
(7) 镶有铁或钢套的铝制缸套

5. Write a 100-word summary according to the text.

## READING MATERIAL

### Engine and Transmission Mountings

1) Inherent Engine Vibrations

The vibrations originating within the engine are caused by both the cyclic acceleration of the reciprocating components and the rapidly changing cylinder gas pressure which occurs throughout each cycle of operation.

Both the variations of inertia and gas pressure forces generate three kinds of vibrations which are transferred to the cylinder block:

vertical and / or horizontal shake and rock,

fluctuating torque reaction,

torsional oscillation of the crankshaft.

2) Reasons for Flexible Mountings

It is the objective of flexible mounting design to cope with many requirements, some having conflicting constraints on each other. A list of the duties of these mounts is as follows:

① to prevent the fatigue failure of the engine and transmission support points which would occur if they were rigidly attached to the chassis or body structure;

② to reduce the amplitude of any engine vibration which is being transmitted to the body structure;

③ to prevent road wheel shocks when driving over rough ground imparting excessive rebound movement to the engine;

④ to reduce noise amplification which would occur if engine vibration were allowed to be transferred directly to the body structure, to reduce human discomfort and fatigue by partially isolating the engine vibrations from the body by means of an elastic media.

3) Axis of Oscillation

The engine and transmission must be suspended so that it permits the greatest degree of freedom when oscillating around an imaginary center of rotation known as the principal axis. This principal axis produces the least resistance to engine and transmission sway due to their masses being uniformly distributed about this axis. The engine can be considered to oscillate around an axis which passes through the center of gravity of both the engine and transmission (Figure 4.13—Figure 4.15). This normally produces an axis of oscillation inclined at about 10°—20° to the crankshaft axis. To obtain the greatest degree of freedom, the mounts must be arranged so that they offer the least resistance to shear within the rubber mounting.

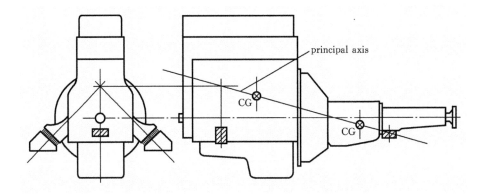

Figure 4.13 Longitudinally mounted power unit with three point support (petrol engine)

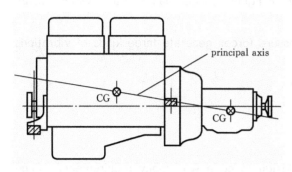 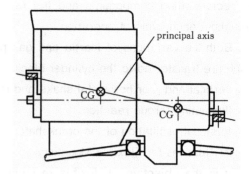

Figure 4.14　Longitudinally mounted power unit with four point support (diesel engine)

Figure 4.15　Transversely mounted power unit with three point support (petrol and diesel engine)

4) Six Modes of Freedom of Suspended Body

If the movement of a flexible mounted engine is completely unrestricted it may have six modes of vibration. Any motion may be resolved into three linear movements parallel to the axes which pass through the center of gravity of the engine but at right angles to each other and three rotations about these axes.

These modes of movement may be summarized as follows (see Table 4.1):

Table 4.1　Six modes of freedom of suspended body

| Linear motions | Rotional motions |
| --- | --- |
| horizontal longitudinal | roll |
| horizontal lateral | pitch |
| vertical | yaw |

# Lesson 28 | Diesel Engine

## TEXT

Diesel engine gets its name from the pioneer work done by Dr. Rudolf Diesel. The diesel is used for the majority of heavy vehicles and the excellent fuel economy makes diesel engine an attractive alternative to the petrol engine for light commercial vehicles, delivery vans and taxis.

Before we see how they differ, let's see how they are alike. Both types of engines run on liquid fuels. Gasoline, kerosene, and diesel oil are all produced from natural petroleum (crude oil), and are distinguished mainly by their volatility. Gasoline is quite volatile, that is, it evaporates or vaporizes at a low temperature. Kerosene needs more heat to make it vaporize, while diesel oil requires still more heat. Both types of engines are internal-combustion engines, that is, they burn the fuel inside their cylinders. Most gasoline engines and many diesel engines work on the four-stroke cycle.

What, then, are the main differences between diesel engines and gasoline engines?

A diesel engine has no distributor, spark plugs, or spark plug wires (see Figure 4.16). The fuel is ignited by heat produced by compressing the air in the cylinders. For this reason, the diesel engine is called a compression ignition engine. (The gasoline engine is a spark-ignition engine.) One of the principles basic to diesel operation is that the temperature of compressed air will rise. The more air is compressed the higher its temperature will be. Here also, a diesel engine differs from a gasoline engine. To get the high temperatures needed to ignite the diesel fuel, higher compression ratios are needed. Diesel car engines have compression ratios between 18 : 1 and 22 : 1. Modern gasoline engines have compression ratios of about 9 : 1, the higher compression ratios mean that the diesel engine must be built stronger to withstand these high pressures. The high compression ratios also give the diesel engine better fuel economy than the gasoline engine.

The diesel engine also differs from the gasoline engine in the way engine speed is controlled. The diesel engine has no throttle plate or similar device to restrict airflow into the engine. Engine speed is controlled only by the amount of fuel put into the cylinders. For this reason, a diesel engine is an unthrottled engine. A gasoline engine has higher vacuum when the throttle is closed and lower or no vacuum when the throttle is open. A diesel engine, because it has no throttle, has no intake manifold vacuum.

Another difference is the range of air-fuel ratios within which they will operate. Remember that a gasoline engine uses air-fuel ratios between 12.5 : 1 and 16 : 1 to 18 : 1. This is because both air and fuel are controlled as they enter the engine. The diesel engine will operate on air-fuel ratios of about 15 : 1 at maximum power and about 100 : 1 at idle. The

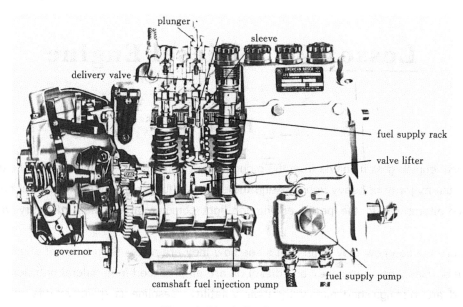

Figure 4.16 A diesel engine

diesel can do this because only the fuel flow is controlled, not the airflow.

The final difference between gasoline engine and diesel engine is the way the fuel is injected. The fuel injection system is the most important part of the diesel engine. Diesel injection must control the quantity of the fuel injected and determine when it is to be injected. The timing of the fuel injection is important, as is the spark timing of a gasoline engine. In a diesel engine, the fuel is injected directly into the cylinder or a prechamber of the engine. The diesel engine uses very high fuel pressures of 27 580 kPa and up at the injection nozzles. This allows the fuel to enter against the high combustion pressures. It also helps vaporize the fuel as it is sprayed in. Diesel injection systems differ, depending on the use or application of the engine. These systems are reviewed below (see Table 4.2).

Table 4.2 Difference between petrol engine and diesel engine

| Petrol engine | Diesel engine |
| --- | --- |
| Exterior mixture formation | Interior mixture formation |
| Externally supplied ignition | Auto-ignition |
| Quantity control | Quality control |
| Regular mixture in the combustion chamber | Irregular mixture in the combustion chamber |
| Engine speed 4 000 r/min—10 000 r/min | Engine speed 1 500 r/min—5 000 r/min |
| $\lambda$ from 0.7 to 1.3 | $\lambda$ always greater than 1 |
| Compression ratio 8—11 | Compression ratio 14—24 |
| Maximum combustion pressure 3 MPa—5 MPa | Maximum combustion pressure 6 MPa—8 MPa |
| Highest combustion temperature approx. 2500℃ | Highest combustion temperature approx. 2000℃ |
| Specific fuel consumption 240 g/(kW·h)—430 g/(kW·h) | Specific fuel consumption 160 g/(kW·h)—340 g/(kW·h) |
| Actual efficiency $\eta$ off to 30% | Actual efficiency $\eta$ off to 45% |

So diesel engine is more efficient, because it has higher compression ratios. Its ratio may be as high as 16 to I. Up to 40 percent of the chemical energy of the burning fuel may be converted into mechanical energy. In addition, the diesel engine runs cooler than the gasoline engine. This advantage is especially obvious at lower speeds. Diesel oil is not only cheaper than gasoline, but also safer to store.

## NEW WORDS AND EXPRESSION

kerosene ['kerəsi:n] *n.* 煤油
volatility [,vɔlə'tiliti] *n.* 挥发性
volatile ['vɔlətail] *a.* 挥发性的
petroleum [pi'trəuliəm] *n.* 石油
evaporate [i'væpəreit] *v.* （使）蒸发，（使）消失

vaporize ['veipəraiz] *v.* （使）蒸发
unthrottled ['ʌn'θrɔtld] *a.* 无节气门的
prechamber [pri:'tʃæmbə] *n.* （柴油机的）预燃室
nozzle ['nɔzl] *n.* 喷嘴
delivery van 运输货车

## NOTES

1) The diesel is used for the majority of heavy vehicles and the excellent fuel economy makes it an attractive alternative to the petrol engine for light commercial vehicles, delivery vans and taxis.
由于柴油具有优良的燃油经济性的吸引力，因此，大部分重型车辆选用柴油发动机，而且，轻型商用车、运输车和的士则选用它来代替汽油发动机。

2) Both types of engines are internal-combustion engines, that is, they burn the fuel inside their cylinders. Most gasoline engines and many diesel engines work on the four-stroke cycle.
两种类型的发动机都是内燃机，也就是说，它们都是在缸套中燃烧燃料的。大多数汽油发动机和许多柴油发动机工作需要完成四个冲程。

3) Diesel car engines have compression ratios between 18∶1 and 22∶1. Modern gasoline engines have compression ratios of about 9∶1; the higher compression ratios mean that the diesel engine must be built stronger to withstand these high pressures. The high compression ratios also give the diesel engine better fuel economy than the gasoline engine.
柴油汽车发动机的压缩比在 18∶1 到 22∶1 之间。而目前汽油机的压缩比大约只有 9∶1。压缩比大就要求柴油发动机的强度要高，以便能够承受高压。同时压缩比大也使得柴油发动机比汽油发动机有更好的燃油经济性。

4) The diesel engine also differs from the gasoline engine in the way engine speed is controlled. The diesel engine has no throttle plate or similar device to restrict airflow into the engine. Engine speed is controlled only by the amount of fuel put into the cylinders.
柴油发动机与汽油发动机另一个不同点在于发动机的速度控制。柴油发动机没有节气板或类似作用的装置来控制空气进入发动机，因此发动机的速度仅根据发动机缸套中的燃油量来调节。

5) In addition, the diesel engine runs cooler than the gasoline engine. This advantage is especially obvious at lower speeds.

另外，柴油发动机运行时发热量没有汽油发动机大。这一优点在较低速运行时表现更加突出。

# EXERCISES

1. After reading the text above, summarize the main ideas in oral.

2. Fill in the blanks with proper words or phrases according to the text (note the proper tense).

(1) Gasoline, kerosene, and diesel oil are all produced f_____ natural petroleum (crude oil), and are distinguished mainly by their v_____.

(2) The diesel engine differs also differs f_____ the gasoline engine i_____ the way engine speed is controlled.

(3) Engine speed is controlled only by the amount of fuel put i_____ the cylinders.

(4) In a diesel engine, the fuel is injected directly i_____ the cylinder or a p_____ of the engine.

(5) Up to 40 percent of the chemical energy of the burning fuel may be converted i_____ mechanical energy.

3. Translate the following phrases into Chinese according to the text.

(1) to enter against the high combustion pressures

(2) higher compression ratio

(3) the range of air-fuel ratios within which the diesel engine will operate

(4) to restrict airflow into the engine

(5) in the way engine speed is controlled

(6) Let's see how they are alike.

4. Translate the following phrases into English according to the text.

(1) 都是从原油生产出来的  (2) 在低温条件下挥发
(3) 压缩点火式发动机  (4) 比汽油发动机具有更好的燃油经济性
(5) 控制喷油量  (6) 取决于发动机的应用场合

5. Write a 100-word summary according to the text.

# READING MATERIAL

## Diesel Fuel-Injection Systems

The fuel-injection system on a diesel engine must do a number of important things. First, it must meter the correct amount of fuel to run the engine at the speed and load demanded by the driver. Then it must deliver the metered fuel equally to all cylinders at exactly the right time. Next, it must inject the fuel at the correct rate and spray pattern for the best burning in the combustion chamber.

An injection system is desirable in which

(1) injection pressure and fuel quantity can be adjusted independently;

(2) the injection pressure is as high and as constant as possible during the entire injection after combustion start;

(3) the injection quantity or injection pressure at the start of injection, i.e. during the ignition lag between the start of injection and start of combustion (depending on engine temperature, several hundreds μs up to over 1 ms) is as low as possible.

Targets 1 and 2 can be achieved by a common rail injection system (CR system) (see Figure 4.17).

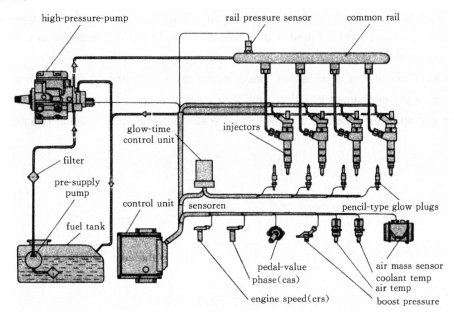

Figure 4.17 A common rail injection system (CR system)

A pressure accumulator is supplied with fuel by a high-pressure pump (common rail). The pressure in the common rail is measured with a pressure sensor and settled to a constant value by a pressure-control valve in the high-pressure pump. Depending on the requirements of combustion, the pressure in the rail can be maintained, largely independent of the engine speed, at a constant value in the range between 15 MPa—140 MPa.

The pressure accumulator is connected to the injectors with short lines. In addition to the injection nozzles, the injectors contain a servo solenoid valve. The control unit initiates the injection by switching on the solenoid valve; injection is terminated by switching it off. The injected fuel quantity is directly proportional to the switch-on time of the solenoid valve and independent of the engine / pump speed (pure time control of the injection quantity).

The point of injection is controlled via an incremental system related to the angle. This process requires an engine speed sensor on the crankshaft plus a phase sensor on the camshaft (second engine speed sensor) for cylinder detection (in four-stroke engines).

Target 3 is not achieved by this system. On the contrary, a high pressure is present even at the start of injection. In order to produce a smooth combustion noise nevertheless, the injection must not be interrupted until the start of combustion. The fuel quantity injected during this pilot injection must be very small (typically approx. 1%—2% of the full-load quantity).

Since the solenoid valves, short switching times (in the range of several hundreds μs) can only be achieved through servo assistance as well as corresponding dimensioning of the solenoid valve control in the control unit, with high voltages and currents.

Further advantages of the common rail injection system are that the space required for mounting on the engine is smaller than for distributor or in-line injection pumps.

Vital for the implementation of the system are the high-pressure sealing of the pressure accumulator and of the injectors, the hydraulic stability at pilot injection and the monitoring of the system for errors in the high-pressure part of the system. A failure of the pressure control loop or of the pressure-control valve with a pressure rise in the common rail is covered by a pressure limitation valve.

A sticking injector or a solenoid valve which does not close (consequence: injection quantity too large, permanent injection) and leakage of the pressure accumulator are detected by the monitoring of the pressure control loop, except for very small leakage quantities.

# Lesson 29  Electronic Fuel Injection System

## TEXT

The carburetor sends the correct air-fuel mixture to the engine. However, not all cars have carburetors. Fuel-injection systems (see Figure 4.18) are used on many modern cars.

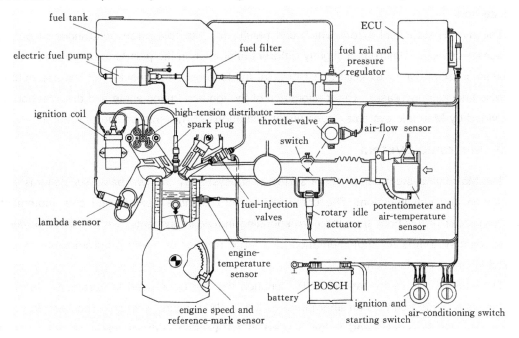

Figure 4.18  The operation of fuel supply system

Fuel-injection systems have many advantages over carburetors. For example, they provide more exact fuel control. Thus, they can better match air-fuel ratios to change engine conditions. They also provide better economy and emission control. Furthermore, fuel-injection systems do not need many pails that carburetors have.

The Motronic system is an engine-management system comprising a control unit (ECU) which implements at least the two basic functions—ignition and fuel injection, but which, however may contain additional subsystems as required for improved engine control.

### 1. Detection of Measured Values

The combustion process in the cylinder is influenced not only by fuel management, mixture quantity and air-fuel ratio, but also by the ignition advance and the energy contained in the ignition spark. An optimized engine control must therefore control the air-fuel ratio $\lambda$ throughout the injection time $t_i$ (i.e. the quantity of injected fuel) as well as the ignition advance angle $\alpha_z$ and the dwell angle $\beta_s$. The main parameters which effect the combustion process are detected as measured values and processed together such that the optimum ignition and injection timing is calculated for instantaneous engine operating conditions.

## 2. Actuating Variables / Sensors

Engine speed and load are the main actuating variables. Because a specific ignition advance angle and a specific injection time correspond to each point of the engine speed / load map, it is important that all variables which pertain to the same point be calculated on the same speed / load area. This is only possible if the ignition advance and the injection time are calculated with the same speed and load values (engine speed detected only once with the same sensors).

This avoids statistical errors which can result, for example, from tolerances of different load sensor devices. Whereas a slightly different allocation in the part-load range normally only increases consumption or exhaust emissions, at full load near the knock limit the susceptibility to engine knocking increases. Clear allocation of the ignition timing angle and the injection time is provided by Motronic systems, even under conditions of dynamic engine operation.

## 3. Motronic System

The Motronic system comprises a series of subsystems, the two basic subsystems which are ignition and fuel injection. The combined system is more flexible and can implement a greater number of functions than the corresponding individual systems. An important feature of the Motronic system is its implementation of a large number of freely programmable maps as desired for most sub-functions.

The exhaust gas recirculation (EGR) function has not been used in Europe to date, and therefore is provided only as an alternative to the lambda control system. The lambda control system can only be considered today if used in conjunction with an adaptive precontrol for reasons of reducing exhaust emissions.

The knock control is either connected to the Motronic system via a defined interface or integrated into the system. This combination of subsystems makes sense from a physical standpoint: it enables a basic system (ignition and fuel injection) with open-loop functional control as well as an expanded system (incorporating knock and lambda controls) with closed-loop functional control in a management system.

The idle speed control is realized by means of data from the ignition system and the fuel injection system and is part of the overall system of control which includes tank ventilation and camshaft control.

Microcomputer-controlled systems today are required to perform self-diagnosis of the control unit itself, as well as of the entire system to a certain extent. Motronic systems of the future will thus include a diagnostic feature.

An engine-management system should include at least those functions described here. The addition of other functions is practical if they can be implemented without the need for a number of additional inputs and outputs. Systems which use input and output signals different from those used by the Motronic system which require very limited data exchange with the Motronic system are not integrated but rather connected with the Motronic system via interfaces. Typical examples of such systems are the transmission control system and the traction control system which access the ignition and injection system via corresponding interfaces.

## 4. System Configuration

Figure 4.18 is a typical Motronic system which shows the fuel circuit and the acquisition of load and temperature data. The system does not include the cold-start valve or the thermo-time switch whose functions are performed by the control unit. The auxiliary-air device has been replaced by the idle-speed actuator. In addition to the ignition coil, the ignition section also includes the high-voltage distributor which is normally mounted directly on the camshaft. In contrast to the conventional ignition distributor, the high-voltage distributor only incorporates the high-voltage distribution function. The control unit electronically determines the proper ignition timing as a function of engine speed and load.

An essential feature of the system is the sensing of engine speed at the crankshaft. An inductive sensor detects crankshaft angular velocity via the modulation of its magnetic field which is induced by the ring gear. The reference mark is detected by an identical inductive sensor. This signal is used to define the ignition advance angle. In some cases only one inductive-type sensor combined with a special toothed disk determines both engine speed and angle reference mark.

## 5. Gasoline Direct Injection (GDI)

Conventional gasoline engines are designed to use an electronic fuel injection system, replacing the traditional mechanical carburetion system. Multi-point injection (MPI), where the fuel is injected through each intake port, is currently one of the most widely used systems. Although MPI provides a drastic improvement in response and combustion quality, it is still limited due to fuel and air mixing prior to entering the cylinder.

Due to the very short time for injection, high-pressure injectors are required. In direct injection engines, injection typically occurs during the intake stroke and a very short time compared to the 720° and MPI engine typically has for fuel delivery.

# NEW WORDS AND EXPRESSIONS

throttle ['θrɔtl] *n.* 节气门
carburetor [kɑːbəˈretə(r)] *n.* 化油器
filter ['filtə] *n.* 滤清器
injection [inˈdʒekʃən] *n.* 喷射
instantaneous [ˌinstənˈteinjəs] *a.* 瞬间的，即时的
susceptibility [səˌseptəˈbiliti] *n.* 易感性

comprise [kəmˈpraiz] *v.* 包含，由……组成
recirculation [ˌriːsəːkjuˈleiʃən] *n.* 再流通，再循环
programmable [ˈprəugræməbl] *a.* 可编程的
traction [ˈtrækʃən] *n.* 牵引
idle speed 怠速
throttle cable 节气门线

advance angle 提前角
dwell angle 持续角
pertain to 适合,和……相称,属于
in conjunction with 与……协力
auxiliary-air device 附加/旁通空气装置

# NOTES

1) The Motronic system is an engine-management system comprising a control unit (ECU) which implements at least the two basic functions ignition and fuel injection, but which, however may contain additional subsystems as required for improved engine control.

Motronic 系统是一种包含一个电子控制装置的发动机管理系统,该装置至少具备点火和燃油喷射控制两个基本功能,还有一些为改善发动机控制功能而设的其他子系统也包含其中。

2) The combustion process in the cylinder is influenced not only by fuel management, mixture quantity and air-fuel ratio, but also by the ignition advance and the energy contained in the ignition spark.

汽缸中的燃烧过程不仅受燃油管理、混合物数量和空气-燃油比等因素的影响,而且受点火提前量和在点火火花中包含的能量的大小的影响。

3) Engine speed and load are the main actuating variables. Because a specific ignition advance angle and a specific injection time correspond to each point of the engine speed / load map, it is important that all variables which pertain to the same point are calculated on the same speed / load area.

发动机速度和负载是主要的调节变量。因为某个特定的点火提前角和某个特定的点火时间在图上对应着每一个发动机的速度/负载,按照某个速度/负载区域计算出所有调节变量,这一点是很重要的。

4) The idle speed control is realized by means of data from the ignition system and the fuel injection system and is part of the overall system of control which includes tank ventilation and camshaft control.

怠速控制是通过利用从点火系统和燃油喷射系统采集的数据实现的,它是包括通风和凸轮轴控制在内的整系统的一部分。

5) Systems which use input and output signals different from those used by the Motronic system but which require very limited data exchange with the Motronic system are not integrated but rather are connected with the Motronic system via interfaces.

一些系统使用的输入和输出信号与那些在 Motronic 系统中使用的不同,这些系统只是与 Motronic 系统有非常有限的数据交换,没有被集成到 Motronic 系统而是通过接口模块与 Motronic 系统连接在一起。

# EXERCISES

1. After reading the text above, summarize the main ideas in oral.
2. Fill in the blanks with proper words according to the text (note the proper tense).

(1) Fuel-insection systems have many advantages o_____ carburetors.

(2) They can better match air-fuel ratios _____ change engine conditions.

(3) The lambda control system can only be considered today if used _____ conjunction with an adaptive precontrol _____ reasons of reducing exhaust emissions.

(4) Figure 4.18 is a typical Motronic system which shows the fuel circuit and the acquisition _____ load and temperature data.

(5) Up to 40 percent of the chemical energy of the burning fuel may be converted i_____ mechanical energy.

3. Translate the following phrases into Chinese according to the text.

(1) an engine-management system comprising a control unit (ECU)

(2) in conjunction with an adaptive precontrol for reasons of reduced exhaust emissions

(3) all variables which pertain to the same point

(4) a slightly different allocation in the part-load range normally

(5) with closed-loop functional control in a management system

(6) the thermo-time switch whose functions are performed by the control unit

4. Translate the following phrases into English according to the text.

(1) 在许多方面超过化油器         (2) 怠速调节器
(3) 发动机瞬时工作条件           (4) 微机控制系统
(5) 开环控制系统
(6) 至少具备点火和燃油喷射控制两方面的功能

5. Write a 100-word summary according to the text.

# READING MATERIAL

## 1. Carburetor

A carburetor delivers fuel in proportion to the amount of air flowing through it. As you press on the accelerator pedal, the throttle valve opens wider to draw more air through the carburetor. The carburetor provides richer or cleaner mixtures, depending on a number of factors: engine speed, load, temperature, and throttle position. To meet complicated demands a carburetor is a highly intricate device, with many internal passages and parts (see Figure 4.19).

## 2. The Venturi

An automobile carburetor is designed with a venturi chamber. The venturi is simply a narrowed portion in the air passage. Air moving through the throat of the carburetor speeds up as it travels through this narrowed passageway.

The increased air speed through the venturi creates a low-pressure area at the opening of the fuel nozzle. Atmospheric pressure pushes down on a fuel reservoir within the carburetor known as the float chamber. Fuel is forced through a tube that extends into the low-pressure

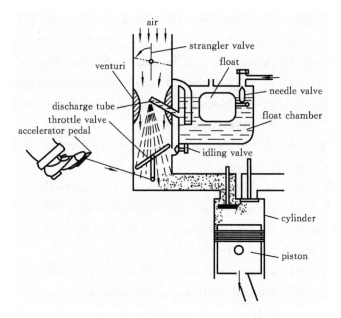

Figure 4.19 Engine carburetor

area of the venturi. Thus, fuel sprays through the end of the tube into the air stream.

### 3. Float Chamber

The float chamber is a reservoir for storing and supplying fuel to the carburetor. As the engine uses fuel, the float chamber replenishes it automatically.

The float chamber works on the same basic principle as the holding tank in a flushing toilet. A float rests on top of the fuel in the reservoir. As fuel is used, the float level drops. When the float drops, a needle valve is opened. The open needle valve permits the flow of fuel from the fuel pump into the carburetor's float chamber. When the chamber is full again, the needle valve is pushed upward and closes the fuel inlet.

### 4. Metering the Fuel

The pressure differential between the float chamber and the venturi causes fuel to flow. However, to maintain the proper air-fuel ratio, the carburetor must provide just the right amount of fuel. To do so, the main discharge tube has a small hole (called a jet or main jet). This allows a precise amount of fuel to enter the air stream. In most cases, this small hole is in the float chamber at the end of the main discharge tube. There, its small size limits fuel flow.

### 5. Need for Cold Starting Arrangement

A carburetor set to give mixture strength of 15 : 1 at a normal engine speed would be unsuitable for starting a cold engine. This is because:

(1) The cold engine will not vaporize the fuel.

(2) The slow cranking speed only gives a small depression and this causes the carburetor to supply a very weak mixture.

## Lesson 29  Electronic Fuel Injection System

(3) Petrol falls out of the slow moving air and is deposited in the walls of the induction pipe.

Shutting off the air supply by means of a strangler valve gives a rich mixture (about 8 : 1) and provides the engine with a sufficient number of fuel particles that vaporize easily.

### 6. Slow Running

The small amount of air passing through the carburetor when the engine is slowly running only produces a very small choke depression. This means that too little fuel will be supplied and the engine will stall.

The slow running system has an outlet in a region where a high depression exists when the engine is idling.

The adjusting screws control the slow running system, one screw sets the idling speed the other enables the slow running mixture to be varied to give the smoothest engine speed.

### 7. The Throttle Mechanism

The throttle mechanism controls the flow of the air-fuel mixture. The throttle has several parts, including the throttle shaft and the throttle plate. By opening and closing, the throttle plate controls the flow of the air-fuel mixture into the engine. More air flows in as the plate opens, less air flows in as the plate closes. The changes in airflow also control gasoline flow. Increased airflow means a greater pressure drop and thus more fuel flow. Decreased airflow means less pressure drop and less fuel flow.

The motion of the throttle shaft turns the throttle plates. The throttle shaft connects to the throttle cable. This throttle cable, in turn, connects to the accelerator pedal inside the car. The driver controls the flow of air-fuel mixture with the pedal.

# Lesson 30  Engine Service and Maintenance

## TEXT

This lesson describes various engine services and explains how various troubles in the engine are corrected. The procedures discussed here are aimed at correcting specific troubles.

The major enemy of good work is dirt. A trace of dirt left on a bearing or a cylinder wall would ruin an otherwise good job. Thus, you must be absolutely sure that you do not leave dirt or abrasive in the engine or on engine parts when you finish a job.

Before any major job, the block should be cleaned. Electrical units should be removed or covered if the engine is steam-cleaned so that moisture does not get into them.

### 1. Cylinder Block Module Service

1) Connecting rods and rod bearings service

Worn bearings greatly increase engine oil consumption. Before the engine is torn down, they can be checked for wear with an oil-leak detector. Now, you can remove the oil pan, connect the detector hose to the oil filter. Then, with the detector filled with oil, apply an air pressure of 175 kPa to the detector tank. The pressure forces oil through the lubricating system. A normal bearing will leak between 20 to 150 drops of oil a minute. If bearings are worn, more oil will leak from them. But if it leaks less than 20 drops, then either the bearing clearance is too small or else the oil line to the bearing is stopped.

2) Piston and rings service

① Piston cleaning. Use solvent, not a caustic cleaning solution or a wire brush, to remove deposits. Ring groove, slots (or holes) must also be cleaned. Be sure, don't remove any metal.

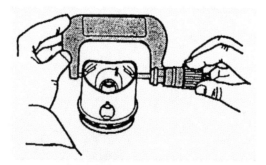

Figure 4.20  Checking for diameter of piston

② Piston inspection. Check them with a micrometer for worn, scored skirt or for cracks at the ring lands, skirts, ring bosses and heads (Figure 4.20). And if the cylinder wall is excessively worn, it will require refinishing. This means that an oversize piston will be required. That is, new pistons are needed.

3) Crankshaft and main bearings service

Many bearing difficulties can be taken care of by means of bearing replacement. If not, then remove the crankshaft from the engine block and check both separately for alignment and for clogged oil passages.

4) Valves and valve mechanisms service

Valves must be properly timed. They must seat tightly and operate without lag. Valve-tappet clearance, as well as the clearance between the valve stems and guides, must be correct. Failure to meet any of these requirements means valve and engine troubles.

Types of valve troubles include sticking, burning, breakage, wear and deposits.

Valve service and maintenance includes adjusting valve-tappet clearance (also called adjusting valve lash), grinding valves and valve seats, installing new seat inserts, cleaning or replacing valve guides, servicing the camshaft and camshaft bearings, and timing the valves.

## 2. Fuel System Maintenance

The fuel system is one place where your attention and periodic action can make a big difference in the economy, reliability and emission levels of your car. Attention to just a few details can help assure trouble-free operation and savings.

1) Fuel tank level

One of the important things to keep your car running smoothly is to pay attention to your fuel gauge. It is not a good practice to let your car run out of gas. You should try to refill the gas tank soon after the gauge falls below the one quarter level.

The danger in letting the fuel tank run low is that all of the contaminants that can damage the fuel system settle to the bottom of the tank. You have no control over impurities you may be buying with your gasoline. There almost always will be some water from condensation and dust or other impurities in the fuel. The lower you let the level of fuel in the tank become, the greater the probability that water or contaminants will be down into the fuel delivery system through the fuel line.

2) Carburetor maintenance

Check the carburetor every time you remove the air cleaner. In inspecting the carburetor, check the following:

① Check the screws that join the top body, main body, and throttle body.

② Inspect all rubber hoses and diaphragms for cracks.

③ Check the fuel line to carburetor fitting to make sure it fits securely and does not leak.

④ Check the entire carburetor body for gasoline leaks and air leaks.

⑤ Check the mating surface between the carburetor and the intake manifold. Two or four bolts hold the carburetor to the manifolds. A gasket between the two parts gives a tight seal. If the gasket is worn, the engine could draw in air. This would result in a lean fuel mixture and poor engine performance.

⑥ Check the carburetor-to-manifold bolts, and make sure no air leaks into the engine. If the carburetor becomes loose, the throttle linkage will not work properly. Loose linkage will also affect the choke system and the accelerator pump system.

3) Air cleaner service

Air cleaners should be removed periodically and the filter element washed, the usual recommendation is that it should be done every time when the engine oil is changed. However, if the car encounters unusually dusty conditions, then the air-cleaner element should be cleaned immediately.

4) Fuel pump service

To check the fuel-pump pressure, use a special gauge. Run the engine at several different speeds and check the fuel pressure on the gauge. Compare the pressure readings against those in the service manual. Low pump pressure will cause fuel starvation and poor engine performance. High pressure will cause an overrich mixture, excessive fuel consumption, and such troubles as fouled spark plugs, rings and valves (from excessive carbon deposits).

5) Fuel filter

Fuel filters require no service except periodic checks to make sure that they are not clogged, and replacement of the filter element or cleaning of the filter, according to type. On many models, the filter is part of the fuel pump and can be removed so that the element can be replaced. Air cleaner is to keep damaging if the element becomes clogged and the engine will suffer.

## NEW WORDS AND EXPRESSIONS

solvent ['sɔlvənt] n. 溶媒，溶剂
caustic ['kɔːstik] a. 腐蚀性的
scored [skɔːd] a. 有伤纹的，刮伤的
crack [kræk] n. 裂缝，裂纹
refinishing ['riːfiniʃiŋ] n. 整修表面
clog [klɔg] v. 障碍，阻塞
valve-tappet [vælv'tæpit] n. 气门挺杆
gauge [gedʒ] n. 标准尺，量规，量表
condensation [kɔnden'seiʃən] n. 浓缩

diaphragm ['daiəfræm] n. 膜片
bolt [bəult] n. 门闩，螺钉
choke [tʃəuk] v. 阻塞
periodically [ˌpiəri'ɔdikəli] ad. 周期性地，定时性地
starvation [stɑː'veiʃən] n. 缺乏，不足
foul [faul] vt. 淤塞
steam-cleaned 蒸汽清洁
oil-leak 油漏检测

## NOTES

1) Use solvent, not a caustic cleaning solution or a wire brush, to remove deposits. Ring groove, slots (or holes) must also be cleaned. Be sure, don't remove any metal.

使用溶剂，但不是带腐蚀性的清洁剂或者钢丝刷来去除沉积物。活塞的环槽、沟槽（或孔）也要清洗干净。注意，不要连金属也洗掉了。

2) Valve service and maintenance includes adjusting valve-tappet clearance (also called adjusting valve lash), grinding valves and valve seats, installing new seat inserts, cleaning

or replacing valve guides, servicing the camshaft and camshaft bearings and timing the valves.

气门的维护与维修包括调整气门挺杆的间隙(也称为调整气门间隙),研磨气门和气门座,安装新的气门座圈,清洁或更换气门导管,维护凸轮轴以及凸轮轴轴承和气门正时调整。

3) The fuel system is one place where your attention and periodic action can make a big difference in the economy, reliability, and emission levels of your car.

你应该关注燃料系统,对其进行周期性的检修将提升你的汽车的经济性、可靠性和排放级。

4) The lower you let the level of fuel in the tank become, the greater the probability that water or contaminants will be down into the fuel delivery system through the fuel line.

燃油箱中的残油量越低,水或沉积物通过油路被抽到燃油系统的可能性就越大。

5) Air cleaners should be removed periodically and the filter element washed, the usual recommendation is that this should be done every time the engine oil is changed.

空气清洁剂应该定期更换,过滤器元件要清洗。通常建议在每次发动机更换机油时做这一工作。

6) Compare the pressure readings against those in the service manual. Low pump pressure will cause fuel starvation and poor engine performance. High pressure will cause an overrich mixture, excessive fuel consumption, and such troubles as fouled spark plugs, rings and valves (from excessive carbon deposits).

将压力表上的读数与服务手册上的数据进行对照。低泵压会造成燃料供给不足和发动机性能差;高泵压会导致混合气体过浓、消耗过多的燃油,还会使火花塞、活塞环和气门淤塞(产生积碳)。

# EXERCISES

1. After reading the text above, summarize the main ideas in oral.

2. Fill in the blanks with proper words or phrases according to the text (note the proper tense).

(1) The procedures discussed here are aimed _____ correcting specific troubles.

(2) And if the cylinder wall is e_____ worn, it will require r_____.

(3) It is not a good practice to let your car run _____ gas.

(4) This would result _____ a lean fuel mixture and poor engine p_____.

(5) The car e_____ unusually dusty conditions, then the air-cleaner element should be cleaned immediately a_____.

3. Translate the following phrases into Chinese according to the text.

(1) ruin an otherwise good job

(2) Check them with a micrometer for worn, scored skirt or for cracks at the ring lands, skirts, ring bosses and heads.

(3) the danger in letting the fuel tank run low

(4) compare the pressure readings against those in the service manual

(5) to check the fuel-pump pressure

(6) to help assure trouble-free operation and savings

4. Translate the following phrases into English according to the text.

(1) 油漏检测器　　　　　　　(2) 一种带腐蚀性的溶剂

(3) 需要一个加大尺寸的活塞　(4) 调整气门间隙

(5) 积聚在油箱底部的沉积物　(6) 每次更换机油时

(7) 积碳

5. Write a 100-word summary according to the text.

# READING MATERIAL

### 1. Engine Cooling

Some forms of cooling must be provided to take away the heat from the cylinder and working parts of an engine. This heat comes from combustion of the fuel and from friction between rubbing parts. An uncooled engine would result in:

① seizure of working parts due to heat expansion;

② excessive wear—the oil would be burnt;

③ pre-ignition of the petrol-air mixture. This means that the mixture would be ignited before time by some red-hot particle in the combustion chamber. There are two methods of cooling: air cooling and liquid cooling.

1) Air Cooling

Most motor-cycle engines are air cooled. The principle is to fin the cylinder so as to increase the area of the hot surface exposed to the flow of cool air. This method of cooling is cheap, light-weight and is not subject to troubles such as leakage and freezing problems.

Airflow for cooling a multi-cylinder engine is provided by a centrifugal fan; this forces the air through ducted passages and over the finned cylinders.

2) Liquid Cooling

This system consists of several interdependent parts that function together to maintain proper engine temperatures. The parts include: radiator, fan, coolant recovery system, coolant pump, water jacket, thermostat, pressure cap, and soft plugs.

To dissipate excess engine heat, the cooling system performs four functions:

① absorption

② circulation

③ radiation

④ control

### 2. Engine Lubrication

The purpose of the lubrication system is to circulate oil through the engine. An engine must have a good lubrication system. Without it, the friction heat from the contact of the moving

## Lesson 30  Engine Service and Maintenance

parts would wear the parts and cause power loss. Oil, when placed between two moving parts, separates them with a film. This oil film prevents the parts from rubbing against each other. This oil film also cushions the parts, giving quieter and smoother engine operation. Besides lubricating engine parts, oil is also used to:

① clean the inside of the engine;

② help cool the engine;

③ form a seal between the cylinder walls and piston rings.

Friction between engine components is reduced by:

① boundary lubrication—relies on oil being splashed up onto the surfaces;

② full film lubrication—an oil film is maintained by forcing the oil between the surfaces by an oil pump.

The system used on a modern engine combines both two methods: pistons are lubricated by splash and bearings which are pressure fed.

The main parts of a lubrication system are: pump, main oil gallery, relief valve and filters.

1) Pump

In most cars, the oil pump is in the crankcase above the sump. It draws oil through a tube that extends downward into the sump. This tube has a filter screen over its bottom end. The screen keeps large pieces of sludge and dirt from being drawn into the pump. The tube may be hinged on the pump end so that it can move up and down as the oil level changes in the sump. Thus, the pump always draws oil from the top of the sump, not from the bottom where the dirt and sludge tend to settle. Modern cars use one of two common types of oil pumps—the gear-type and the rotor-type.

2) Main Oil Gallery and Relief Valve

The main oil gallery runs the length of the engine. Drillings from the gallery allow oil to be supplied to the bearing surfaces.

Generally the relief valve fitted in the gallery, this spring loaded valve opens when the pressure reaches the maximum allowed.

3) Filters

Besides the gauze screen that prevents pieces of metal entering the pump there is an external filter which can be renewed periodically. A modern engine uses a full-flow filtering system. In this system, the output of the oil pump flows through the oil filter before moving through the engine. In other words, the oil is filtered and cleaned before each trip through the engine. When an engine runs at 3 000 r / min, its entire five quarts of oil passes through the filter at least once every minute. Thus the oil filter ensures that only clean oil enters the engine.

# Lesson 31  Clutchs and Transmissions

## TEXT

### 1. Elements of the Power Train

The elements of the power train (Figure 4.21) must meet the following requirements:

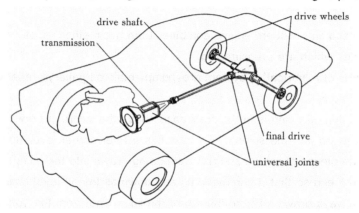

Figure 4.21  Power train system

① enable driving away;

② convert torque and speed;

③ enable different directions of rotation for driving forward and backward;

④ transmit attractive and pushing forces;

⑤ permit different rotational speeds of the drive wheels when cornering;

⑥ guarantee optimum operation of the engine (or electric motor) in terms of fuel consumption and exhaust emissions.

### 2. Clutch

In order to transmit the power of the engine to the road wheels of a car, a friction clutch and a change-speed gearbox are normally employed. The former is necessary in order to enable the drive to be taken up gradually and smoothly, while the latter provides different ratios of speed reduction from the engine to the wheels, to suit the particular conditions of running.

A clutch performs two tasks:

① it disengages the engine from the gearbox to allow for gear changing;

② it is a means for gradually engaging the engine to the driving wheels.

When a vehicle is to be moved from rest the clutch must engage a stationary gearbox shaft with the engines; this must be rotating at a high speed to provide sufficient power or else the load will be too great and the engine will stall (come to rest).

To start the engine, the driver must depress the clutch pedal. This disengages the transmission from the engine. To move the car, the driver must reengage the transmission to the engine. However, the engagement of the parts must be gradual. An idle engine develops little power. If the two parts were connected too quickly, the engine would stall. The load must be applied gradually to operate the car smoothly.

A driver depresses the clutch pedal to shift the gears inside the transmission. After the driver release the clutch pedal, the clutch must act as solid coupling device. It must transmit all engine power to the transmission, without slipping.

### 3. Gearbox

The modern automobile engine is a powerful, light weight, and dependable power plant. However, it is not perfect for three reasons. First, modern engines do not produce much torque at low engine speeds. Second, engines produce maximum torque between 2 000 rpm and 3 000 rpm. As a result, engines operate best only within this fairly narrow range. Third, much more force is needed to move a car from rest than to keep it moving once it is started. Thus, the vehicle needs a wider range of torque than what is available from the engine.

For the above reasons, cars need a device that makes better use of engine power and torque. The gearbox is this device.

There are two types of gearboxes: manual and automatic.

In simple terms, a gearbox multiplies engine torque and—through gears—sends that power to the drive axle. A driver shifts or changes the gears to increase or decrease the torque produced by the engine. In a car with a manual gearbox a driver shifts the gears manually. In a car with an automatic gearbox, the gears shift automatically.

The gears reduce engine speed in the gearbox so that engine torque increases. These speed decrease and torque increases are needed so that the engine can run at higher speeds. At such speeds, it produces more torque and is more efficient. In other words, the gearbox allows higher engine speeds allow vehicle speeds and multiplies torque to help move the car.

An automatic gearbox is a device that provides gear reduction, with resulting multiplication of torque. The gear ranges are automatically selected to provide the most efficient operation and the best torque output.

Automatic gearboxes have three basic systems—a torque converter, a gear system, and a hydraulic system. These fit together in a unit that fastens directly behind the engine. The front section of the gearbox houses the torque converter. The torque converter is like the clutch in a manual gearbox. It is the coupling between the engine and drive train that transmits power to the drive wheels.

### 4. Propeller Shafts and Universal Joints

The propeller shaft transmits the drive from the gearbox main shaft to the final drive pinion. The shaft is long so it is made of tubular section and balanced to reduce vibration.

The drive shaft is not solidly bolted to the gearbox and the final drive. There must be some allowance for motion between the final drive and the gearbox.

The gearbox and engine mount firmly to the car. However, the final drive mounts on springs as part of the rear suspension system. The suspension provides a flexible coupling between the wheels and car body. This flexible coupling insulates the car body from the jolts of the road surface. In most automobiles, the rear wheels mount firmly to the axle shafts. The suspension connects the final drive assembly to the car body. The final drive moves up and down in relation to the engine and gearbox. A coupling is needed that permits movement between the final drive and gearbox. The universal joints (U-joints) and sliding joints (see Figure 4.22) provide this coupling. There are two types of universal joints: cross type joint and constant-velocity universal joint.

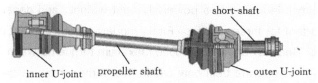

Figure 4.22  Propeller shafts and universal joints

## 5. Final Drive

To avoid loss of power the top gearbox ratio is 1 : 1, i.e. direct; this means that the propeller shaft rotates at engine speed. The duty of the final drive gears is to gear down the speed to suit the road wheels and to redirect the line of drive (see Figure 4.23).

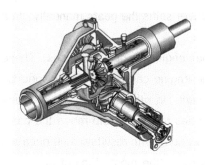

Figure 4.23  Final drive

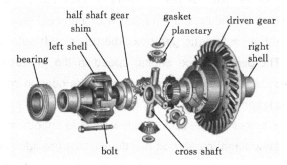

Figure 4.24  Differential

## 6. Differential

When a vehicle is cornered the inner wheel moves through a shorter distance than the outer wheel. This means that the inner wheel must slow down and the outer wheel must speed up. During this period it is desirable that each driving wheel maintains its driving action. The differential performs these two tasks.

The principle of the bevel type differential can be seen if the unit is considered as two discs and a lever (see Figure 4.24).

## Lesson 31  Clutchs and Transmissions

# NEW WORDS AND EXPRESSIONS

disengage [ˈdisinˈgeidʒ] v. 脱离
pedal [ˈpedl] n. 踏板
coupling [ˈkʌpliŋ] n. 联结，接合，耦合
slipping [ˈslipiŋ] n. 滑动，打滑，空转
multiplication [ˌmʌltipliˈkeiʃən] n. 增加
power plant [ˈpauə plɑːnt] n. 动力设备
countershaft [ˈkauntəʃɑːft] n. 中间轴
converter [kənˈvəːtə(r)] n. 转换器

pinion [ˈpinjən] n. 小齿轮，副齿轮
tubular [ˈtjuːbjulə] a. 管状的
jolt [dʒəult] n. 颠簸
shim [ʃim] n. 薄垫片
redirect [ˌriːdiˈrekt] vt. 使改变方向
final drive 主减速器，后桥
tubular section 管状的截面
gear down 降速

# NOTES

1) In order to transmit the power of the engine to the road wheels of a car, a friction clutch and a change-speed gearbox are normally employed. The former is necessary in order to enable the drive to be taken up gradually and smoothly, while the latter provides different ratios of speed reduction from the engine to the wheels, to suit the particular conditions of running.

为了把发动机的动力传递给与路面接触的车轮，正常情况下都会用到摩擦离合器和变速箱。为了使行驶过程逐渐地、平缓地进行，摩擦离合器是必要的；而变速箱以不同的减速比将发动机速度传给车轮，以适应特定的行驶条件。

2) When a vehicle is to be moved from rest the clutch must engage a stationary gearbox shaft with the engines. This must be rotating at a high speed to provide sufficient power, otherwise the load will be too great and the engine will stall (come to rest).

当汽车启动时，离合器就要使一对固定的齿轮轴与发动机一起工作；此时为保证有足够的动力必须运转在高速挡，否则路面摩擦力太大，发动机会熄火（停止）。

3) The gears reduce engine speed in the gearbox so that engine torque increases. This speed decreases and torque increases are needed so that the engine can run at higher speeds. At such speeds, it produces more torque and is more efficient. In other words, the transmission allows higher engine speeds at low vehicle speeds and multiplies torque to help move the car.

啮合的齿轮降低发动机齿轮箱的速度使得发动机的扭矩增加。而速度的降低和扭矩的增加是必要的以便发动机可以以较高的速度运转。以这样的速度，发动机产生更大的扭矩，效率也更高。换句话说，传动系统允许车辆行驶在较低的速度而发动机运行在较高的速度来增大扭矩，推动车辆行驶。

4) The gearbox and engine mount firmly to the car. However, the final drive mounts on springs as part of the rear suspension system. The suspension provides a flexible coupling between the wheels and car body.

变速箱和发动机都是固连到车上的。而后桥却是装在弹簧上作为后悬挂系统的一部分。

悬挂系统使得车轮与车体之间的连接是柔性的。

5) When a vehicle is cornered the inner wheel moves through a shorter distance than the outer wheel. This means that the inner wheel must slow down and the outer wheel must speed up. During this period it is desirable that each driving wheel maintains its driving action. The differential performs these two tasks.

当车辆转弯时，内侧的车轮移动的距离比外侧的要短。这意味着，内侧的车轮必须减速而外侧的车轮必须加速，也就期望在此期间每侧的车轮都要保持其应有的驱动动作，差速器就是用于完成这两项任务的。

## EXERCISES

1. After reading the text above, summarize the main ideas in oral.

2. Fill in the blanks with proper words or phrases according to the text (note the proper tense).

   (1) This disengages the transmission f_____ the engine.

   (2) The load must be applied g_____ to operate the car s_____.

   (3) It must transmit all engine power to the transmission, w_____ slipping.

   (4) _____ a result, engines operate best only within this fairly narrow range.

   (5) The front section of the gearbox h_____ the torque converter.

   (6) The final drive mounts _____ springs _____ part of the rear suspension system.

   (7) This flexible coupling insulates the car body f_____ the jolts of the road surface.

3. Translate the following phrases into Chinese according to the text.

   (1) different rotational speeds of the drive wheels when cornering

   (2) in terms of fuel consumption and exhaust emissions

   (3) a means for gradually engaging the engine to the driving wheels

   (4) to shift the gears inside the transmission

   (5) to act as solid coupling device

   (6) with resulting multiplication of torque

   (7) the coupling between the engine and drive train that transmits power to the drive wheels

4. Translate the following phrases into English according to the text.

   (1) 摩擦离合器

   (2) 变速箱

   (3) 适应特定的行驶条件

   (4) 踩下离合器踏板

   (5) 在三个方面表现不佳

   (6) 仅仅在一个十分狭窄的范围内

   (7) 扭矩转换器

   (8) 用螺栓固连到变速箱和后桥上

5. Write a 100-word summary according to the text.

# READING MATERIAL

## Network Application on Automotive Control

### 1. Automotive Controller Area Network Applications

The controller area network (CAN) is a serial, asynchronous, multi-master communication protocol for connecting electronic control modules in automotive and industrial applications (Figure 4.25). CAN was designed for automotive applications which need high levels of data integrity and data rates of up to 1Mb/s.

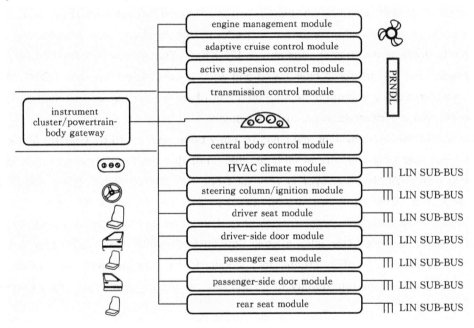

Figure 4.25  Automotive CAN Network

1) Key Benefits

■ The automotive networking standard protocol for Europe

■ Supports the US automakers migration to CAN for body electronics busses

2) Main Design Notices

Not all CAN networks are created equally. In the automotive environment, CAN networks can be split into two distinct categories based on the nature of the traffic in the network. Body control networks, dealing with passenger comfort and convenience systems for example, deal with a wide range of message identifiers that not appear in particular order or frequency. In contrast, power train networks that pass information related to engine and transmission control have a much lower number of different messages to deal with, but the messages appear very rapidly and very regularly. These differences in messaging result in very different approaches to designing hardware and software systems to deal with the demands that each type of network places on each node in that network.

CAN, like all major networking protocols, requires a physical layer device to communicate. This physical layer comes from the ISO/OSI seven layer stack model and is responsible for current and voltage control for the bus. It deals with current and voltage transients and signaling bus (line) faults and works to possibly correct them. The Bosch CAN specification does not dictate physical layer specifications for anyone implementing a CAN network. This is both a blessing and a curse to the designer. Over the course of the last decade, two major physical layer designs have come to the forefront and become the basic physical layer designs used in most CAN applications. They both communicate using a differential voltage on a pair of wires and are commonly referred to as a high-speed and a low-speed physical layer respectively. The low-speed architecture has the ability to change to a single-wire operating architecture (referenced off ground) when one of the two wires is faulted through a short or open. Because of the nature of the circuitry required to perform this function, this architecture is very expensive to implement at bus speeds above 125 Kb/s. This is why 125 Kb/s is the dividing line between what is considered high-speed and what is considered low-speed CAN. Although both architectures use a voltage difference on a pair of wires, the termination methods for each are different and incompatible in production systems.

One additional CAN physical layer has recently been developed by General Motors. This physical layer uses only one wire at all times that limits its speed performance to 33.33 Kb/s. This single-wire CAN physical layer is very different from the other two types and is not yet widely accepted. Because there are no requirements on the physical layer in the CAN specification, other standards organizations have developed standards to help designers create compatible CAN devices. The International Standards Organization (ISO) and Society of Automotive Engineers (SAE) create the standards for Europe and the United States respectively to ensure interoperability of components at the physical layer and recommended design practices.

## 2. Automotive Local Interconnect Network Applications

Local interconnect network (LIN) is a UART-based, single-master, multiple-slave networking architecture originally developed for automotive sensor and actuator networking applications (Figure 4.26). LIN provides a low-cost networking option for connecting motors, switches, sensors and lamps in the vehicle. The LIN master node connects the LIN network with higher-level networks, like controller area network (CAN), extending the benefits of networking all the way to the individual sensors and actuators.

1) Key Benefits

LIN physical layer has critical wave shaping that aids EMC problems by reducing radiated emissions.

Mechatronics smart connector solutions offer increased integration of connectors and silicon for greater design flexibility and added feature content.

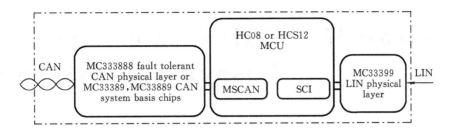

**Figure 4.26　Typical LIN Master Module**

2) Main Design Notices

Form factor, manufacture capability, load control and diagnostics

Challenges exist when integrating UN networking into an automotive environment. Most applications, where LIN could be used, are currently implemented using discrete, point-to-point wiring systems, with no allocation for silicon, circuits or components at the load. The load, whether a lamp, motor or sensor, is usually connected with a simple connector to wires in the tangle of the wiring harness. As a result, little room remains to incorporate the components to enable LIN. For example, in a power mirror, a supplier might place as many as three motors, heater element, electrochromic glass and multiple lamps. These components do not leave much room for other potential requirements. The capability to manufacture control modules is another significant challenge to automotive electronics manufacturers. This problem is not unique to UN developers but it is a problem not always faced by manufacturers of motors, sensors and actuators. Finally, when distributing the intelligence of the system using LIN, new options become available to designers. Motor, lamp and solenoid loads can now be controlled at the origin. Diagnostic data can be easily rejected through the UN network providing an unprecedented level of control and system level information. The challenge is how to provide the silicon content to control and diagnose these loads in a small form factor that can fit in a very small space.

Stringent EMC radiated emissions requirements

Electromagnetic Compatibility (EMC) deals with how multiple electronic devices interact based on the electromagnetic emissions they radiate (radiated emissions) and how they respond to radiated emissions from outside sources (susceptibility). This is of enormous concern in the automotive environment due to the close proximity of a very wide range of electronic systems and devices. It is very important that the LIN network does not radiate very much energy, since these busses pass information through long wires that result in antennae that send emissions to the rest of the vehicle. LIN is designed as a single-wire bus, switching from ground to battery-level voltages. This large voltage swing can be a potential source of large amounts of radiated emissions, particularly if little care or attention is paid to physical layer device design.

# Lesson 32 Drive Axles and Suspension Systems

## TEXT

### 1. Basic Parts of the Steering System

The function of the steering system is to provide the driver with a means for controlling the direction of the vehicle when it moves.

The basic steering systems in most cars are the same. The steering gear of steering box is the heart of the steering system. This is usually next to the engine. A shaft extends from the back of the steering gear. This shaft is connected to the steering column or steering shaft. The steering wheel is at the top of the steering column. Another shaft comes from the bottom of the steering gear. This shaft connects to the arms, rods, and links. This parts assembly, called the steering linkage, connects the steering gear to the parts at the wheels. The wheels and tires mount to the steering knuckles. As shown in Figure 4.27, the knuckles are pivoted at the top and bottom. Thus, the wheels and tires can turn from side to side.

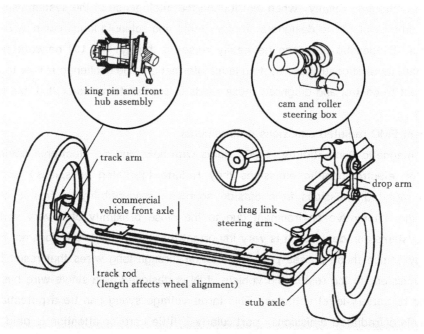

Figure 4.27 Basic parts of commercial steering system

While the steering system may look complicated, it works quite simply. When a driver drives a car straight down the road, the steering gear is centered. The gear holds the linkage centered so that the wheels and tires point straight ahead. When the driver turns the steering wheel, the steering shaft rotates and the steering gear moves toward that side. The shaft coming out the bottom of the steering gear turns as well. When the shaft turns, it pulls the linkage to one side and makes the steering knuckles turn slightly about their pivot points. Thus, the steering knuckle, spindle, wheels, and tires turn to one side, causing the car to turn.

The type of steering layout depends on the suspension system. The beam axle used on heavy commercial vehicles has a king pin fitted at each end of the axle and this pin is the pivot which allows the wheels to be steered (Figure 4.28). Cars have independent suspension and this system has ball joints to allow for wheel movement (Figure 4.28).

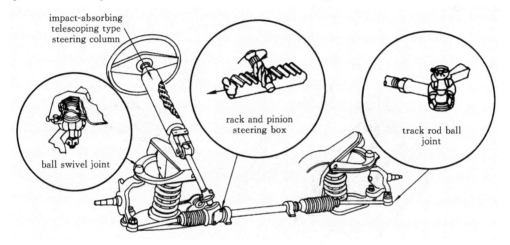

Figure 4.28 Basic parts of the steering system (independent suspension)

The requirements in terms of steering behavior can be summarized as follows.

① Jolts from irregularities in the road surface must be damped as much as possible in being transmitted to the steering wheel. However, such damping must not cause the driver to lose contact with the road.

② The basic design of the steering kinematics must satisfy the Ackermann conditions: the extensions of the wheel axes of the left and right front wheels, when at an angle, intersect on an extension of the rear axle.

③ By means of suitable stiffness of the steering system (particularly if rubber-elastic connections are used) the vehicle must react to minute steering corrections.

④ When the steering wheel is released, the wheels must return to the straight-ahead position automatically and must remain stable in this position.

⑤ The steering should have as low a ratio as possible (number of steering-wheel turns from lock) in order to obtain ease of handling. Thereby the occurring steering forces are determined not only by the steering ratio, but also by the front-axle loading, the size of the turning circle, the wheel suspension (caster, steering-axis inclination, steering roll radius) and the tire tread.

## 2. An Overview of Suspension

The suspension covers the arrangement used to connect the wheels to the body. The purpose of suspension is to prevent large shocks, caused by the wheels striking bumps in the road, from being passed to the vehicle occupants and components; otherwise discomfort and damage would occur.

The deflection of a pneumatic tire takes most of the impact from a road bump but some form of springing is still needed to give a satisfactory ride. Unfortunately the release of the energy contained in a spring when it has been deflected by a road bump will cause the vehicle to bounce, so a shock absorber is fitted to overcome this.

The suspension system has two subsystems—the front suspension and the rear suspension (Figure 4.29).

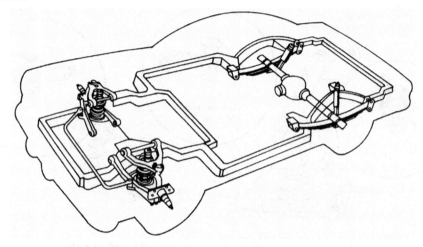

Figure 4.29　The suspension system

1) Front Suspension

The front suspension is more complicated than the rear suspension because the front wheels must move in several different directions. The wheels must move up and down with the suspension and turn left to right with the steering. Since the car goes in the direction in which the front wheels point, the alignment of the front wheels is important. The wheels must point in just the right direction for the car to move straight down the road and turn properly.

Modern cars use an independent front suspension. In the system, each wheel mounts separately to the frame and has its own individual spring and shock absorber(Figure 4.30). Thus, the wheels act independently. When one wheel hits a bump or hole in the road, the other wheel does not deflect.

When the vehicle is traveling straight, the lever will divide the driving force equally and both discs will move in the same amount.

When the vehicle corners, the driving force will still be divided equally but the inner disc will now move through a smaller distance; this will cause the lever to pivot about its center which will prize forward the outer disc to give it a greater movement. This action shows that the torque applied to each driving wheel is always equal—hence the differential is sometimes called a torque equalizer.

2) Rear Suspension

The purpose of the rear suspension is to support the weight of the rear of the vehicle. As

## Lesson 32  Drive Axles and Suspension Systems

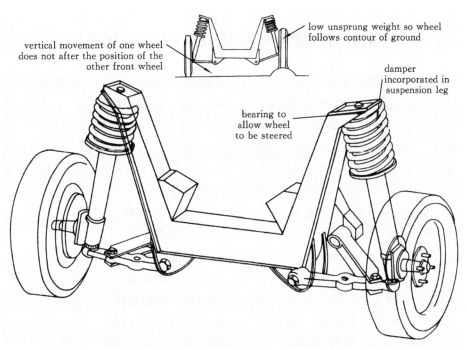

Figure 4.30  Independent suspension system

with the front suspension, this system contributes to the stability and ride of the vehicle. Rear suspension may be of the solid axle or independent design. Many cars have solid axle rear suspension. Either design may have different kinds of springs, including torsion bars. However, the coil spring and leaf spring types are most popular (Figure 4.31).

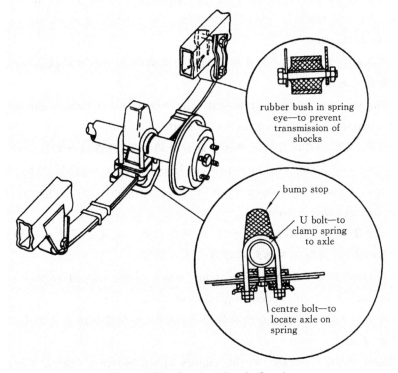

Figure 4.31  Laminated or leaf spring

# NEW WORDS AND EXPRESSIONS

knuckle ['nʌkl] *n.* 指节，关节
pivot ['pivət] *vi.* 在枢轴上转动 *n.* 枢轴
spindle ['spindl] *n.* 转向节（轴端）
irregularity [iˌregju'læriti] *n.* 不规则，不平整
damp [dæmp] *n.* 阻尼 *vt.* 使衰减，制动，抑制
kinematics [ˌkaini'mætiks] *n.* 运动学
minute [mai'nju:t] *a.* 微小的
inclination [ˌinkli'neiʃən] *n.* 倾斜
tread [tred] *n.* 轮胎面
bump [bʌmp] *n.* 撞击
occupant ['ɔkju:pənt] *n.* 车里的人，乘客
deflection [di'flekʃən] *n.* 偏斜，偏差
bounce [bauns] *v.* （球）反弹，跳起

laminated ['læmineitid] *a.* 薄板状的，薄片状的
steering column 转向柱管
steering linkage 转向传动机构
steering knuckle 转向节
king pin and front hub assembly 主销和前毂装配件
track arm 转向臂
track rod 转向杆
drop arm 摇臂
stub axle 转向轴
drag link 摇臂连杆
steering box 转向器
ball swivel joint 球形转向节
pneumatic tire 充气轮胎

# NOTES

1) Jolts from irregularities in the road surface must be damped as much as possible in being transmitted to the steering wheel. However, such damping must not cause the driver to lose contact with the road.

由路面的不规则带来的摇晃必须在传递到方向盘的过程中尽可能减弱。然而，这样的减弱不能使驱动轮脱离地面。

2) When the steering wheel is released, the wheels must return automatically to the straight-ahead position and must remain stable in this position.

当方向盘释放后，车轮必须自动地转到直线前进的位置，并在这样的位置稳定保持住。

3) The purposes of suspension is to prevent large shocks, caused by the wheels striking bumps in the road, from being passed to the vehicle occupants and components. Otherwise discomfort and damage would occur.

车轮撞击地面隆起之处会引起较大的振动，避振的目的就是为了不让这种振动传递给车辆中的乘客和零部件，否则会使人感到不舒服或造成危害。

4) The deflection of a pneumatic tire takes much of the impact from a road bump but some form of springing is still needed to give a satisfactory ride.

充气轮胎的变形克服了许多地面冲击的影响，然而，要想获得满意的驾乘，还需要有不同结构形式的弹簧（来减振）。

5) Unfortunately the release of the energy contained in a spring when it has been deflected by a road bump will cause the vehicle to bounce, so a shock absorber is fitted to

overcome this.

不幸的是,当弹簧受到地面冲击变形时,变形产生能量的释放会使车辆产生反弹,安装减振器就是为了克服这一情形的。

# EXERCISES

1. After reading the text above, summarize the main ideas in oral.

2. Fill in the blanks with proper words or phrases according to the text (note the proper tense).

(1) This shaft is connected _____ the steering column or steering shaft.

(2) The wheels and tires mount to the steering k_____.

(3) The shaft coming _____ the bottom of the steering gear turns as well.

(4) This is because the front wheels must move _____ several different directions.

(5) The wheels must point in just the right direction for the car to move straight _____ the road and turn properly.

(6) The final drive mounts _____ springs _____ part of the rear suspension system.

3. Translate the following phrases into Chinese according to the text.

(1) the extensions of the wheel axles of the left and right front wheels

(2) by means of suitable stiffness of the steering system

(3) in order to obtain ease of handling

(4) the purposes to prevent large shocks

(5) to move in several different directions

(6) a torque equalizer

4. Translate the following phrases into English according to the text.

(1) 与发动机相邻　　　　　　(2) 方向盘

(3) 转向传动机构　　　　　　(4) 测定微小的方向调整

(5) 传递给车厢中的乘客和零部件　(6) 独立的前悬挂系统

5. Write a 100-word summary according to the text.

# READING MATERIAL

## Gas (Pneumatic) Suspension

This type of suspension system is usually used in purely pneumatic form in buses and commercial vehicles. It is used in hydropneumatic form for passenger cars.

### 1. Pure Pneumatic Suspension

In a purely pneumatic suspension (Figure 4.32), rubber air-spring bellows with fabric inserts are maintained at an air pressure according to the load.

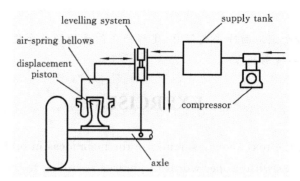

Figure 4.32  Pure pneumatic

## 2. Hydropneumatic Suspension

A hermetically sealed quantity of gas is used for suspension and is compressed by means of hydraulic oil according to the load (Figure 4.33). The gas and hydraulic oil are separated by a rubber diaphragm. The suspension element assumes the additional function of a shock absorber via throttle valves in the oil chamber.

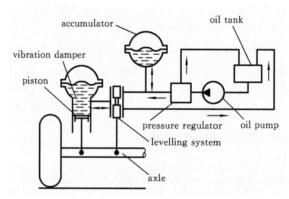

Figure 4.33  Hydropneumatic suspension

## 3. Leveling Control

In a pneumatic and hydropneumatic suspension, the vehicle body can be maintained at the same height irrespective of the load; in many cases the height of the vehicle body can also be varied at will by the driver. For this purpose the quantity of air or hydraulic oil supplied to the suspension elements is increased or reduced by the leveling control. Some leveling controls are hydraulically damped in order to reduce the energy required while the vehicle is in motion. Leveling systems with transverse shut-off or restriction are used to increase roll stability. If additional demands are made on the leveling control system which cannot be fulfilled by mechanical control elements, the electronic leveling control system is used (Figure 4.34).

## 4. Advantages of Electronic Leveling Control for Passenger Cars

(1) Speed-dependent control of vehicle tilt and vehicle body level in order to reduce fuel

## Lesson 32  Drive Axles and Suspension Systems

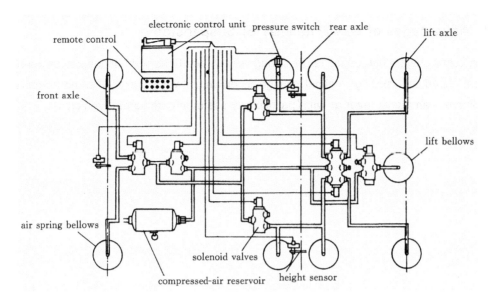

Figure 4.34  Electronic leveling control, automatic axel lift system for commercial vehicles

consumption.

(2) Increase in vehicle body level when traveling on uneven road surfaces.

(3) Improved cornering stability through absolute transverse shut-off of the pneumatic springs.

(4) Switch-off of the control system when braking, accelerating and cornering in order to reduce energy required by the suspension system.

### 5. Advantages of Electronic Leveling Control for Commercial Vehicles

(1) Reduce air consumption through optimum damping.

(2) Improve cornering stability through absolute transverse shut-off of the pneumatic springs on axle.

(3) Automatic stroke limitation for interchangeable open bodies and containers.

(4) Quick adjustment.

(5) Automatic adaptation of height of bed to height of loading platform (height of bed level desired).

(6) Safe operation (remote control).

(7) Lift-axle control (level increases automatically when lift axle is raised).

(8) Automatic dropping of the lift axle when the permissible load (10 t) at the drive axle is exceeded.

(9) Increase pull-away traction by increasing the load on the driving axle, limitation of load to the maximum value (15 t), increased load on driving axle for pulling away is limited to 2—3 min.

### 6. Pneumatic Spring Combined with Shock Absorber

In the case of purely pneumatic suspension, the actual suspension element can also be combined with the shock absorber to form one unit.

## 7. Advantages of Gas (Pneumatic) Suspension

Constant body height (thus large spring wheel positions with independent suspension) deflection, headlamp setting minimal change in driving always correct, same comfort due to cargo. Driver can adjust level at will (particularly useful in commercial vehicles).

# Lesson 33 Brake System

## TEXT

### 1. An Overview of the Braking System

Drum brakes have a drum attached to the wheel hub, and braking occurs by means of brake shoes expanding against the inside of the drum. With disc brakes, a disc attached to the wheel hub is clenched between two brake pads. On light vehicles, both of these systems are hydraulically operated. The brake pedal operates a master cylinder. Hydraulic lines and hoses connect the master cylinder to brake cylinders at the wheels. Most modern light vehicles have either disc brake on the front and drum brakes on the rear or disc brakes on all 4 wheels. Disc brakes require greater force to operate them. A brake booster assists the driver by increasing the force applied to the master cylinder when the brake is operated.

Air operated braking systems are used on heavy vehicles. Compressed air operating on large diameter diaphragms provides large force to the brake assembly that is needed. An air compressor pumps air to storage tanks. Driver controlled valves then direct the compressed air to different wheel units to operate the friction brakes. On articulated vehicles, any delay in applying the trailer brake should be minimized. This is achieved by using a relay valve and a separate reservoir on the trailer. This arrangement also applies the brakes if the trailer becomes disconnected from the prime mover.

All vehicles must be fitted with at least 2 independent systems. They were once called the service brake and the emergency brake. Now they are usually referred to as the foot brake and the park brake. Most light vehicles use a foot brake that operates through a hydraulic system on all wheels and a hand operated brake that acts mechanically on the rear wheels only. One common use of the hand brake system is to hold the vehicle when it is parked. The systems are designed to be independent so that if one fails, the other is still available.

### 2. Basic Features of Braking System

Energy is required when a vehicle is accelerated from rest to a certain speed. A proportion of that energy is now stored in the vehicle and is called kinetic energy. In order to reduce the speed of the vehicle, the brakes have to convert the kinetic energy to heat energy, the speed of conversion governs the rate at which the vehicle slows down.

A braking system consists of an energy-supplying device, a control device, a transmission device and the brake.

Braking systems are differentiated according to the types of energy used: muscular energy braking system, energy-assisted braking system, non-muscular-energy brake system, inertia braking system and gravity braking system. The difference between these braking systems is primarily the way in which energy is used in braking-system control. A portion of the controlled working force is used as the operating force in an energy-assisted braking system, for example, but not in a non-muscular-energy braking system. Energy-assisted braking systems and non-muscular-energy braking systems also use different energy media. Energy is generated primarily by vacuum, compressed air or hydraulic power (sometimes also electric power).

Two types of brakes are used in modern cars: drum brakes and disc brakes. Since 1976 cars have used disc brakes on the front wheels. Most cars use drum brakes on the rear wheels (Figure 4.35). In both drum and disc brakes, a hydraulic system applies the brakes. The hydraulic system connects the brake pedal to the brake parts at each wheel.

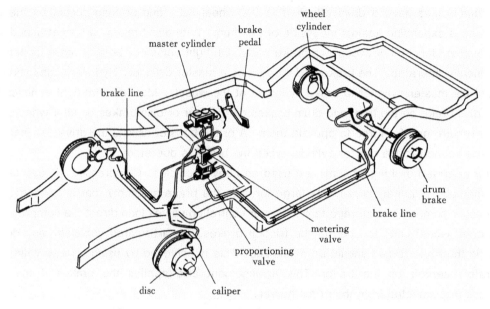

Figure 4.35  The principal parts of the brake hydraulic system

Two types of hydraulic brake systems are used. The manual brake system is the simplest. Here, the force of the driver's foot on the pedal applies all the force to the hydraulic system. Another system, the power brake system, uses parts that assist a driver in applying force to the hydraulic system. There is also an antiskid system that prevents the brakes from locking up the wheels causing skidding.

Braking systems are differentiated according to transmission devices: single-circuit braking system (No longer permissible for service braking systems above 25 km/h) and multi-circuit braking system, as well as:

① braking system with mechanical force transmission;
② braking system with hydraulic force transmission;
③ braking system with pneumatic force transmission;
④ braking system with electrical force transmission.

## 3. Types of Brake

There are two main types of brake: drum brake (see Figure 4.36) and disc brake (see

Figure 4.37).

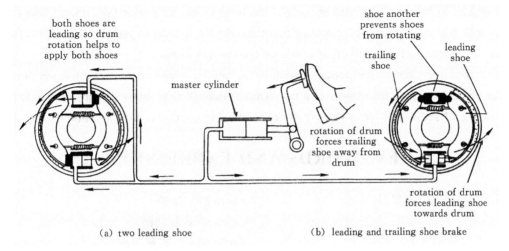

(a) two leading shoe    (b) leading and trailing shoe brake

**Figure 4.36　Drum brake**

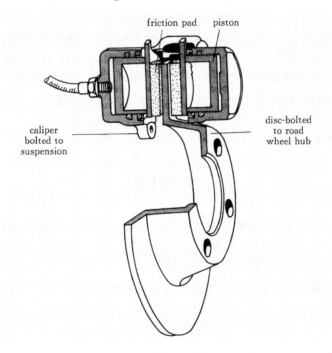

**Figure 4.37　Disk brake**

1) Drum brakes

Drum brakes have two shoes, anchored to a stationary back-plate, which are internally expanded to contact the drum by hydraulic cylinders or a mechanical linkage.

The end at which the shoe is anchored affects the retarding force it applies to the drum; the rotation of the drum gives a self-energizing action called self-servo which causes:

① the leading shoe to be forced towards the drum,

② the trailing shoe to be forced away from the drum.

The leading shoe is the first shoe after the expander in the direction of rotation.

2) Disc Brakes

Exposed to the air, disc brakes radiate the heat to the air better than drum brakes. This means that the brake can be operated continuously for a longer period, i. e. they have a greater resistance to fade (fall-off in brake efficiency due to heat).

This fade resistance, and features such as automatic adjustment, make the disc brake a popular choice for the front wheels of a car. One drawback with many designs of disc brake is the absence of self-servo, so a vacuum servo is fitted to boost the effort applied by the driver.

## NEW WORDS AND EXPRESSIONS

clench [klentʃ] *n.* 捏紧,钉牢
pad [pæd] *n.* 垫,衬垫
booster ['buːstə] *n.* 调压器
kinetic [kai'netik] *a.* 运动的,动力的,与运动有关的
skid [skid] *n.* 打滑,滑行
antiskid ['ænti'skid] *a.* 防滑的
caliper ['kælipə] *n.* 制动钳体
anchor ['æŋkə] *v.* 抛锚,固定
expander [ik'spændə(r)] *n.* 扩大器
drum brake 鼓式制动器

wheel hub 轮毂
brake shoe 制动蹄
disc brake 盘式制动器
kinetic energy 动能
service braking 行车制动
parking braking 驻车制动
retarding braking 缓速制动
no-muscular energy brake 动力制动
leading shoe 领蹄
trailing shoe 从蹄

## NOTES

1) Most light vehicles use a foot brake that operates through a hydraulic system on all wheels and a hand operated brake that acts mechanically on the rear wheels only.

大多数轻型车辆用的是一个脚刹和一个手刹。脚刹是通过安装在所有车轮上的一个液压系统来操作的,而手刹是仅靠装在后轮上的机械装置来进行操作。

2) Braking systems are differentiated according to the types of energy used: muscular energy braking system, energy-assisted braking system, non-muscular-energy brake system, inertia braking system and gravity braking system.

制动系统根据其使用的能量不同可以分为人工制动系统、助力制动系统、动力制动系统、惯性制动系统和重力制动系统。

3) The difference between these braking systems is primarily the way in which energy is used in braking-system control. A portion of the controlled working force is used as the operating force in an energy-assisted braking system, for example, but not in a non-muscular-energy braking system.

这些制动系统的区别主要在于用在制动系统控制的能量的不同。例如,在助力制动系统中,一部分的控制用的力被作为操作力,而在动力制动系统中就不是这样。

4) These have two shoes, anchored to a stationary back-plate, which are internally

expanded to contact the drum by hydraulic cylinders or a mechanical linkage.

这些有两个制动蹄，它们安装在一个固定的支承板上，通过液压缸或者一个机械连杆从内部延伸接触到制动鼓。

5) Exposed to the air, disc brakes radiate the heat to the air better than drum brakes. This means that the brake can be operated continuously for a longer period, i.e. they have a greater resistance to fade (fall-off in brake efficiency due to heat).

由于暴露在空气中，碟片式制动器比鼓式制动器更容易散热。这意味着碟式制动器可以连续更长时间制动，即可获得较大的制动阻力（由于发热，制动效率会下降）。

# EXERCISES

1. After reading the text above, summarize the main ideas in oral.
2. Fill in the blanks with proper words or phrases according to the text (note the proper tense).

(1) Compressed air operating on large diameter d_____ provides large forces to the brake assembly that is needed.

(2) Now they are usually referred _____ as the foot brake and the park brake.

(3) The hydraulic system c_____ the brake pedal to the brake parts at each wheel.

(4) There is also an a_____ system that prevents the brakes from locking _____ the wheels causing skidding.

(5) The leading shoe is the first shoe after the e_____ in the direction of rotation.

3. Translate the following phrases into Chinese according to the text.

(1) a drum attached to the wheel hub

(2) to consist of an energy-supplying device, a control device, a transmission device and the brake

(3) the way in which energy used in braking-system control

(4) the power brake system

(5) braking system with pneumatic force transmission

4. Translate the following phrases into English according to the text.

(1) 动能      (2) 脚刹和驻刹
(3) 人工制动系统      (4) 动力制动系统
(5) 应急制动系统      (6) 助力制动系统
(7) 液压制动系统

5. Write a 100-word summary according to the text.

# READING MATERIAL

## 1. Electrohydraulic Braking

Electrohydraulic braking (EHB) systems (see Figure 4.38) are designed to allow electronic control of vehicle braking while retaining a reduced hydraulic system. The hydraulic system functions as a reserve in the event of a failure in the electronic control. The EHB control unit receives inputs from sensors connected to the brake pedal. In normal operation, a backup valve is closed and the controller activates the brakes of the wheel through an electric motor driven hydraulic pump. When the controller goes into a fail-safe mode, the backup valve is opened, which allows the brakes to be controlled through a conventional hydraulic circuit.

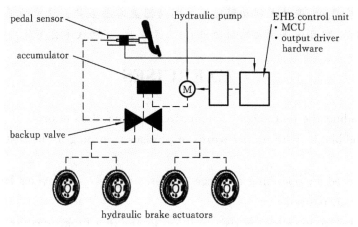

Figure 4.38 Electrohydraulic braking system

1) Key Benefits

① Reusing hydraulic system technology while incrementally built on the development of advanced electronic systems, such as electronic stability programs (ESP), traction control and brake assist.

② Using software updates to simplify the calibration process by adjusting brake response and pedal feel.

③ Improving connectivity with other emerging systems, such as adaptive cruise control.

④ Removing the large vacuum servo to allow flexible installation.

⑤ Featuring an anti-lock braking system (ABS) without feedback from the pedal.

2) Main Design Notices

Electrohydraulic braking is based on existing ABS systems with the addition of several enhancements. The inclusion of analog electrohydraulic valves requires closed-loop, current-controlled pulse width modulation (PWM) outputs from the electronic control unit (ECU). An EHB system is required to incorporate a fail-safe state in the event of a fault occurring. To correctly initiate the fail-safe state, the system relies on its electronic components to provide a high level of operational fault coverage.

## 2. Electromechanical Braking (Brake by Wire)

Electromechanical braking systems (EMB) (see Figure 4.39), also called brake by wire, replace conventional hydraulic braking systems with completely "dry" electrical component systems by replacing conventional actuators with electric motor-driven units. This move to electronic control eliminates many of the manufacturing, maintenance, and environmental concerns associated with hydraulic systems. Because there is no mechanical or hydraulic back-up system, reliability is critical and the system must be fault-tolerant. Implementing EMB requires features such as a dependable power supply, fault-tolerant communication protocols, and some level of hardware redundancy. As in electrohydraulic braking (EHB), EMB is designed to improve connectivity with other vehicle systems, thus enabling simpler integration of such higher-level functions as traction control and vehicle stability control. This integration may vary from embedding the function within the EMB system, as with ABS, to interfacing to these additional systems using communication links.

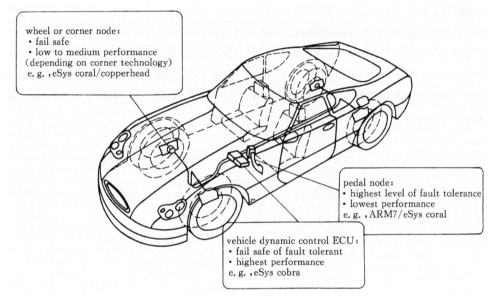

**Figure 4.39 Control package**

Both EHB and EMB systems offer the advantage of eliminating the large vacuum booster found in conventional systems. Along with reducing the dilemma of working with increasingly tighter space in the engine bay, this elimination helps simplify production of right-and left-hand drive vehicle variants. When compared to those of EHB, EMB systems offer increased flexibility for the placement of components by totally eliminating the hydraulic system.

The benefits of EMB are:

① connecting with emerging systems, such as adaptive cruise control,

② reducing system weight to provide improved vehicle performance and economy,

③ assembling the system into the host vehicle simpler and faster,

④ reducing pollutant sources by eliminating corrosive, toxic hydraulic fluids,

⑤ removing the vacuum servo and hydraulic system for flexible placement of components,

⑥ reducing maintenance requirements,

⑦ supporting features such as "hill hold",

⑧ removing mechanical components for freedom of design.

EMB systems represent a complete change in requirements from previous hydraulic and electrohydraulic braking systems. The EMB processing components must be networked using high-reliability bus protocols that ensure comprehensive fault tolerance as a major aspect of system design. The use of electric brake actuators means additional requirements that include motor control operation within a 42 V power system and high temperature and high density to the electronic components. In addition to supporting existing communications standards such as CAN and K-line, EMB systems require the implementation of deterministic, time-triggered communications, such as those available with FlexRay, to assist in providing the required system fault tolerance. The EMB nodes may not need to be individually fault tolerant, but they help to provide fail-safe operation and rely on a high level of fault detection by the electronic components.

These new system requirements must be met using high-end components at very competitive prices to replace established, cost-effective technology while maintaining strict adherence to the automotive qualification. Delivering the large current requirements to stop a large SUV may cause limited adoption initially. The first implementation will be on small car platforms.

# Part V

# Management of Enterprise

# Lesson 34 | Productivity in Manufacturing

## TEXT

Productivity is a simple concept. It is the amount of output produced per unit of input. While it is easy to define, it is notoriously difficult to measure, especially in the modern economy. In particular, there are two aspects of productivity that have increasingly defied precise measurement: output and input. Properly measured, output should include not just the number of widgets coming out of a factory, or the lines of code produced by a programming team, but rather the value created for consumers. Fifty years ago, tons of steel or bushels of corn were a reasonable proxy for the value of output. In today's economy, value depends increasingly on product quality, timeliness, customization, convenience, variety and other "intangibles".

Productivity can be defined in two basic ways. The most familiar, labor productivity is simply output divided by the number of workers or, more often, by the number of hours worked. Output can be anything from tons of steel to airline miles flown, but more generally it is some very broad aggregate like gross domestic product. Measures of labor productivity, however, actually capture the contribution to output of other inputs and hours worked.

Total factor productivity, by contrast, captures the contribution to output of everything except labor and capital: innovation, managerial skill, organization, even luck.

The two productivity concepts are related. Increases in labor productivity can reflect the fact that each worker is better equipped with capital—a supermarket clerk who has an automatic scanner instead of old-fashioned cash register—or, alternatively, gains in total factor productivity. Thanks to specialization, for example, Adam Smith's pin factory turned out more pins with the same number of craftsmen and identical tools. And General Motors' Fremont, California, plant—once one of the worst in the company—had a productivity turnaround when it required its workers to use Japanese manufacturing methods.

While factors of production like land will always be scarce, the potential for increasing total factor productivity is limitless. At least half, if not more, of the growth in labor productivity in the post-World War II period has been due not to the use of added capital, but to making better use of these inputs. The United States produced 65 percent more in 1981 than in 1948 from the same quantity of labor and capital resources.

Gains in living standards are tied to productivity gains. There are only three ways that a nation can enjoy a rising level of per capital consumption. First, a bigger proportion of the population can go to work. Second, a country can borrow from abroad or sell assets to foreigners to pay for extra imports. Third, the nation can boost productivity—either by investing a bigger share of national income in plant and equipment or by finding new ways to increase efficiency.

Productivity isn't everything. However, in the long run it is almost everything. Productivity growth determines our living standards and the wealth of nations. This is because the amount a nation can consume is ultimately closely tied to what it produces. By the same token, the success of a business generally depends on its ability to deliver more real value for consumers without using more labor, capital or other inputs.

Similarly, a proper measure of inputs includes not only labor hours, but also the quantity and quality of capital equipment used, materials and other resources consumed, worker training and education, even the amount of "organizational capital" required, such as supplier relationships cultivated and investments in new business processes. The irony is that while we have more raw data today on all sorts of inputs and outputs than ever before, productivity in the information economy has proven harder to measure than it ever was in the industrial economy.

## NEW WORDS

widget ['wɪdʒɪt] *n.* 小器具，装饰品
intangible [ɪn'tændʒəbl] *a.* 难以确定的，无形的
stagnate [stæɡneɪt] *v.* 停滞，不流动，不发展
exaggerate [ɪɡ'zædʒəreɪt] *v.* 夸大，夸张
aggregate ['æɡrɪɡeɪt] *n.* 合计，总计，集合体
craftsman ['krɑːftsmən] *n.* 手艺人，工匠
Fremont [fri'mɔnt] *n.* 弗里蒙特（美国城市名）
domestic [də'mestɪk] *a.* 家庭的，国内的

turnaround ['tɜːnəˌraʊnd] *n.* （尤指美国行市）突然好转
irony ['aɪərəni] *n.* 反话，讽刺，讽刺之事
historical [hɪs'tɔrɪkəl] *a.* 历史的，与历史有关的
innovation [ˌɪnəu'veɪʃən] *n.* 改革，创新
cultivated ['kʌltɪveɪtɪd] *a.* 有教养的，栽植的
investment [ɪn'vestmənt] *n.* 投资，可获利的东西

## NOTES

1) Properly measured, output should include not just the number of widgets coming out of a factory, or the lines of code produced by a programming team, but rather the value created for consumers.

适当地讲，产出不仅应包括某个工厂生产的产品数量，或者某个程序团队编写的程序代码行数，还应包括为消费者创造的价值。

2) Total factor productivity, by contrast, captures the contribution to output of everything except labor and capital: innovation, managerial skill, organization, even luck.

相对来说，在生产力的所有因素中，创新、管理技能、组织能力甚至是运气等因素的影响更为重要，而不仅仅是劳动力和资金。

3) By the same token, the success of a business generally depends on its ability to deliver more real value for consumers without using more labor, capital or other inputs.

出于同样的原因，一个企业的成功取决于它能否在使用较少劳动力、资金以及其他投入的前提下获得更多的价值。

4) Similarly, a proper measure of inputs includes not only labor hours, but also the quantity and quality of capital equipment used, materials and other resources consumed, worker training and education, even the amount of "organizational capital" required, such as supplier relationships cultivated and investments in new business processes.

同样地,正确的衡量投入不仅包括工作时间,还包括固定设备的质量和数量、原材料和其他已消费的资源、工人培训与教育,甚至是需要的"管理费用",例如培养的与供应商的关系、在新的商业领域的投资。

## EXERCISES

1. After reading the text above, summarize the main ideas in oral.
2. Fill in the blanks with proper words or phrases according to the text (note the proper tense).

(1) In p_____, there are two aspects of productivity that have increasingly defied precise measurement: o_____ and i_____.

(2) While factors of production like land will always be s_____, the p_____ for increasing total factor productivity is l_____.

(3) The most f_____, labor productivity, is simply output divided by the number of workers or, more often, by the number of hours worked.

(4) Thanks to s_____, for example, Adam Smith's pin factory t_____ o_____ more pins with the same number of craftsmen and identical tools.

(5) B_____, the success of a business generally depends on its ability to deliver more real value for consumers without using more labor, capital or other inputs.

(6) The irony is that while we have more r_____ today on all sorts of inputs and outputs than ever before, productivity in the i_____ has proven harder to measure than it ever was in the industrial economy.

3. Translate the following phrases into Chinese according to the text.

(1) economic welfare      (2) labor productivity
(3) productivity gain     (4) productivity growth
(5) by the same token     (6) organizational capital

4. Translate the following phrases into English according to the text.

(1) 投入产出        (2) 总产值
(3) 原材料          (4) 国民收入
(5) 信息经济时代    (6) 工业经济时代

5. Write a 100-word summary according to the text.

## READING MATERIAL

Productivity—the amount of output per unit of input—is a basic yardstick of an economy's health. When productivity is growing, living standards tend to rise. When productivity is stagnating, so, generally, is well-being. It can be said without exaggeration that in the long run probably nothing is as important for economic welfare as the rate of productivity growth.

As a consequence of slower productivity growth in the past two decades, average compensation has edged up only slightly faster than the price level. Living standards have increased largely because more Americans, especially mothers, have been working, and because the United States has been able to attract capital from abroad to offset a persistent trade deficit. "Most of the growth slowdown [in per capita income]," states the Economic Report of the President, "can be traced to a slowdown of productivity growth".

Other industrial countries have also experienced a productivity slowdown, most even sharper, suggesting that worldwide forces rather than local ones were to blame. Despite two decades of speculation and study, however, the reasons for the worldwide productivity slump remain a mystery. A host of explanations have been proposed, including some that suggest that productivity growth is likely to revive spontaneously. Harvard economist Dale W. Jorgenson, for example, blames the sudden surge in oil prices in 1973, which claims made much of the existing capital stock obsolete. His colleague Zvi Griliches points a finger at the slower growth of aggregate demand by consumers for goods and services, which, he argues, has kept a great deal of productive capacity idle and hence inputs underemployed. But Edward Denison, an emeritus fellow of the Brookings Institution who conducted a comprehensive analysis of seventeen suggested causes, has concluded that much, if not most, of the slowdown remains unexplained.

Most of the focus in recent years has been on three suspects:

1) Lagging investment

How much a country invests matters, many economists have decided, because more capital per worker should lift output per day? In stock brokerage, for example, the latest computer not only lets a broker execute more trades every day, but also embodies technological breakthroughs that allow new products to be traded.

2) Innovation

The rate of return to capital invested in research and development is very high, averaging more than 20 percent a year. But the United States spends a smaller fraction of its GDP on civilian R&D than Germany or Japan. And Zvi Griliches points out that the number of new patents granted each year began to decline as far back as the sixties.

Some economists think the spurt of productivity growth after World War II was due to the backlog of ideas and technology and investment projects that were put on hold during the depression and World War II. Pent-up consumer demand and the rebuilding of Japan and Germany, according to this thinking, created tremendous demand for new construction and equipment. This explanation is consistent with the decline in productivity growth that started in 1973. Thus, part of the decline may have been simply a return to more normal growth rates.

3) Skills

About 10 to 15 percent of the growth in productivity over the post-World War II era can be traced to more and better schooling. But average years of schooling have not increased since 1976, when it peaked at 12.9 years. Moreover, the quality of basic elementary and secondary education has stagnated or even declined in the past two decades.

Many economists focused in the 1980s on the apparently divergent behavior of productivity in manufacturing and in services. (The Bureau of Labor Statistics publishes separate measures of productivity in manufacturing despite Edward Denison's warnings that measuring productivity below the level of the economy as a whole is tricky.) From 1948 to 1973, manufacturing and services productivity grew more or less in tandem and then, from 1973 to 1979, stagnated in tandem. In the eighties productivity growth in manufacturing snapped back. Tougher foreign competition and deregulation led to a wave of mergers and acquisitions, which in turn led to plant modernizations and streamlined production processes. Productivity growth in services, by contrast, slowed even more in the eighties. Outside of manufacturing—from government to construction to retailing—productivity growth has come to a standstill despite huge investments in information—processing technology.

Some economists have concluded that industrialized countries are specializing in what they do best. While Japan and Germany have surged ahead in some industries, the United States has widened its lead in others and stayed ahead, if by a narrower margin, in still others.

Stagnating pay and greater income inequality have focused renewed public attention on slow productivity growth. Policy prescriptions range from tax cuts on capital gains and more deregulation to industrial policy and government backing for commercially promising technologies. Most economists support closing the federal budget deficit and maintaining low inflation because they believe a stable macroeconomic environment is good for productivity growth. But the major focus of current discussion is on how to raise investment in people and machines and how to get more bangs for the buck from that investment.

# Lesson 35  Product Quality Control and Quality Assurance

## TEXT

"Quality control (QC)" refers to the actions taken throughout the engineering and manufacturing of a product to prevent and detect product deficiencies and product safety hazards. The American Society for Quality Control (ASQC) defines quality as the totality of features and characteristics of a product or service that bear on ability to satisfy a given need. In a narrower sense, "quality control" refers to the statistical techniques employed in sampling production and monitoring the variability of the product. Quality assurance refers to those systematic actions vital to provide satisfactory confidence that an item or service will fulfill defined requirements.

Quality control received its initial impetus in the Unite States in World War II when war production was facilitated and controlled with QC methods. The traditional role of quality control has been to control the quality of raw materials, control the dimensions of parts during production, eliminate imperfect parts from the production line, and assure functional performance of the product. With increased emphasis on tighter tolerance levels, slimmer profit margins, and stricter interpretation of liability laws by the courts, there has been even greater emphasis on quality control. More recently the heavy competition for U. S. markets from overseas producers who have emphasized quality in the extreme has placed even more emphasis on QC by U. S. producers.

An appropriate engineering viewpoint of quality is to consider that it is fitness for use. The consumer may confuse quality with luxury, but in an engineering context quality has to do with how well a product meets its design and performance specifications. With that concept in mind, the various components for achieving quality can be listed as follows (Figure 5.1).

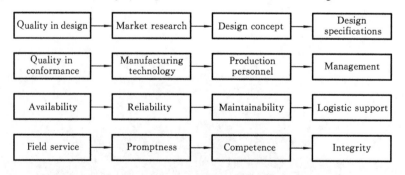

Figure 5.1  The list of various components for achieving quality

## Lesson 35  Product Quality Control and Quality Assurance

### 1. Quality control concepts

A basic tenet of quality control is that variability is inherent in any manufactured product. Someplace there is an economic balance between reducing the variability and the cost of manufacture. Statistical quality control considers that part of the variability is inherent in the materials and process and can be changed only by changing those factors. The remainder of the variability is due to assignable causes that can be reduced or eliminated if they can be identified.

The basic questions in establishing a QC policy for a part are four in number:

1) What to inspect

The objective should be to focus on a few critical characteristics of the product that are good indicators of performance. This is chiefly a technique-based decision. Another decision is whether to emphasize nondestructive or destructive inspection. Obviously, the chief value of an NDI technique is that it allows the manufacturer to inspect a part that will actually be sold. Also, the customer can inspect the same part before it is used. Destructive tests, like tensile tests, are done with the assumption that the results derived from the test are typical of the population from which the test samples were taken. Often it is necessary to use destructive tests to verify that the nondestructive test is measuring the desired characteristic.

2) How to inspect

The basic decision is whether the characteristic of the product to be monitored will be measured on a continuous scale (inspection by variables) or by whether the part passes or fails some go no-go test. The latter situation is known as measurement by attribute. Inspection by variables uses the normal, lognormal, or some similar frequency distribution. Inspection by attributes uses the binomial and Poisson distributions.

3) When to inspect

The decision on when to inspect determines the QC method that will be employed. Inspection can occur either while the process is going on (process control) or after it has been completed (acceptance sampling). A process control approach is used when the inspection can be done nondestructively at low unit cost. An important feature of process control is that the manufacturing conditions can be continuously adjusted on the basis of the inspection data to reduce the percent defectives. Acceptance sampling often involves destructive inspection at a high unit cost. Since not all parts are inspected, it must be expected that a small percentage of defective parts will be passed by the inspection process. The development of sampling plans for various acceptance sampling schemes is an important aspect of statistical quality control.

4) Where to inspect

This decision has to do with the number and location of the inspection steps in the manufacturing process. There is an economic balance between the cost of inspection and the cost of passing defective parts to the later stages of the production sequence or to the customer. The number of inspection stations will be optimal when the marginal cost of another inspection exceeds the marginal cost of passing on some defective parts. Inspection operations should be conducted before production operations that are irreversible, i.e., such that rework is impossible, or very costly. Inspection of incoming raw materials to a production process is one such place. Steps in the process that are most likely to generate flaws should be followed by an inspection. In a new process, inspection operations might take place after every process step, but as experience is gathered, the inspection would be maintained only after steps that have been shown to be critical.

## 2. Quality Assurance Concepts

Quality assurance is concerned with all corporate activities that affect customer satisfaction with the quality of the product. There must be a quality assurance department with sufficient independence from manufacturing to act to maintain quality. This group is responsible for interpreting national codes and standards in terms of each purchase order and for developing written rules of operating practice. Emphasis should be on clear and concise written procedures. A purchase order will generate a great amount of in-plant documentation, which must be accurate and be delivered promptly to each workstation. Much of this paper flow has been computerized, but there must be a system by which it gets on time to the people who need it. There must also be procedures for maintaining the identity and traceability of materials and semi-finished parts while in the various stages of processing. Definite policies and procedures for dealing with defective material and parts must be in place. There must be a way to decide when parts should be scrapped, reworked, or downgraded to a lower quality level. A quality assurance system must identify which records should be kept, and establish procedures for accessing those records as required.

(http://ebusiness.mit.edu/erik/bpp.pdf
http://www.econlib.org/library/Enc/Productivity.html
http://brainstorm.itweb.co.2a/online/ReadStory.asp? StoryID = 133510)

# NEW WORDS

fulfill [ful'fil] vt. 实践,履行,完成
inherent [in'hiərənt] a. 固有的,与生俱来的
statistical [stə'tistikəl] a. 统计的,统计学的
variability [ˌvɛəriə'biliti] n. 可变性,变率
tensile ['tensail] a. 可拉长的,可伸长的
lognormal ['lɔgnɔːməl] a. 对数正态的

binomial [bai'nəumiəl] a. 二项的,二项式的
scheme [skiːm] n. 安排,体制,计划
eliminate [i'limineit] vt. 排除,清除
traceability [ˌtreisə'biləti] n. 可描绘,可追溯
semi-finished ['semifiniʃ] a. 半完成的

# NOTES

1) With increased emphasis on tighter tolerance levels, slimmer profit margins, and stricter interpretation of liability laws by the courts, there has been even greater emphasis on quality control.

## Lesson 35  Product Quality Control and Quality Assurance

随着日益苛刻的公差标准的提出、逐渐减缩的利润空间以及严厉的关于(生产者)义务的法律的颁布,质量控制越来越受到重视。

2) Statistical quality control considers that part of the variability is inherent in the materials and process and can be changed only by changing those factors.

统计质量控制理论认为,这种可变性是在加工过程和原材料中固有的特性,只能通过改变这些因素来改变。

3) The basic decision is whether the characteristic of the product to be monitored will be measured on a continuous scale (inspection by variables) or by whether the part passes or fails some go no-go test.

检测方法是指待检测的产品是否可以在一个持续的数值范围内被测量(通过某个变量)或者这个零件在某种试验中通过或者失败。

4) There is an economic balance between the cost of inspection and the cost of passing defective parts to the later stages of the production sequence or to the customer.

在后续生产阶段以及消费者使用阶段中偶尔出现的不合格产品的成本和检测的成本从经济学的角度来看是平衡的。

## EXERCISES

1. After reading the text above, summarize the main ideas in oral.

2. Fill in the blanks with proper words or phrases according to the text (note the proper tense).

(1) In a narrower sense, "quality control" refers to the s_____ techniques employed in sampling production and m_____ the variability of the product.

(2) The traditional role of quality control has been to control the quality of r_____, control the d_____ of parts during production, eliminate i_____ parts from the production line, and assure f_____ of the product.

(3) Someplace there is an economic balance between reducing the v_____ and the c_____ of manufacture.

(4) The objective should be to focus on a f_____ critical characteristics of the product that are g_____ indicators of performance.

(5) The number of inspection stations will be optimal when the m_____ cost of another inspection exceeds the marginal cost of passing on some d_____ parts.

(6) Quality assurance is concerned with all c_____ a_____ that affect customer s_____ with the quality of the product.

3. Translate the following phrases into Chinese according to the text.

(1) quality control       (2) quality assurance
(3) profit margin         (4) marginal cost
(5) Poisson distribution
(6) American Society for Quality Control (ASQC)

4. Translate the following phrases into English according to the text.

(1) 有损检测　　　　　　　　　(2) 无损检测
(3) 拉伸实验　　　　　　　　　(4) 边际成本
(5) 泊松分布　　　　　　　　　(6) 过程控制
5. Write a 100-word summary according to the text.

# READING MATERIAL

## 1. Views of Quality and Quality Control

What is quality? Garvin (1988) offers five definitions of quality, which we summarize as follows:

1) Transcendent

Quality refers to an "innate excellence" which is not a specific attribute of either the product or the customer, but is a third entity altogether. This is "I can't define it, but I know it when I see it" view of quality.

2) Product-based

Quality is a function of the attributes of the product (the quality of a rug is determined by the number of knots per square inch, or the quality of an automobile bumper is determined by the dollars of damage caused by a five-mile-per hour crash). This is something of a "More is better" view of quality (more knots, more crashworthiness, etc.).

3) User-based

Quality is determined by how well customer preferences are satisfied; thus, it is a function of whatever the customer values (features, durability, aesthetic appeal, and so on). In essence, this is the "Beauty is in the eye of the beholder" view of quality.

4) Manufacturing-based

Quality is equated with conformance to specification (e.g., is within dimensional tolerances, or achieves stated performance standards). Because this definition of quality directly refers to the processes for making products, it is closely related to the "Do it right the first time" view of quality.

5) Value-based

Quality is jointly determined by the performance or conformance of the product and the price (e.g., a \$1 000 compact disk is not high quality, regardless of performance, because few would find it worth the price). This is a "Getting your money's worth" or "affordable excellence" view of quality.

Above definitions bring up two points. First, quality is a multifaceted concept that does not easily reduce to simple numerical measures. We need a framework within which to evaluate quality polices, just as we need one (i.e., factory physics) for evaluating operations management policies. Indeed, the two frameworks are closely related. Second, the definitions are heavily product-oriented. This is the case with most of the TQM literature and is a function of the principle that quality must ultimately be "customer-driven". Since what the customer sees is the product, quality must be measured in product terms. However, the quality of the

## Lesson 35  Product Quality Control and Quality Assurance

product seen by the customer is ultimately determined by a number of process-oriented factors, such as design of the product, control of the manufacturing operations, involvement of labor and management in overseeing the process, customer service after sale, and so on.

### 2. Quality Control

Quality control has traditionally been the liaison between manufacturing and design. This function interprets design's specifications for manufacturing and develops the quality plan to be integrated into manufacturing engineering's methods and planning instructions to operations. Quality control is also responsible for recommending to management what level of manufacturing losses (cost of mistakes in producing the product) can be tolerated. This is based on the complexity of the product design; specifically the degree of preciseness necessary in tolerances. Quality control traditionally monitors manufacturing losses by setting a negative budget that is not to be exceeded, and establishes routines for measurement and corrective action.

Within the past decade or two, quality control has become increasingly involved with marketing and customers in establishing documentation systems to ensure guaranteed levels of product quality. This new role has led to the new title quality assurance, to differentiate it from traditional in-house quality control.

Quality assurance strives through documentation of performance and characteristics at each stage of manufacture to ensure that the product will perform at the intended level. Whereas quality control is involved directly with manufacturing operations, quality assurance is involved with the customer support responsibilities generally found within the marketing function. Many industrial organizations have chosen to establish an independent quality assurance sub-function within the manufacturing function and have placed the technical responsibilities of quality control, namely process control, within the manufacturing engineering organization.

# Lesson 36 | ISO 9000

## TEXT

The ISO 9000 families are among ISO's most widely known standards ever. ISO 9000 standards are implemented by some 887 770 organizations in 161 countries. ISO 9000 has become an international reference for quality management requirements in business-to-business dealings.

Quality management principles introduce the following eight quality management principles on which the quality management system standards of the revised ISO 9000:2000 series are based. These principles can be used by senior management as a framework to guide their organizations towards improved performance. The principles are derived from the collective experience and knowledge of the international experts who participate in ISO Technical Committee.

### 1. Customer Focus

Organizations depend on their customers and therefore should understand current and future customer needs, should meet customer requirements and strive to exceed customer expectations.

Increased revenue and market share obtained through flexible and fast responses to market opportunities. Increased effectiveness in the use of the organization's resources to enhance customer satisfaction. Improved customer loyalty leading to repeat business. Applying the principle of customer focus typically leads to: researching and understanding customer needs and expectations; ensuring that the objectives of the organization are linked to customer needs and expectations; communicating customer needs and expectations throughout the organization; measuring customer satisfaction and acting on the results; systematically managing customer relationships; ensuring a balanced approach between satisfying customers and other interested parties (such as owners, employees, suppliers, financiers, local communities and society as a whole).

### 2. Leadership

Leaders establish unity of purpose and direction of the organization. They should create and maintain the internal environment in which people can become fully involved in achieving the organization's objectives. People will understand and be motivated towards the organization's goals and objectives. Activities are evaluated, aligned and implemented in a unified way. Miscommunication between levels of an organization will be minimized. Applying the principle of leadership typically leads to: Considering the needs of all interested parties including customers, owners, employees, suppliers, financiers, local communities and society as a whole. Establishing a clear vision of the organization's future. Setting challenging goals and targets. Creating and sustaining shared values, fairness and ethical role models at all levels of the organization. Establishing trust and eliminating fear. Providing people with the required resources, training and freedom to act with responsibility and accountability. Inspiring, encouraging and recognizing people's contributions.

### 3. Involvement of People

People at all levels are the essence of an organization and their full involvement enables their abilities to be used for the organization's benefit. Motivated, committed and involved people within the organization. Innovation and creativity in furthering the organization's objectives. People being accountable for their own performance. People eager to participate in and contribute to continual improvement. Applying the principle of involvement of people typically leads to: people understanding the importance of their contribution and role in the organization; people identifying constraints to their performance; people accepting ownership of problems and their responsibility for solving them; people evaluating their performance against their personal goals and objectives; people actively seeking opportunities to enhance their competence, knowledge and experience; people freely sharing knowledge and experience; people openly discussing problems and issues.

### 4. Process Approach

A desired result is achieved more efficiently when activities and related resources are managed as a process. Lower costs and shorter cycle times through effective use of resources. Improved, consistent and predictable results. Focused and prioritized improvement opportunities. Applying the principle of process approach typically leads to: systematically defining the activities necessary to obtain a desired result; establishing clear responsibility and accountability for managing key activities; analysing and measuring of the capability of key activities; identifying the interfaces of key activities within and between the functions of the organization; focusing on the factors such as resources, methods, and materials that will improve key activities of the organization. Evaluating risks, consequences and impacts of activities on customers, suppliers and other interested parties.

### 5. System Approach to Management

Identifying, understanding and managing interrelated processes as a system contributes to the organization's effectiveness and efficiency in achieving its objectives. Integration and alignment of the processes that will best achieve the desired results. Ability to focus effort on the key processes. Providing confidence to interested parties as to the consistency, effectiveness and efficiency of the organization. Applying the principle of system approach to management typically leads to: structuring a system to achieve the organization's objectives in the most effective and efficient way; understanding the interdependencies between the processes of the system; structured approaches that harmonize and integrate processes; providing a better understanding of the roles and responsibilities necessary for achieving common objectives and thereby reducing cross-functional barriers; understanding organizational capabilities and establishing resource constraints prior to action; targeting and defining how specific activities within a system should operate. Continually improving the system through measurement and evaluation.

### 6. Continual Improvement

Continual improvement of the organization's overall performance should be a permanent objective of the organization. Performance advantage through improved organizational capabilities. Alignment of improvement activities at all levels to an organization's strategic intent. Flexibility to react quickly to opportunities. Applying the principle of continual improvement typically leads to: employing a consistent organization-wide approach to continual improvement of the organization's performance; providing people with training in the methods and tools of continual improvement; making continual improvement of products, processes and systems an objective for every individual in the organization; establishing goals to guide, and measures to track, continual improvement. Recognizing and acknowledging improvements.

### 7. Factual Approach to Decision Making

Effective decisions are based on the analysis of data and information. An increased ability to demonstrate the effectiveness of past decisions through reference to factual records. Increased ability to review, challenge and change opinions and decisions. Applying the principle of factual approach to decision making typically leads to: Ensuring that data and information are sufficiently accurate and reliable. Making data accessible to those who need it. Analyzing data and information using valid methods. Making decisions and taking action based on factual analysis, balanced with experience and intuition.

### 8. Mutually Beneficial Supplier Relationships

An organization and its suppliers are interdependent and a mutually beneficial relationship enhances the ability of both to create value. Key benefits: Increased ability to create value for both parties. Flexibility and speed of joint responses to changing market or customer needs and expectations. Optimization of costs and resources. Applying the principles of mutually beneficial supplier relationships typically leads to: Establishing relationships that balance short-term gains with long-term considerations. Pooling of expertise and resources with partners. Identifying and selecting key suppliers. Clear and open communication. Sharing information and future plans. Establishing joint development and improvement activities. Inspiring, encouraging and recognizing improvements and achievements by suppliers.

# NEW WORDS

implement ['implimənt] n. 贯彻，实现，执行
framework ['freimwə:k] n. 构架，结构
revenue ['revinju:] n. 国家收入，税收
accountability [əkauntəbiliti] n. （对……）负有责任，负有义务
involvement [in'vɔlvmənt] n. 连累，包含

committed [kə'mitid] *a.* 效忠的，忠于的
approach [ə'prəutʃ] *vt.* 接近，动手处理
evaluate [i'væljueit] *v.* 评估，评价，评测
constraint [kən'streint] *n.* 约束，强制，局促

harmonize ['hɑːmənaiz] *v.* 协调
permanent ['pəːmənənt] *a.* 永久的，持久的
strategic [strə'tiːdʒik] *a.* 战略的，战略上的
factual ['fæktjuəl] *a.* 事实的，实际的

## NOTES

1) Organizations depend on their customers and therefore should understand current and future customer needs, should meet customer requirements and strive to exceed customer expectations.

经营机构以消费者为中心，因此应该了解消费者现在和未来的需求，以满足消费者的需求为目标，并且力争超过他们的期望。

2) People at all levels are the essence of an organization and their full involvement enables their abilities to be used for the organization's benefit.

不同等级的员工是一个公司的基本构成，他们的参与和能力的发挥有利于实现公司利益的增长。

3) Identifying, understanding and managing interrelated processes as a system contributes to the organization's effectiveness and efficiency in achieving its objectives.

将企业作为一个系统来对其相关过程进行识别、理解和管理，这样能够使企业更为高效地达到其目标。

4) An organization and its suppliers are interdependent and a mutually beneficial relationship enhances the ability of both to create value.

一个企业与其供应商之间是相互依赖的关系，这种互相都得利的关系能促进他们之间双赢。

## EXERCISES

1. After reading the text above, summarize the main ideas in oral.

2. Fill in the blanks with proper words or phrase according to the text (note the proper tense).

(1) ISO 9000 has become an international reference for q_____ requirements in business-to-business dealings.

(2) Increased effectiveness in the use of the organization's resources to enhance c_____ s_____.

(3) M_____, c_____ and i_____ people within the organization.

(4) Continually improving the system through m_____ and e_____.

(5) Effective decisions are based on the analysis of d_____ and i_____.

(6) F_____ and s_____ of joint responses to changing market or customer needs and expectations.

3. Translate the following phrases into Chinese according to the text.

(1) quality management　　　　(2) ISO Technical Committee
(3) customer focus　　　　　　(4) strategic intent
(5) responsibility and accountability　(6) a mutually beneficial relationship

4. Translate the following phrases into English according to the text.

（1）ISO 9000 标准　　　　（2）风险评估
（3）团队利益　　　　　　（4）道德规范
（5）双赢　　　　　　　　（6）短期效应

5. Write a 100-word summary according to the text.

# READING MATERIAL

The ISO 9000 family is primarily concerned with "quality management". This means what the organization does to fulfill: the customer's quality requirements, and applicable regulatory requirements, while aiming to enhance customer satisfaction, and achieve continual improvement of its performance in pursuit of these objectives.

The vast majority of ISO standards are highly specific to a particular product, material, or process. However, the standards that have earned the ISO 9000 families a worldwide reputation are known as "generic management system standards". "Generic" means that the same standards can be applied: to any organization, large or small, whatever its product, including whether its "product" is actually a service, in any sector of activity, and whether it is a business enterprise, a public administration, or a government department.

## 1. ISO 9000 Standards

ISO 9001:2000 is used if you are seeking to establish a management system that provides confidence in the conformance of your product to established or specified requirements. It is now the only standard in the ISO 9000 family against whose requirements your quality system can be certified by an external agency. The standard recognizes that the word "product" applies to services, processed material, hardware and software intended for, or required by, your customer.

There are five sections in the standard that specify activities that need to be considered when you implement your system. You will describe the activities you use to supply your products and may exclude the parts of the product realization section that are not applicable to your operations. The requirements in the other four sections—quality management system, management responsibility, resource management and measurement, analysis and improvement—apply to all organizations and you will demonstrate how you apply them to your organization in your quality manual or other documentation.

Together, the five sections of ISO 9001:2000 define what you should do consistently to provide products that meet customer and applicable statutory or regulatory requirements. In addition, you will seek to enhance customer satisfaction by improving your quality management system.

ISO 9004:2000 is used to extend the benefits obtained from ISO 9001:2000 to all parties that are interested in or affected by your business operations. Interested parties include your employees, owners, suppliers and society in general.

ISO 9001:2000 and ISO 9004:2000 are harmonized in structure and terminology to assist you to move smoothly from one to the other. Both standards apply a process approach. Processes are recognized as consisting of one or more linked activities that require resources and must be managed to achieve predetermined output. The output of one process may directly form the input to the next process and the final product is often the result of a network or system of processes. The eight Quality Management Principles stated in ISO 9000:2000 and ISO 9004:2000 provide the basis for the performance improvement outlined in ISO 9004:2000.

The nature of your business and the specific demands you have will determine how you apply the standards to achieve your objectives.

## 2. Examples

Example 1: A metal parts fabricating company used ISO 9000:2000 to develop a plan to implement their quality management system. When they were ready, they prepared a quality manual and quality system procedures as required by ISO 9001:2000, excluding the requirements covering product design and development because their products are made to designs prepared by their customers. Later, in order to bid on the supply of parts to a major automotive company, they adapted their quality system to meet the sector specific requirements of ISO/TS 16949.

Example 2: A welfare agency decided to establish a quality improvement strategy. It adopted ISO 9004:2000 as the basis for planning and implementing its system. The agency found that ISO 9000:2000 provided very useful additional guidance and plans to seek certification to ISO 9001:2000 to gain more credibility.

Example 3: A washing machine manufacturer had a well-established company culture of continual improvement and effective production control. The management decided to improve the company's development processes and to implement ISO 9001:2000 to obtain certification for commercial purposes. The company used ISO 9004:2000 to guide its improvement processes and ISO 10006:1997 to develop a project management plan.

Example 4: A large chemical processing company was required by its major customers to gain registration/certification to ISO 9001:2000. In order to obtain additional benefits, company leadership planned a comprehensive management strategy based on ISO 9000:2000 and ISO 9004:2000. A thorough review of their business processes indicated that all elements of ISO 9001:2000 were applicable to their quality management system. The company used ISO 10013:1999 to guide the development of quality documentation in its various production divisions and ISO 10015:1999 for guidance in the preparation of training plans for their employees.

# Lesson 37  E-business

## TEXT

E-business means companies make use of Internet and information technologies, aiming at raising operation efficiency, to carry out every phase of business procedures automatically, electronically and with paper documents eliminating. These phases include: market researching, negotiating, delivering, producing, money transferring and after-sale services providing and so on.

E-business is not a kind of pure technique itself, but an application process of Internet and information technologies in doing business. In such process, the tools used for information exchanging, transmitting, processing and storing based on paper media are replaced by the tools based on electronic media.

Let us see what the difference between traditional business and electronic business is:

In traditional business surroundings, a company should spend quite a lot of time and effort to investigate and decide what and how to produce, then, advertise in mediums (such as TV, radio, bulletin board on street and so on), contact the buyer through phone, fax, mail or face to face. After looking at the goods, the buyer bargains, places the order or signs the agreement with the seller. The seller prepares the goods and finally sends the goods to the buyer. The buyer pays for the deal in cash or by check. In the above procedure all information are exchanged by phone, mail, fax or telegraph, and in resent decades—in EDI(electronic data interchange). EDI is a computer network system dealing with some special data exchange such as invoices, contracts, credited letters and so on between certain partners. Building an EDI system costs a lot of money and it is rather complicated to use it. So, as you can see, in traditional business surroundings, people spend more time and efforts to do business. Sometimes mistakes or delays will happen.

In e-business surroundings, people use Internet or WWW to do business. The contact between the buyer and the seller is no longer face to face, but through Internet, on which both the buyers and the sellers have far more changes to know each other, not only one to one, but many to many. No geographical constrains, no time limited, all of them can find satisfied partners. The buyer uses browser to seek out the product list on the home page of the website or on-line shops based on the wanted domain names, and see the packing, outlook, style, color and price of products, sometimes, even can bargain on-line. If he is satisfied with the goods, he can place an order by click the keyboard or by e-mail. The seller immediately receives the message. If he accepts the order, he can use Internet or WWW to arrange goods production, distribution as well as payment (called electronic funds transfer (EFT)). All data is transmitted just in time and business operation becomes more efficient. The procedure shows in

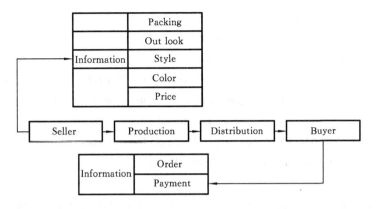

**Figure 5.2    The procedure of E-business**

Figure 5.2.

You can see that e-business has changed the way of doing business and the way of consuming.

Does it mean that company do not need as many people as before? The answer is not absolute. But one thing is sure that the company can utilize the human resource better and make operations more efficient, because e-business let the data be processed and transmitted automatically, immediately and turn out the data for further business decision making in real time. But anyway, the whole e-business system needs men to maintain and manipulate. Daily business decisions can't be made without experienced and capable men. So we must realize one thing: even in e-business environment, business still plays the major role, modern electronic transmission mediums are only the tool that can be more efficient, provide faster and better customer service, lower production cost and reduce business cycle time.

The concept of e-business was first emerged at the beginning of 1990s. In 1980s, some large companies and banks exchanged business data and information with each other by using their own computer systems through connected network. This system is called EDI (Electronic Data Interchange) system. During the past 20 years, the application of EDI in advanced countries had increased rapidly, almost in every business field, and it had actually shortened the time taken for order-ship-bill cycle and reduced the mistake and delays. The EDI's wide application has also promoted the development of information technologies. That was the primary stage of e-business. EDI only allowed pre-established trading partners to exchange business data. To use EDI, the company must equip with a rather expensive electronic translation system. Many small or middle-sized companies can't afford to use it. Another restraint is that EDI system belongs to certain companies, a new partner can't use it before being approved. Besides, the application of EDI doesn't lead to some great changes in traditional business.

In 1995, the business application of Internet and the invention of World Wide Web (WWW) brought the true meaning to e-business. Internet or WWW doesn't belong to any person or company. It somewhat likes highways. You can use it if you pay the fee. Sometimes it is free. So you don't need to build up an expensive system, you only need to buy a computer, a modem and browser software, open an account on Internet or WWW. From this point, e-business is viewed as a new generation of EDI, and e-business can do more.

WWW is only invented a few years ago, but it has developed so fast that no one can ignore it. It provides the basic condition to business for applying e-business, and opens a new channel of sales, distribution and cooperation to business. A piece of news from newspaper said, 34% of American families have the experience of using Internet, among them 54 million people use Internet or WWW to do business. Although the situation in China is not so optimistic as that in U.S.A., but it is true that e-business becomes one of the hot topics in the year of 2000.

Those above facts have improved that e-business is not the flash in the pan, but a trend, a great innovation of the way of people's working and living. The potential capability and future market of e-business is great, and it will be a main business channel in the next century.

(http://www.iso.com/)

## NEW WORDS

eliminate [i'limineit] vt. 消除,排除
negotiate [ni'gəuʃieit] vi. 谈判,协商
medium ['miːdjəm] n. (复 media)中间,媒介
utilize ['juːtilaiz] vt. 利用
surroundings [sə'raundiŋz] n. 环境
geographic [ˌdʒiə'græfik] a. 地理的,地区性的
browse [brauz] n. 浏览
domain [dəu'mein] n. 领域,领土,域,域名
click [klik] vt. 点击,敲击
distribution [ˌdistri'bjuːʃən] vt. 分发,配送,发布
advertise ['ædvətaiz] vt. 为……做广告,通知
manipulate [mə'nipjuleit] vt. 操纵

## NOTES

1) E-business means companies make use of Internet and information technologies, aiming at raising operation efficiency, to carry out every phase of business procedures automatically, electronically and with paper documents eliminating.

电子商务是指企业利用因特网与信息技术,以提高经营效率为目标,在企业经营全过程的各个环节实现自动化、电子化和无纸化。

2) E-business is not a kind of pure technique itself, but an application process of Internet and information technologies in doing business. In such process, the tools used for information exchanging, transmitting, processing and storing based on paper media are replaced by the tools based on electronic media.

电子商务本身不是一种纯技术,而是因特网与信息技术在商务中的运用过程。在这个运用过程中,以纸介质为基础的用于信息交换、传递、处理及存储的工具被以电子媒介为基础的工具所取代。

3) So we must realize one thing: even in e-business environment, business still plays the major role, modern electronic transmission mediums are only the tool that can be more efficient, provide faster and better customer service, lower production cost and reduce

business cycle time.

所以我们必须认识到，即使是在电子商务环境里，商务仍是主角，现代电子传输媒介只是一个更有效率，提供更好和更快的顾客服务，并能降低生产成本以及减少经营周转时间的工具而已。

4) WWW is only invented a few years ago, but it has developed so fast that no one can ignore it. It provides the basic condition to business for applying e-business, and opens a new channel of sales, distribution and cooperation to business.

万维网虽仅在几年前问世，但它已发展如此之快以至于无人能忽略它。它向企业提供了开展电子商务的基本条件，并且为其打开了一个新的销售、配送与合作的渠道。

## EXERCISES

1. After reading the text above, summarize the main ideas in oral.

2. Fill in the blanks with proper words or phrases according to the text (note the proper tense).

(1) E-business is an application process of I_____ and i_____ technologies in doing business.

(2) In e-business surroundings, people use I_____ or W_____ to do business.

(3) The contact between the buyer and the seller is no longer f_____, but t_____.

(4) No g_____ constrains, no t_____ limited, all of them can find satisfied partners.

(5) If he is satisfied with the goods, he can place an order by click the k_____ or by e_____.

(6) The whole e-business system needs men to m_____ and m_____.

3. Translate the following phrases into Chinese according to the text.
(1) place an order        (2) market research
(3) distribution          (4) in cash
(5) by check              (6) order-ship-bill cycle
(7) win/win relationship  (8) Internet and information technologies

4. Translate the following phrases into English according to the text.
(1) 谈判               (2) 传统商务
(3) 电子商务           (4) 电子资金
(5) 信息技术           (6) 调制解调器
(7) 经营渠道

5. Write a 100-word summary according to the text.

## READING MATERIAL

### E-Business / E-Commerce in the New Economy

E-business and e-commerce are both products of the Internet. The Internet is basically a vast and even increasing network of computers across the globe that are interconnected over existing telecommunication networks. Simply described, it is a, or the, network of networks. It is estimated that the number of persons connected to the Internet today well surpass 500 million, closing the gap on the 700 million or so connected to the telephone. It is calculated that there are over 90 million Internet hosts worldwide, facilitating a dramatic increase in the volume of trade and information available online. The economic rationale of the Internet comes from e-business and its developmental and moral platform will come from its impact in areas such as e-government.

It is important to elaborate on the definitions of e-commerce and e-business as that will help determine the scope and perspective of this analytical paper. E-commerce has been simply defined as conducting business on-line. In the World Trade Organization (WTO) Work Programmer on Electronic Commerce, it is understood to mean the production, distribution, marketing, sale or delivery of goods and services by electronic means. Broadly defined, electronic commerce encompasses all kinds of commercial transactions that are concluded over an electronic medium or network, essentially, the Internet. Electronic commerce is a new way of doing business. It is transacting or enabling the marketing, buying, and selling of goods and/or information through an electronic media, specifically the Internet.

From a business point of view, e-commerce is not limited to the purchase of a product, it includes, besides e-mail and other communication platforms, all information or services that a company may offer to its customers over the Net, from pre-purchase information to after-sale service and support. There are essentially two major uses of e-commerce. The first is to use it to reduce transaction costs by increasing efficiency in the use of time and procedures and thus lowering costs. The other is to use it both as a marketing tool to increase sales (and customer services) as well as to create new business through it—for example, IT-enabled business, call centers, software and maintenance services, etc. as well as "digital commerce". It is thus a tool for both existing business as well as an opportunity for new business, both for existing companies as well as for new entrants. E-commerce is seen as being B2C (business to consumer), B2B (business to business) and B2G (business to government). Of these three, B2B has been the most successful though recent reverses in the stock market valuations of high-tech stocks and the slowing down of the U. S. economy in particular is casting doubts on this. In future perhaps the major gains and usage of e-commerce and the Internet will come from "old economy" enterprises using it, governments using it (e-government), and social sectors using it (e-education and e-health).

E-business is the application of Internet technologies to business processes. However it is more than information technology tools or straight e-commerce. It also implied that the organization, especially its managers, are willing and receptive to radical changes that such new business techniques and tools bring. It implies organizational process and organizational culture re-engineering, for a true transition into the new economy. Its benefits come not just from the efficiencies and automation of a company's internal processes but from its ability to spread the efficiency gains to the business systems of its suppliers and customers.

## Lesson 37  E-business

An E-enterprise (participating in E-business) is defined as an enterprise prepared to conduct commerce in this new economy. This means it has created and embraced a business strategy informed by changing economics, new opportunities, and new threats. It has laid down the necessary technology infrastructure to support new business processes. It has used information technology to hone internal process such as human resources, workflow management, and training. Thus prepared, the enterprise is able to conduct e-commerce: "the commercial exchange of value (money, goods, services, or information) between an enterprise and an external entity (an upstream supplier, a partner, or a down-stream customer) over a universal, ubiquitous electronic medium."

In order to appreciate the relevance of e-business and its potential to impact on business and development, it is important to understand that e-commerce and e-business are more than just electronics and commerce/business added together. They represent an entirely new way of doing business (including that of government) over a medium that changes the very rules of doing that business. There are therefore far more about strategy and management than what are about technology. In order to appreciate the importance of e-business, it is important to see it from the perspective of the transactional aspects of e-business, those that represent the business between the different players.

Therefore, e-business is taken as the extension of business on to the Internet; the re-engineering of business processes for digitizing of the transactions; the restructuring of the frameworks, both private and public to carry out the transactions seamlessly; and the development of the capacity in society and enterprises for this.

# Part VI

## Practical English

# Lesson 38 | Writing Skills in Application Articles

### A. 书信的写作(Letter Writing)

书信是人们交流思想、情感与信息的最重要的方式之一,它在社会生活中的地位也是十分重要的。书信分为社交书信(Social Correspondence)、私人书信(Private Letters)和商务书信(Business Letters)三大类。

按照一般的格式,英文书信通常由以下几个部分组成:

信头(Heading)
信内地址(Inside address)
称呼(Salutation /Greeting)
正文(Body of the letter/Message)
结句(Complimentary Closure)
签名(Signature)
附言和附件(Postscript and Enclosure)

### 1. 信头(Heading)

英语书信的信头与常见的中文书信在格式上有较大的区别。在开始正文写作之前应详细写明写信人的地址与写信日期。虽然也有只在信封上注明地址的情况,但这仅限于非常熟悉的朋友之间的日常信件,一般不用在正规的公务与商务信件中,这样会给复函与存档带来很大的麻烦,因此尤其应该避免。另一种情况是,有些事务性信件的信纸上本来就印有详细的地址、邮政编码、电话号码、电报挂号与传真号,这时写信人的地址可以从略,只需注明写信日期。

信头分为地址和日期两部分,置于信纸的右上角,一般分为四行:第一行为门牌号码、街道名与邮政信箱,第二行为寄信人所在的市(县)省(州、郡)名与邮政编码,第三行为所在的国家名,第四行为写信日期(见例 6-1)。如果是寄给某一单位的则第一行为单位名称,信头共五行(见例 6-2)。如果有更详细的地址可在前面再加一行。

**例 6-1**

　　　　311 Nestor Street (门牌号及街名)
　　　　West Lafayette(城镇名),IN 4790222 (州名与邮政编码)
　　　　U.S.A. (国名)
　　　　June 6,2001(日期)

**例 6-2**

　　　　Shanghai Normal University
　　　　　　100 Guilin Road
　　　　　　　　Shanghai 200234
　　　　　　　　　　P. R. China
　　　　　　　　　　　　October 12th, 2000

信头有斜列式(indented form)与齐头式(block form)两种。斜列式就是从第二行开始依次向里缩进一至两个字母的空间(例 6-2),这是相对较传统的信头排列方式。齐头式则是每行开头齐平的排列方式(例 6-1)。随着计算机打印的日益推广,齐头式运用得越来越多。

在实际的运用中,信头的写法有可能在遵循一般规则的前提下还有不少的变化。如美国人的门牌号码前不加 No,而英国人则往往加 No;有的人用逗号将大小地址分隔开来,有的人只留下相应的空格。日期有的人用简写,如将"1999 年 8 月 21 日"简写为"Aug. 21,1999","21st Aug,1999"或"8/21/1999"。但由于与中文的日期排列方式不同,英国人和美国人也可能有不同的理解,最后一种简写方式很容易出错,建议最好不用,尤其是初写英文信的读者要慎用,不如按规范的方式写成"August 21st,1999"。此外,有的人还将地名也缩写,如将"Street"缩写为"St",或者将"Avenue"缩写为"Ave",将"English Department"缩写为"English Depart"等等,在正式的书信中最好不采用。

例 6-3

  School of Education
  Sproul Hall 1207
  Univ. of California
  Riverside,CA92521
  U.S.A.
  Aug. 3,2000

例 6-4

  International Academy of Cytology
  Depart of Surgery
   Tokyo Medial Univ.
    Shinjuku,Tokyo 160,Japan
     11 June,2001

在正式的信件中一般不用缩写,而且还应注明电话号码、电报挂号、传真号和收信人姓名;现在,随着电子邮件应用的日益普及,还可注明电子邮箱。

例 6-5

Shanghai Normal University
The School of Mechanical Engineering
1550 Pudong Avenue Haisi Road 100
Shanghai 201418,China
Tele 86-21-57122370
Fax 86-21-57122370
E-Mail abc@shnu.edu.cn
October 25th,2006
Mr. Jonathan Evans
Manager of Human Resources
Scientific Research Inc.
4000 International Parkway

Atlanta, GA3907, USA

## 2. 信内地址(Inside Address)

信内地址也是收信人的地址,一般置于信纸的左上角,从低于写信人地址最后一行的一至二行的位置开始写起。一般先写收信人的头衔与姓名,然后按照从小到大的顺序写地址。其排列方式与信头一致,也可以有齐头式和斜列式两种。需要注意的是,信内地址应与信封上的地址保持一致。有时,在比较随便的私人信件中,信内地址也可以从略,但在外交、礼仪等正规的邀请信函中,信内地址则通常置于写信人签名下方左侧的空白处。

**例 6-6**

  Mr. Rame(姓名), CEO(头衔)
  11th Main Street(门牌号及街道名)
   Chikkadapally(城镇名)
    Hyderrabad 500020(省/州名及邮政编码)
     AP India(国名)

**例 6-7**

  Dr. R. D. Stewart, Director
  Univ. of Wisconsin-Superior Transportation & Logistics Research Center
  Erlanson Hall, Room 301
  Superior, WI54880, USA

需要注意的是信内地址中的称谓问题。英文书信中的称谓和中文书信中的一样比较复杂,而且比较讲究,因此使用时千万不可出错。英文书信中的称谓一般可分为以下几类:

(1) 用于个人的称谓。成年男性都可以称 Mr.(先生),如 Mr. Farnworth。对青少年可以称为 Mr., 也可以称 Master(相当于汉语中的"少爷",在现代英语中不常用),如 Master Mark。英国人在很正规的书信中,称成年男性 Esq.(即 Esquire,先生),如 Abraham Grey, Esq.;对未婚女性一般称 Miss(小姐),如 Miss Rose Tailor;对已婚女性一般称 Mrs.(即 Mistress,夫人),对不知是否已婚的女子则可称 Miss,也可称 Ms.,尤其是在现代美国英语中,更常用 Ms.,如 Ms. Linda Smith。

(2) 用于团体的称谓。对男性组成的团体可称 Messrs(由法文 Messieurs 缩写而来),也可称为 Gentlemen(先生们)。对女性组成的团体则可称 Mmes(由法文 Mesdames 缩写而成,夫人们、女士们)或 Madams。对男女混合团体也可称 Messrs.。

(3) 用于有头衔和职务的有关人员的称谓。有博士学位的可称为 Dr.(doctor 的缩写,置于姓名之前),如 Dr. Gordon;也可以写明具体的学位名称,置于姓名之后,如 E. P. Gibbs, LL. D.(法学博士),Sigmund Freud, M. D.(医学博士)。在神职人员的姓名前加 Rev(revered 的缩写),如 Rev. John。有教授职称的可用 Prof.(professor 的缩写),如 Prof. Takeshita。对有军衔的可在姓名前冠以军衔名,如 General Marshall Captain Shaw。在总裁、会长、大学校长等人士的姓名前冠以 President,如 President Samson Wakefield。可在大使、政府官员、议员、法官等的姓名前可加 H. E.(His Excellency 的缩写,阁下)或者 The Honourable 等尊称,如 Governor Jeb Bush,The Honourable, H. E. Jiang Zemin。在有爵位的人的姓名前加爵位名,如 Lord G. Byron, Sir John, Duke Wellington。如果收信人有双重头衔,也可以采取一前一后并列使用、中间用逗号隔开的方式,如 Dr. William Coleman,President。虽然英文中的称谓和汉语中的称谓一样丰富多彩,但要记住,并不是所有中文中的称谓都可以用在英文书信中。

### 3. 称呼(Salutation)

称呼位于收信人之下的一至二行,顶格写,且自成一行。英国英语中称呼后面用逗号,美国英语中称呼后面用冒号。称呼是一封信的正式开始,绝对不可以省略。选择何种称呼主要视与收信人的关系而定。主要可分为以下几种。

(1) 一般的称呼:Dear Sir, Dear Madam, Dear Manager。

(2) 比较熟悉的称呼:Dear Mr. Smith, Dear Mrs. Smith, Dear Miss John, Dear Dr. Wang。

(3) 亲密的称呼:My Dear Mr. Rose, My Dear Kennedy, My Dear John。

(4) 正式的称呼:My Dear Sir, Dear Sir, Gentlemen, Ladies, Your Excellency。

### 4. 正文(The Body of the Letter)

虽说书信都有一定的格式需要遵循,但那毕竟只是一些表面的东西,比较随便的信件根本就不必拘泥于形式,而只有信的正文才是应该慎重考虑的内容。因此,无论是何种书信,均应将重点放在这一部分上。当然,正如我们在前面说过的,书信的内容因人而异,就像人们常说的:文如其人。不必也根本不可能拘泥于特定的格式或者规范。尽管如此,我们还是要在这里添上几句建议,对初学写英文信的人来说或许有些帮助。

首先,要注意礼貌。礼貌不仅体现在具体的内容之中。在信件的正文写作中不仅要注意语气的礼貌得体,不使用粗俗的词语,在安排信件内容时也应充分尊重对方,可以先回答对方在信中提到的问题,在关键的地方还可以引用对方的某些词语,以表明你认真的态度,再写自己要表达的内容。这时,你不要只顾说自己的东西,而应充分考虑对方能否接受。尤其是当你生气时,不要不假思考地就将信寄出去,最好是等第二天你冷静下来将信重读一遍后再做处理。

其次,要安排好信的整体布局。动笔之前,应理清思路。为了保险起见,亦可将要写的主要事情用一张纸列出来,以免遗漏。写信时,可按照事情的重要性安排先后,把最重要的放在最前面以示强调,然后依次展开。段落的安排与书信的篇幅也应和谐一致,如果信不长,段落也不宜过长。可在写完一件事后另起一行写另一件事,当然,这并不是说每件事都要自成一段,应视具体情况具体安排。

再次,一些看似无关紧要的细节也应注意。比如用何种信纸。私人信件不必在乎这些,但正规的事务信件应用 A4 纸,既显得慎重又便于对方存档。如果不是写给经常通信的人,最好留份底稿,以备将来查对。

正文的起首与结束部分有一些约定俗成的格式和套语,这也是英文书信的习作者应该掌握的。

"万事开头难。"写信也一样,这是由于信的第一句话在一定程度上决定了整封信留给收信人的印象,是烦琐还是简洁,是幽默还是庄重,第一句话都能定下基调。所以写信人应根据书信的内容、与收信人的关系以及自己的风格来选择适当的开头。如下面的示例:

(1) Your letter of June 21st,2001 was received and carefully read.(您/贵公司 2001 年 6

月 21 日的来信已收悉并仔细拜读。）

(2) In accordance with the request made in your letter of Feb. 2nd, we enclose in this letter the invoice of the goods you lately purchased.（根据贵公司 2 月 2 日来信中的要求,现将贵公司上次所购货物的发票附在信中。）

(3) We regret our inability to accept the quoted prices put forward in your letter on October 7th,1999.（你方在 1999 年 10 月 7 日的信中的报价我方无法接受,对此我方深感遗憾。）

(4) It is with the greatest pleasure that introduce Mr. Moss Armstrong, the former executive of my company.（兹向您介绍我公司的前任总经理 Moss Armstrong 先生,深感高兴之至。）

(5) The purpose of this letter is to inform you that …（……特寄此函告知。）

显然,以上均为正规的商务或者公务信函的起首,语言规范,语气庄重,而且逻辑性强。但如果用在私人信件中就不妥,它会使书信显得冷漠,令人敬而远之。而下面的示例尽管在内容上大致相似,同样是书信起首,但语气随和,用词简单,形式上截然不同。

(1) How are things recently?（最近过得还好吗?）

(2) I'm very pleased to tell you that …（我很高兴地告诉你……）

(3) As I haven't heard of you recently, I feel anxious.（久未与你通信,深感挂念。）

(4) I gave my pleasure to introduce Miss Ross Wordsworth.（很高兴向你介绍 Ross Wordsworth 小姐。）

(5) Much to our regret that we have to inform you …（非常遗憾,我们不得不告诉你……）

书信的起首一般很简洁。即使是很正规的书信,也只需一两句话说明信的大意,私人信件则只需一两句寒暄,然后就另起一段进入信的正文,切忌洋洋洒洒地写一大段,那样反而会使书信显得累赘烦琐。

## 5. 结尾(The Complimentary Close)

和书信的起首一样,书信的结束部分的重要特点也是简洁流畅,其目的或是为了给对方留下深刻和美好的印象,或是强调前文的重要内容,或是表达一种希望或者良好的祝愿,等等。如下面示例:

(1) Hope to hear from you soon.（盼你早日来信。）

(2) We are looking forward to your early reply.（望你早日来信。）

(3) Your prompt reply will be greatly appreciated.（望您尽快回信,我们将不胜感激。）

(4) Your prequalification documents for this tender for construction are to arrive before the date of January 20th, 2001.（你方参加此次施工投标的资格预审证明文件务必在 2001 年 1 月 20 日之前送到。）

(5) Please look into this case at your earliest convenience and kindly let us know any possible result.（请您在方便的时候尽早对这一案件进行调查,无论结果如何,请务必告知我们。）

(6) Any further information about the samples will be sent to you at the earliest time at your request.（这批样品有详细资料备索,如有需要,我们将尽早奉寄。）

(7) Thank you very much for your patronage in the past and we look forward to your help in the future.（感谢您在过去对我们的资助,也希望您将来能继续给予我们支持。）

(8) Please accept my apology for the trouble I have brought you during my last visit.

（上次出访给你带来了不少麻烦,请接受我的歉意。）

　　需要注意的是,结束部分一定要与起首以及正文在内容、语调等方面相吻合,不可游离正文之外,更不可矫揉造作。书信的结尾往往有一个表示礼貌、客气、谦恭、尊敬等语气的短句,相当于汉语中的"此致"、"敬上"、"谨启"之类的话。其在信中的位置一般是正文结束隔两行起,独立成行,位于信笺的右角,也可以略居中右方。下面是写信人的签名。和中文书信一样,英文书信中的结尾句视写信人与收信人的关系可分为以下几种：

　　(1) 写给很熟悉的朋友或者亲人的,可用以下类型：

Yours,

With love,

With best wishes,

Yours affectionately,

Yours sincerely,

　　(2) 写给一般的朋友或者熟人,可用以下结尾：

Yours sincerely,

Cordially, yours,

Always truthfully, yours,

With best wishes,

As ever, yours,

　　(3) 写给上级或长者,可用以下类型：

Yours respectfully,

Obediently yours,

Your obedient/humble servant,

It's my honor to remain yours truthfully,

Very respectfully yours,

　　(4) 写给陌生人、团体,或者在公务与商务信件中可用以下类型：

Faithfully, yours,

Yours truly,

Faithfully,

Very sincerely, yours,

　　以上类型只是相对而言的,并非不可变通。假如收信人既是上级又是很熟悉的朋友,结尾语采用比较随便一点的口吻也许更合适。英国人和美国人的习惯不同,比如英国人常用"Yours faithfully,"而美国人常用"Yours sincerely,"美国人往往比较随便而英国人则一般比较正统,等等；因此,使用何种结尾语主要视写信人与收信人的关系而定。

## 6. 签名(Signature)

　　写信人的姓名一般签在结尾语之下一至两行处,这是任何书信都必不可少的一个部分。在私人信件中,只需亲笔签名就可以了,而在公务与商务信件中,除了亲笔签名之外,还应在下面打印出写信人的姓名,往往还在其下一行标明写信人的职务,有时还可将职务与单位名称一起署上。如果写信人是女性,最好还在姓名之前标明"Miss"或者"Mrs."或者"Ms.",以免收信人复信时出错。中国人写的英文信还可签中文名字,但此时务必在下面一行打印出名字的拼音。

**例 6-8**

    Love,
    （签名）
    Eddie(Mrs.)

**例 6-9**

    Sincerely yours,
    （签名）
    Margaret Jones

**例 6-10**

    Sincerely,
    （签名）
    Michael W. Moore
    Secretary（职务名称）

**例 6-11**

    Yours very truly,
    STERN & BROTHERS CO., LTD(公司名称)
    （签名）
    John Howard

## 7. 附言与附件(Postscript and Enclosure/Attachment)

附言一般见于私人信件中，常用 P.S.（postscript 的缩写）表示。附言一般是在写完信之后又想起了什么别的东西时附在信后的几句简短的话。有时是因为另有一点内容要补充，而这点内容又并不重要或者与信的正文毫无关系，也可采用这种补遗式的方式。由于附言的这种性质，在正式的信件中应避免使用，否则会给收信人一种考虑不周全的印象，其结果会适得其反。如果添加附言，可在签名之下两行的位置开始顶格写起，结束后无须另行签名。

附件则与附言相反，一般出现在正式的信函之中，常用 Enclosure 的缩写 Encl. 或 Enc. 表示，如附件不止一件还应标明附件的数量，以便收信人查收。如：

**例 6-12**

Encl. Health Certificate for Mr. Li Chunlin（李春林先生的健康证明）

**例 6-13**

Two Enclosures：
1. The Invoice of This Batch of Computers（本批电脑的发票）
2. A List of Quoted Prices for Legend Computers（联想电脑报价单）

## B. 履历表(C.V.)

履历表的英文是 Curriculum vitae，简称C.V.，是求职申请表的一种比较简单的形式。有些企业或雇主在招聘时，可能会要求应聘者提供求职信和履历表。履历表主要由一些与个人的生活和经历有关的事实性信息组成，因此，它应当是非常客观的，但客观并不意味平淡无奇，或纯粹事实的堆砌。一份好的履历表与一份优美的求职信一样能打动招聘者的心。

## 1. 写作注意事项(Points to Note)

写履历表之前,要按照履历表的格式,逐项填写。漂亮整洁的格式和编排无疑会给人办事井井有条的印象。目前,求职信和履历表一般都是用 A4 纸,排版、间距和字体都要便于读者阅读,切不可排得过分紧密,也不可过分花哨。即使是再好的应聘条件,如果没人阅读或者仔细阅读,也不可能有成功的胜算。

其实,文无定法,履历表也一样,但一些基本的部分是应该有的。这些部分可以根据不同的读者对象进行繁简调整,这就要根据应聘的职位和性质来定了。如果你是去应聘金融业的职位,你就必须重点描述你在这个领域的学识背景、从业情况及管理才能,而应聘金融业监管机构的职位,则要着重描述对这个职位的了解程度及对相关法规的熟悉程度了。

另有一点要特别提请注意:履历表一定要附在求职信后。通常情况下,履历表是不单独使用的。

## 2. 履历表的构成(Ingredients)

履历表一般由如下内容组成:姓名、地址、电话号码、年龄(或出生年月)、性别、婚姻状况、国籍、教育背景、工作经历(如果没有工作经历,社会活动也可)、个人爱好兴趣、技能等。下面部分要特别留心。

(1) 个人信息(Personal Details)

这一部分如实列出即可,请参考文后的格式和范例。

(2) 教育背景(Educational Background)

要确保中小学和大学接受教育的起讫日期、考试成绩和科目(课程)准确无误。

(3) 工作经历(Work Experience)

英文履历表,工作经历应从最近的一次工作岗位和任职时间起进行排列。

(4) 其他(Other Information)

这一部分可以包括一些可以进行取舍的信息,如除了应聘职位要求的技能外,应聘者所具有的其他技能获资格证书、个人爱好和兴趣、个人品行与能力的证明书或介绍信之类,这其中可包括在校导师的介绍信或证明信、前任雇主开具的证明信等。这些信件可以作为履历表的附件一并寄给招聘单位。

## 3. 履历表参考样本与范例

(1) 履历表参考格式(一)(Reference Format 1)

CURRICULUM VITAE

Personal Details     Name:_____

                         Date of Birth:_____

                         Address:_____

                         Tel:_____

Position Applied for:_____

Education

    19__ to 19__                  University, Shanghai

|  |  |  |
|---|---|---|
|  | BS in Electronic Engineering | |
| 19 __ to 19 __ | _____ High School, Shanghai | |
|  | Graduation Certificate | |
|  | Chinese | B |
|  | Mathematics | A |
|  | Physics | A |
|  | English | B |
|  | Chemistry | B |

Work Experience

19 __ to 19 __  Company:_____  
Post:_____  
Responsibilities:_____  
_____

19 __ to 19 __  Company:_____  
Post:_____  
Responsibilities:_____  
_____

Other Information

Referees

[name]  
[Designation]  
[company/address]

[name]  
[Designation]  
[company/address]

(2) 履历表参考格式（二）(Reference Format 2)

Curriculum Vitae

A. PERSONAL INFORMATION

    Name:_____  
    Address:_____  
    _____

Telephone:_____

    Date and Place of Birth: May 25, 1967 Nanjing  
    Nationality: Chinese

B. EDUCATION

Higher Education:

1988—1993　　University of ＿＿＿＿＿＿，Shanghai
Ph. D. in Systems Engineering
1984—1988　　＿＿＿＿＿＿ University，Shanghai
BSc in Computer Sciences

C. EMPLOYMENT
1998—Present　　＿＿＿＿＿＿ Systems，Shanghai：
　　　　　　　　Software Development Manager
1996—1998　　＿＿＿＿＿＿ Electronics，Shanghai：
　　　　　　　　Control Systems Supervisor
1993—1996　　＿＿＿＿＿＿ Telecom，Shanghai：
　　　　　　　　Systems Analyst
Current Salary：　＿＿＿＿＿＿ plus bonuses

D. OTHER INFORMATION
Language：Chinese (native)
　　　　　English (fluent，spoken/written)
　　　　　German (fairly fluent)

E. REFEREES
Mr. ＿＿＿＿＿＿
General Manager，Research and Development
＿＿＿＿＿＿ Systems Ltd.
No. 100，＿＿＿＿＿＿ Street
Shanghai 200000
Telephone：(021) 0000-0000
　　(names of other referees will be supplied on request)

(3) 履历表范例(中英混合式)(C. V. Sample)

David Lee　　1200 Overview ＃12 ＿＿＿＿＿＿
李大卫　　　Arlington, t ＿＿＿＿＿＿-＿＿＿＿＿＿ USA
　　　　　　Phone：(817) 123-＿＿＿＿＿＿　Fax：(817) 234 -＿＿＿＿＿＿
E-mail：＿＿＿＿＿＿@＿＿＿＿＿＿. com
URL：http：//www. ＿＿＿＿＿＿. com

Gender　　Age　　Location　　性别　　年龄　　工作地点
Male　　　33　　　　　　　　　男　　　33

Work Objective　　应聘职务
　●Project Manager/Financial　　专案经理/财务部门
Professional Skills　　专业技能
　●Accounting (G/L，A/R，A/P and more)
　●Purchasing (contracting and acquisition)
　●Assets and Capital Expenditure Management
　●Local and Wide Area Network，Hardware and Software
　●Employees training materials preparation，including video production

## Lesson 38  Writing Skills in Application Articles

- Human Resources: laws interpretation, daily management, traditional and internet recruiting
- I am hardworking, detail oriented and loyal to work.
- 会计(总账,应收账款,应付账款等)
- 采购(外包及内外购)
- 资产及资本支出管理
- 区域网络系统,硬件及软件
- 员工培训教材制作（包括录像带制作）
- 人力资源管理:法律规章、日常管理、传统及网上招聘
- 本人工作认真,做事仔细,对工作忠诚。

Computer Skill    电脑技能
- Windows NT, Windows 95, Windows 3.1, Dos, UNIX
- Microsoft Word, Microsoft Excel, Microsoft PowerPoint, Microsoft Exchange, Lotus WordPro, Lotus 1-2-3, Lotus Notes, WordPerfect
- SBT Accounting, ADP Payroll for Windows, Label Designer.
- Netscape, Internet Explorer, Microsoft Frontpage, Hardware, Internet and Intranet, Extensive E-mail User, and more.

Work Experience 工作经验

ABC INC. , DALLAS, TX                           February 1995—Present
Administrative Manager

A $40 million company with 15 U.S. and 2 international locations, and 270 employees. ABC is a world leader in hard, thin-film coating services for industrial, medical, wear and decorative components.

- Manage all accounting functions at a local level including monthly P&L, balance sheet, accounts payable/receivable, general ledger, budgeting collections, sales tax, credit verification, assets management, etc. Work closely with and provide necessary information to corporate office.
- Responsible for all aspects of human resources at a local level including payroll, recruiting, employee orientation, benefits, employee relations, staff training, unemployment claims, employee surveys, management of personnel files, etc. Provide necessary information to corporate office.
- Provide computer administration and support to local office including NT server administration, daily backups, networking, and software and hardware installation and support.
- Lead local offices Y2K compliance efforts and transition to new, Y2K compliant hardware and manufacturing software including database conversion.
- Intranet Team Contributor and 1 of 3 company employees with rights to and responsibility for adding material to and updating company Intranet using MS FrontPage.
- Purchasing including purchase order management and contract negotiations.

- Manage all functions of office including petty cash, telephones, office equipment, file storage, supplies, etc.
- Directly supervise office support staff including accounting clerks and office support staff.
- ISO 9002 Management Representative and perform ISO administrative functions.
- Act as a support person and advisor to the General Manager.

ABC INC., Dallas, TX                    1995年2月至今

行政经理

营业额 4 000 万美元的公司,有 15 家美国分公司及 2 家海外工厂,270 名员工。ABC 公司是全球著名的工业用、药用硬纸薄膜的涂层加工工厂。

- 管理分公司全部会计事务,包括月结损失表、资产负债表、应付账款、应收账款、总账、预算管理、货款回收、销售税务、信用查核、资产管理等;并就各项事务与总公司保持密切联系及提供必要资料。
- 负责分公司有关人事资源的所有事项,包括薪资发放、员工招募、职务分配、福利、员工关系、员工培训、解雇赔偿、员工意见调查、人事档案等。提供必要资料给总公司。
- 提供分公司电脑的管理及支持,包括 NT 服务器管理、每日建立备份档案、网络运作、软件/硬件的支持及安装。
- 领导分公司应 Y2K 并转换 Y2K 无碍的硬件,生产制造使用的软件及资料库。
- 参与 Intranet 的建立,并引导公司 1/3 的员工,有权有责使用 MS FrontPage 添加资料到公司的内部网络。
- 采购事项包括采购单的管理及外包事项的谈判。
- 办公室事务的管理包括零用金、电话、办公设备、档案存储及办公文具等。
- 直接管理包括会计职员等办公室职员。
- ISO 9002 管理代表并执行 ISO 规定的管理机能。
- 总经理直属部属,就职责项下所有事务向总经理负责。

Newstart Construction Corp., Fort Worth, TX

February 1992—January 1995

Manager

A $2 million, painting and remodeling of residential and commercial properties.

- Provide customer service and support.
- Calculate estimates and present sales proposals to potential customers.
- Conduct follow-up sales and visits.
- Coordinate and distribute direct mail to target areas.
- Manage Lotus Notes database for customer and service provision information.
- Responsible for all aspects of human resources including payroll, quarterly and annual payroll reports, recruiting, benefits, employee relations, workers compensation, staff training, unemployment claims, policies and procedures etc.
- Perform most accounting functions including AR, AP, purchase orders, general

ledger and collection.

Newstart Construction Corp., Fort Worth, TX

1992年2月至1995年1月

经理
一家年营业额200万美元的公司,从事商店及住宅的装潢油漆工程。
- 提供客户服务及支持。
- 对潜在客户提出工程概要及估价。
- 指导电话询问或到访,进行客户跟催。
- 协调及分发DM到锁定的区域。
- 为客户管理Lotus Notes资料库,服务作预准备。
- 负责人力资料的所有管理事项,包括薪金发放、薪资季报、年报、员工招募、福利、员工关系、工作津贴、员工培训、解雇赔偿、人事政策及程序等。
- 处理所有会计事务,包括应付应收账款、请购单、总账及贷款回收等。

Educational Background 教育背景

Texas Christian University
Bachelor of Science Degree, Major in Psychology; Minor in Marketing
得克萨斯州基督教大学,BS学士学位,主修心理学,辅修营销学。
Fort Worth, TX
1985—1991
Dale Carnegie Leadership Course
Recognition for perfect attendance, a 30 hours seminar
Fort Worth, TX
May 1—July 31, 1996

For more information or to schedule an interview, e-mail me to:××××@×××××××.com
  如需更详细资料或安排面谈来信:××××@×××××××.com

## C. 论文写作(Writing Research Papers)

### 1. 论文概念和写作要求(The Research Paper and Writing Requirement)

论文是指论文写作者在导师的指导下,通过选题和查阅大量相关的参考资料,针对某一领域的某一课题进行认真、深入的学习和研究之后而写成的非常正式的、带有一定学术研究性质的文章,它是写作者所获取的新知识和新理解的书面表现形式。由于论文本身的性质和要求,论文写作所要花费的时间和精力是其他文章(如记叙文、说明文和议论文)写作所不及的。

毫无疑问,不同领域的论文在内容、形式与风格等方面或多或少都存在着不同的要求。但是,无论什么样的论文,它们在以下三个方面的写作要求是一致的:

(1) 论文写作一定要有充分的文献资料。除了查阅如书籍、杂志、报纸等资料以外,必要的话,还可以从调查或访问中收集第一手资料。

(2) 论文应带有一定的研究性质。论文必须有明确的观点、充分的论据、严密的逻辑和系统的论证与说明过程。

(3) 论文要有一定的格式。

## 2．论文的格式（Formats）

同正式的分析类报告一样，论文也有非常严格的格式要求。一般说来，一份完整的论文主要由以下这些部分构成：

(1) 标题页（Title Page）

标题页应包括论文题目、写作者姓名、论文性质、导师姓名、写作地点、完成时间等。例如：

Eastern Philosophy and Jack Kerouac's Postmodern Poetry

By

Christopher R. Smith

B. A. Indiana University，1993

A Thesis Submitted in Partial Fulfillment of the Requirements for

the Degree of Master of Arts

(in English)

The Graduate School University of Maine

December，1997

Advisory Committee

　Burton Hatlen，Professor of English，

Advisor Ken Norris，Professor of English

(2) 摘要（Abstract）

摘要是论文主要内容的缩写。写摘要时，要从作者的角度出发，紧扣论文原文的风格、形式和重点内容，省去具体细节，表达力求简洁扼要，字数一般在 200 字左右。注意：摘要并不等同于概要。其原因主要表现在三个方面：第一，概要是概述者从读者的角度出发，通过自己的语言将原文的主要内容概述出来，因而在语言风格和用词上可以进行适当的调整（如可以用 According to the writer...，As the writer says...等）。第二，虽说概要也是对文章主要内容的缩写，但概要长短非常灵活，它可以是一个或几个句子，也可以是一个或几个段落。第三，概要常常作为议论文引用是一种非常有效的手段而运用于论文写作当中。

(3) 致谢（Acknowledgment）

致谢就是对在论文写作过程中给自己提供过帮助的人或机构（如出版社）表示感谢，多用 to be thankful to...，to be grateful to...，to be indebted to...等表达。致谢时语气应该真诚、自然。例如：

Acknowledgment

I would first like to express my deepest gratitude to John H. Mitford for his unwavering support and editorial skill on this project. Also, I would like to give a warm thank you to Linda Hackler, who saw the ideas through from beginning to end with me and patiently listened to me construct and reconstruct my arguments. Finally, I'd like to thank my family, whose persistent encouragement was often the sustaining force that kept me writing.

(4) 目录(Table of Contents)

目录应当包括致谢、引言、正文、结论(或后记)、注释和参考书目录等。目录的顺序、层次和页码编排一定要清晰无误,要与论文正文一致。

(5) 引言(Introduction)

引言部分主要介绍该论文写作的背景信息,以便使读者能够有准备地进入正文。该部分应陈述论文所要解决或说明的问题、前人对此所做过的研究、论文的目的、论证的方法(或过程)、论文的结构、论文的结论和意义等。不过,引言中的结论只能作简略的介绍,因为在论文的结论部分会有详细的阐述。

(6) 正文(Body)

论文的正文部分是重点,要求论点明确、层次清晰、论证严密、方法得当、论据充分、引文正确、注释明确、语言规范。值得注意的是,在整个论文的写作过程中,要合理地运用和调整英语动词的时态,即概述、转述或者引用参考资料原文以及论文写作者在分析、论证时要用现在时态,而论及过去的历史事实或论文写作者自己的阅读经历时则要用过去时态。

(7) 结论(Conclusion)

结论是通过严密的论证过程得出的,所以,结论部分不应该再有进一步的论证。写作时,结论必须明确、简要,总结性要强。

(8) 注释(Notes)

注释是论文不可缺少的重要组成部分。论文的注释一般包括脚注(footnotes)、尾注(endnotes)或括号注(parenthetical in-text citation),写作时可以根据具体情况或导师的要求选择不同的注释。文科论文的注释格式应遵循 MLA(Modern Language Association of America)所规定的格式。

(9) 参考文献(Bibliography)

同注释一样,参考文献也是论文必不可少的重要组成部分。论文参考文献的名称有多种,如 Bibliography, References, Literature Cited 和 Works Cited 等,但现在一般用 Works Cited。文科论文的参考文献的写作格式也要遵循 MLA 所规定的格式。

(10) 附录(Appendix)

在论文的论述过程中,有些参考资料,如数据、图表或报告等,具有非常重要的引证或说明的作用,但是,由于论文的篇幅和结构等原因,其内容细节无法全部在文章中呈现出来。这样的话,如果有必要,可以将这些资料作为附录放在论文的最后,以供读者参考。附录在科技工程论文中是常见的。

当然,根据写作的具体情况和导师的要求,论文中的有些部分(如标题页、致谢、附录等)可以适当省略。同时,论文的各部分的结构编排要清晰、合理,各部分的内容最好分开书写或打印。

# Lesson 39　Translating Skills

## A. 专业英语的特点

专业英语以普通英语为基础,隶属于科技英语(English for Science and Technology,缩写为 EST)。专业英语应用于科技专业领域,一般要求语言表述准确、简明、严谨,常通过大量的专业术语、数学公式、各式图表等来完成专业理论知识及应用实例的表达。因此具有以下特点:

(1) 专业英语与相关专业知识联系紧密,理论知识多,内容枯燥,不像基础英语那样生动、有趣。

(2) 专业英语的文学修辞手法较少。科技文章注重事实和逻辑,所用资料、公式仅限专业领域知识,要求文体清晰、准确、严谨规范、客观。

(3) 专业英语文章句子比较长,但结构严密紧凑。专业英语中的句子为了保证内容的完整和严谨,常采用并列谓语结构、定语从句、状语、分词短语等,与日常用语、文学语言比起来结构严密且显得较为冗长,而篇幅却比较节省。

### 1. 专业英语词汇的特点

专业英语词汇由半专业技术词汇和专业技术词汇组成。

(1) 半专业词汇一般各行业通用,但在各行业中有不同的意义,具有常用词汇专业化及同一词语词义多专业化的特点。例如:

常用词汇专业化

spring:春天,弹簧

bed:床,机床床身

bus:汽车,总线

同一词语词义多专业化

clamp:[电子]接线夹,[机械]夹具,[矿业]夹板,[计算机]钳位,钳位电路

(2) 专业技术词汇词义狭窄,专业性很强,只能在各自的专业范围内使用。专业英语词汇的另一个重要特点是大量的词汇都是由构词法派生、合成、转化、混成、缩略而来的。

(i) 派生法(Derivation)

在一个单词的前面或者后面加上词缀来构成一个新词的方法称为"派生法"。词缀分前缀与后缀两种。

前缀:一般词义变化,词性不变。如:

anti-反,防:antiknock 抗震的,antinoise 抗噪声的,抗噪音的

dis-不,相反:discharge 放电

pre-预先,在前:preheat 预热,preamplifier 前置放大器

semi-半:semiconductor 半导体,semiautomatic 半自动的

后缀:一般词义基本不变,词性变化。如:

-ance(附在动词或形容词后面构成名词),表示"性质,状态"。如 resistance(电阻)。

-ive(附在动词后构成形容词),表示"……的"。如 conductive(传导的),resistive(电阻

的)。

(ii) 合成法(Compounding)

由两个或两个以上的词合成一个新词的构词方法就叫合成法。用合成法构成的词叫做复合词。复合词有以下三种书写形式:连起来写(如手册 handbook);分开写(如汽车站 bus stop);用连字符连在一起(如动力驱动的 power-driven)。合成词的前一个词常用来说明后一个词。例如:波长 wave-length;硬件 hardware。

(iii) 转化法(Conversion)

一些单词可以从一种词类转换到另一种词类,这叫"转化"。转化后的词义往往与原来的词义有密切的联系。如:

machine($n.$ 机器)—to machine($v.$ 机加工)

format($n.$ 格式)—to format($v.$ 格式化)

to coordinate($v.$ 协调)—coordinate($n.$ 坐标)

(4) 混成法(Blending)

混成词是取两个词中在拼写上或读音上比较合适的部分组成一个新词。如:

mechatronics= mechanical+ electronics　机电一体化

esclift= escalator+ lift　自动电梯

(5) 缩略法(Shortening)

缩略词是将较长的英语单词取其首部或主干构成与原词同义的短单词,或者将组成词汇短语的各个单词的首字母拼接成一个大写字母的字符串。如:

lab=laboratory　实验室

IC=integrated circuit　集成电路

## 2. 专业英语语法的特点

(1) 时态使用有限

使用最多的时态是一般现在时,其次是一般将来时和现在完成时,再次是一般过去时和现在进行时,其他时态用得不多。

(2) 被动句多

描述客观事实,而对动作执行者不关心。

(3) 简略表达多,后置定语多

名词词组或动词非限定形式代替从句。名词化把大量原来使用动词短语的句子变成名词短语,原来的动作转化为事物,使句子比较简练,包含信息量大,并着重强调存在的事实。动词非限定形式包括动名词、动词不定式和分词短语。使用动词非限定形式可在句子中担任不同成分,使句子结构更加紧凑、表达的内容更加准确、客观。

后置定语出现在名词之后,对所叙述的事实在范围上进行限制,以使专业内容表达精确。

(4) 陈述句多

在专业英语中,为了描绘真实的事物,多采用陈述语气。其次出现较多的有虚拟语气与祈使语气。表示条件假设多用虚拟语气,用于强调怀疑或不可能。祈使语气多用于对操作者提出指示或说明,在产品使用说明书中经常出现,用于表达命令。

(5) 复杂长句多

英语重结构,汉语重语意。在专业英语中,为了严谨地表达复杂的思想,能够准确、严密、不带感情色彩地表达时间、条件、原因、结果、目的、对比等关系,就必然形成长句。而如果把一个句子分成几个独立的句子,就有可能影响到句子之间的密切联系。使用长句,实现了对严谨的推理和准确的叙述的要求。

### 3. 专业英语的翻译要求

专业英语文章主要是论述事理的,其逻辑性强,结构严谨,术语繁多,所以译文必须概念清晰,条理分明,逻辑正确,数据无误,文字简练,通顺易懂,尤其是术语、定义、定理、公式、算式、图表、结论等更要准确恰当。

(1) 对译者的要求
- 有较好的英语基础
- 有较高的汉语修养和中文书面表达能力
- 有丰富的专业知识
- 掌握一定的翻译技巧

(2) 翻译标准:信、达、雅
- 准确(忠于原著,符合科技界习惯、规范和约定,不产生歧义)
- 通顺(汉语句子不宜太长,修饰成分过多会造成喧宾夺主、语意混乱)
- 简练(言简意赅,保持文章的严谨性)

## B. 专业英语词汇的翻译技巧

### 1. 词义选择

单词是句子的基础,英语单词绝大多数为多义词,准确选择词义并与句中的其他词汇的确切的搭配是正确翻译句子的基础。

(1) 根据词类选择词义

对于不同词类表现有不同词义的单词,应先依据单词在句子中的词性及所搭配的词汇来确定词义。如 like。

(i) Like charges repel, while unlike charges attract.
同性电荷相斥,异性电荷相吸。(形容词)

(ii) Things like air, water or metals are matter.
像空气、水或金属之类的东西都是物质。(介词)

(iii) We study mechanics, electronics and the like.
我们学习机械学、电子学及其他同类学科。(名词)

(iv) I hope I can use the computer like you do.
我希望我能如同你一样使用计算机。(连接词)

(v) Do you like this color TV set?
你喜欢这台彩电吗?(动词)

(2) 根据学科领域确定词义

同一个单词在不同学科领域中所表达的含义不同。应在充分了解该学科专业知识后,进行准确的翻译。如 base。

(i) The lathe should be set on a firm base.

车床应安装在坚实的底座上。

(ii) As we all know, a base reacts with an acid to form a salt.

众所周知,碱与酸反应生成盐。

(iii) A transistor has three electrodes, the emitter, the base and the collector.

晶体管有三个电极,即发射极、基极和集电极。

(iv) Line AB is the base of the triangle ABC.

线段 AB 是三角形 ABC 的底边。

(3) 根据上下文及搭配的词语选择词义

单词不是独立的,单词与单词连接构成句子,多个句子构成文章。因此词义的选择还需在理解上下文的含义后,经多次的提炼才能得出准确的翻译。如 light。

(i) The instrument is light. 这台仪器很轻。

(ii) The cover of meter is light blue. 这个仪表盖是浅蓝色的。

(iii) The lamp is light. 这盏灯很亮。

## 2. 词义搭配

同一个词与不同的词搭配时,应贴近其中的主要词语灵活翻译,按照逻辑关系和译文的语言习惯,适当地调整单词的原意,否则译文会很生硬而且不专业。如 universal。

(i) universal meter 万用表

(ii) universal motor 交直流两用电动机

(iii) universal valve 万向阀

(iv) universal grinding machine 万能磨床

有时,在一个句子中多次出现同一个单词,也需要注意词义的搭配。

搭配原则:多次出现的同一个单词的翻译应根据与它搭配的不同词语的含义来变化。

如:

(i) 多个主语共用一个表语,则要考虑该作表语的副词与多个作主语的名词的搭配。

Tensile strength, elasticity and abrasion resistance and compression deformation are relatively low.

抗拉强度较低,弹性及耐磨损性较差,压缩变形较小。(如果都翻译成"较低"则不够专业。)

(ii) 一个谓语带多个宾语,则要考虑谓语动词与名词的搭配。

You cannot build a ship, a house, or a machine tool if you don't know how to make a design or how to read it.

如果你不知道怎样制图或识图,你就不可能建船、盖房或制造机床。

(iii) 一个定语修饰多个中心词及多个定语修饰同一个中心词,则要考虑定语与中心词的搭配。

Engine must breathe freely to provide maximum power and performance.

发动机必须通风良好,以便提供最大的动力和最佳的性能。

Making a visual inspection of the vessel to conform that there are no material or dimensional defects.

对容器进行外观检查,以确保其材料没有缺陷,尺寸符合要求。

### 3. 词义引申

不同的语言在表达上差别很大。要使译文贴切生动,符合本国语言习惯,有时需要对词义进行引申,即再创造。但引申是有原则的,应该遵循:①基于原词义;②根据上下文的逻辑关系进行引申;③符合汉语的搭配习惯;④符合专业领域的规范。

(1) 基本词义明确化(根据上下文及逻辑关系引申)

There is a wide area of performance duplication between numerical control and automatics.

欠佳译法:在数控和自动化机床之间,有一个性能重复的广阔地带。

引申译法:数控和自动化机床有很多相同的性能。

(2) 基本词义具体化(将英文中笼统抽象的词,根据汉语习惯引申为明确具体的词义)

There is no physical contact between tool and workpiece.

欠佳译法:在工具和工件之间没有有形的接触。

引申译法:工具和工件不直接接触。

(3) 基本词义抽象化(将英文中具体形象的词,根据汉语习惯引申为抽象的词义)

High speed grinding machine does not know this disadvantage.

欠佳译法:高速磨床不知道这一缺点。

引申译法:高速磨床不存在这一缺点。

(4) 本词义专业化(即引申出普通单词的专业词义)

The grains are everywhere in intimate contact with one another in metal.

欠佳译法:这些颗粒在金属内部各处紧密地接触。

引申译法:这些晶粒在金属内部各处紧密地接触。

### 4. 词性转译

由于英汉两种语言的表达方式不同,有些词在译文中需要转换词性,才能使译文通顺自然。如:

(i) The instrument is characterized by its compactness and protability.

这台仪器的特点是结构紧凑、携带方便。(将动词译成名词)

(ii) The cutting tools must be strong, tough, hard and wear resistant.

刀具必须有足够的强度、韧性、硬度,而且耐磨。(将形容词译成名词)

(iii) The image must be dimensionally correct.

图形的尺寸必须准确。(将副词译成名词)

(iv) The application of electronic computers makes for a tremendous rise in labor productivity.

使用电子计算机可以大大提高劳动生产率。(将名词译成动词)

(v) Scientists are confident that all matter is indestructible.

科学家们深信一切物质是不灭的。(将形容词译成动词)

(vi) It is a fact that no structural material is perfectly elastic.

事实上,没有一种结构材料是十全十美的弹性体。(将副词译成形容词,将形容词译成名词)

(vii) A continuous increase in the temperature of a gas confined in a container will lead to continuous increase in the internal pressure within the gas.

不断提高密封容器内气体的温度,会使气体的内部压力不断增大。(将形容词译成副词)

### 5. 专业术语的翻译

专业术语有些是普通词汇的专业化,有些是随着学科发展创造出的新词,要将其准确翻译成既符合专业学科规范又符合中国学者要求的汉语术语,可采用以下方法:

(1) 直译

直译即按照每个词的专业词义直接翻译,这样便于读者理解术语的确切含义。如:

gear pump 齿轮泵

CNC(computer numerical control) 计算机数字控制

掌握一定的构词法,如转化法、合成法、派生法、混成法、缩略法,对专业词汇的构成进行分析,对专业词汇的准确翻译以及大量出现的新词的识别十分有效。如:

ultrashort waves 超短波(前缀 ultra-,派生法)

wireless 无线的(后缀-less,派生法)

heat-treatment 热处理(合成法)

cermet(= ceramics+metal)金属陶瓷(混成法)

(2) 音译

音译即根据词汇的发音来翻译。

(i) 由单词首字母缩略组成的新词,若用意译,则译名太长,这时可采用音译。如:

radar (radio detection and ranging):雷达,无线电探测及测距设备

sonar (sound navigation and ranging):声呐,声波导航与测距设备

(ii) 计量单位,如:

bit 比特    hertz 赫兹    watt 瓦特

(iii) 新材料或化学品名

Vaseline 凡士林    nylon 尼龙(酰胺纤维)

(iv) 有些词采用音、直合译法。如:

nanophase 纳米相    Morse code 莫尔斯电码    permalloy 坡莫合金

(v) 随着历史的发展有些术语已为人们熟悉,可由直译代替音译或二者兼用。

motor 马达,电动机    turbine 透平(机),涡轮(机)

(vi) 科学发现或技术创新词

quark 夸克    Darlington 达林顿

(3) 形译

T-square 丁字尺    I-steel 工字钢    V-slot V形槽

## C. 专业英语句子的翻译技巧

### 1. 增减译法

由于英汉两种语言的差异,在翻译过程中,需要适当地增加或者减少相应的词汇,保持译文的通顺,满足英、汉语各自的习惯。通常采用的方法有增词译法、减词译法、句子的分译法和合译法。

(1) 增译法

增译法即在译文中增加原文中无其形而有其义的词。英语中有时为了避免重复，常常省略不影响全句意义的词汇，为确切表达原文意思，翻译成汉语时，需采用增词译法。

(i) 将英语中省略的词翻译出来。

High voltage is necessary for long transmission while low voltage for safe use.

远距离输电需高电压，安全用电则需要低电压。

(ii) 用汉语动词补充英语名词、动名词或介词的意义，以使译文通顺。

The world needn't be afraid of a possible shortage of coal, oil, natural gas or other sources of fuel for the future.

世界无需担心将来可能出现煤、石油、天然气或其他燃料来源短缺的问题。

(iii) 用汉语名词对表示动作意义的英语名词进行补充，使其含义完整。

This lack of resistance in very cold metals may become useful in electronic computers.

这种在超低温中金属没有电阻的现象，可能对电子计算机很有作用。

(iv) 增加表示名词复数的词。

The first electronic computers used vacuum tubes and other components and these made equipment very large and bulky.

第一代电子计算机使用电子管和其他元件，这些使设备又大又笨。

(v) 增加某些被动语态或动名词中没有具体指出的动作执行者或暗含的逻辑主语。

The material is said to behave elastically.

我们说，这种材料具有弹性。

(vi) 在形容词前加名词。

According to Newton's Third Law of Motion action and reaction are equal and opposite.

根据牛顿运动第三定律，作用力和反作用力是大小相等方向相反的。

(vii) 增加表示数量意义的概括性助词，以起修饰润色的作用。

This report summed up the new achievements made in electron tubes, semiconductors and components.

这篇报道总结了在电子管、半导体和元件三方面所取得的新成就。

(viii) 增加使译文语气连贯的词。

In general, all the metals are good conductors, with silver the best and copper the second.

一般说来，金属都是良导体，其中银最佳，铜次之。

(ix) 语法加词。

The development in science to be brought about due to a fuller knowledge of atom are expected to be even more extensive and fundamental.

可以预料，由于对原子的更加充分的认识而引起的科学的发展必将更加广泛，更加重要。

(x) 分词独立结构后分词短语的加词。

Steam still provides power, of which electricity is the obedient carrier, it being capable of transmitting power in any desired amount and to any place where it is necessary to use it.

蒸汽依旧是提供动力，而电则是动力的驱动载体，因为它能够把任何数量的动力传输到任何需要的地方。

(2) 减译法

英语中有大量的虚词,如冠词、介词、连词等,在汉语译文中并不需要一一对应译出,在保证英文原文内容的前提下通常可以省略。

(i) 省略冠词。

用在如固定短语中、形容词最高级前及固定用法中的冠词一般可省略。

The alternating current supplies the greatest part of the electric power for industry today.

如今交流电占了工业用电的绝大部分。

(ii) 省略代词。

英文中的代词通常代替重复的部分,译成汉语不必将重复的地方译出。

The volume of the sun is about 1 300 000 times that of the earth.

太阳的体积约为地球的 130 万倍。

(iii) 省略介词。

介词通常可用来表示原因、状态、结果、位置等,在翻译中可借助其他词表达这些关系时即可省略。

Most substances expand in heating and contract in cooling.

大多数物质热胀冷缩。

(iv) 省略连词。

在翻译中可借助词序表达连词所表达的逻辑关系时即可省略。

If there were no heat-treatment, metals could not be made so hard.

如果没有热处理,金属就不会变得如此坚硬。

(v) 省略非人称代词或先行词 it。

在这种结构中,it 没有具体的汉语含义,只是表示一种英语结构,可以不译。

I think it unnecessary to go on with the measurement.

我认为没有必要再继续测量了。

(vi) 省略逻辑上或修辞上不需要的词。

A generator can not produce energy, what it does is to convert mechanical energy into electrical energy.

发电机不能产生能量,它只能将机械能转换为电能。

(3) 分译法

专业英语中的长句或不易安排的句子成分,可拆开来译成汉语的分句,使译文层次分明,符合汉语的表达习惯。

(i) 单词分译:将单词译为分句。

The time could have been more profitably spent in making a detailed investigation.

当初时间如果花在细致的调查上,好处就更大了。

(ii) 短语分译:如分词短语、介词短语、名词短语、动词不定式短语等,它们表示一定的逻辑关系,译成分句后表达的意思更加清晰。

The wrong power-line connections will damage the motor.

如果把电源线接错,就会损坏电动机。

(iii) 句子分译:使译文层次分明。

Two of the advantages of the transistor are its being small in size and its being able to put close to each other without overheating.

晶体管有两个特点:一是体积小,二是相互能靠近放置而不过热。

(4) 合译法

合译法可省略一些重复或含义相近的词语或句子成分,使译文更加紧凑。

(i) 简单句合译。

Generally speaking, the typical metal conducts electricity and heat. It shows lustrous surface, usually with white, or so-called metallic luster. It is ductile and malleable.

一般说来,典型的金属能导热导电,表面有金属光泽,具有延展性和可锻性。

(ii) 复合句合译。

Welding is used where a tight seal is desired and weight increases cannot be tolerated.

在要求接缝紧密而又不允许增加重量的地方就使用焊接。

(iii) 并列句合译。

Sulphuric-acid enters into the manufacture of explosives, dyestuffs and drugs; it is used in sugar refining and in the preparation of fertilizers.

硫酸被用来制造炸药、染料、药物、食糖和化肥等。

## 2. 反译法

为了达到一定的修辞效果,从与原文相反的角度翻译,称为反译法。

(1) 否定译为肯定

一般将双重否定译为肯定,表示语气的加重。

(i) We can not go until Friday.

我们直到周五才能走。

(ii) There is no material but will deform more or less under the action of force.

在压力的作用下,各种材料或多或少都要变形。

(2) 肯定译为否定

英语中有很多词汇在意义上包含否定的语气,出现在肯定句中,翻译时则需要把否定语气翻译出来。

(i) Worm gear drives are quiet.

涡轮传动没有噪音。

(ii) As rubber prevents electricity from passing through it, it is used as insulating material.

由于橡胶不导电,所以可用作绝缘材料。

(iii) On freezing water expands instead of contracts.

水在结冰时要膨胀而不是收缩。

(3) 肯定译为双重否定

同双重否定译为肯定一样,肯定译为双重否定表示语气的加重,有时也表示"减弱"或含有"贬义"。

(i) We must put the factors into account.

我们不得不将这些因素考虑进去。

(ii) The problem remains to be discussed in detail.

这个问题不得不详细讨论。

### 3. 句子成分的转换

由于英汉两种语言在表达方式和语言结构方面各有特点,不能完全对等翻译,所以将英语译成汉语时,不可硬译、死译,需要适当地转变句子成分。

(1) 英语中的宾语、表语、定语、状语和谓语等转变为汉语中的主语

英语中常见的一些结构,如:to have a height of ..., to have a density of ...等,如果按字面意思直译,很生硬,一般将这些表示事物性质、特征的词转化为主语。

(i) The generator possesses an efficiency of 90% at full load.

这台发电机的满载效率是 90%。(英语的宾语转译成汉语的主语)

(ii) Aluminium is very light in weight, being only one-third as heavy as iron.

铝的重量很轻,只有铁的三分之一。(英语的介词宾语转译成汉语的主语)

(iii) Two widely used alloys of copper are brass and bronze.

黄铜和青铜是两种广泛使用的铜合金。(英语的表语转译成汉语中的主语)

(iv) The renovations of this lathe have been made, and production is on the increase.

这台车床经过革新,生产量增加了。(英语的定语转译成汉语的主语)

(v) In size and appearance Mercury is very much like our moon.

水星的大小和外观很像月亮。(英语的状语转译成汉语的主语)

(vi) A highly developed physical science is characterized by an extensive use of mathematics.

一门高度发展的自然科学的特点是广泛地应用数学。(英语的谓语转译成汉语的主语,常见于 act, behave, feature, characterize, relate, load, conduct 等动词,转化为名词后,作为句子主语)

(2) 英语的主语转变为汉语的宾语、定语和谓语

(i) Considerable use has been made of these data.

这些资料得到了充分的应用。(英语的主语转译成汉语的宾语,常用于被动语态的翻译)

(ii) These instruments differ widely in their precision after operation.

经过操作,这些仪器的精度大不相同。(英语的主语转译成汉语的定语)

(iii) Improvement is needed for our experimental work.

我们的实验工作需要改进。(英语的主语转译成汉语的谓语,常见于 care, need, attention, emphasis, improvement 等名词及名词化结构作主语时)

(3) 英语的定语转变为汉语的谓语、状语

(i) There is a large amount of energy wasted owing to friction.

由于摩擦而损耗了大量能量。(英语的定语转译成汉语的谓语)

(4) 英语的状语转变为汉语的补语

This problem seems much more difficult than that one.

这个问题似乎比那个问题难得多。

## 4．被动语态的翻译

专业英语的语法特点之一就是大量使用被动语态，这是因为专业文章多是论述学科理论、生产实践、科研开发等专业领域的知识，不着重说明从事这些活动的动作者。汉语表示被动语态有很多方法，因此灵活翻译被动语态，才能使译文不死板。

（1）译成汉语主动句

(i) 原文主语仍作汉语主语。

在这种翻译方法中，实际上仍是无"被"字的汉语被动语态，只是用主动语态的形式表达出来，使用"加以"、"经过"、"用……来"等表示。

The plan is going to be examined first by the research group.

计划将先由研究小组加以研究。

(ii) 将由 by 引导的短语中的宾语译为汉语的主语。

The lathe is adjusted by the operator.

操作员正在调试这台车床。

(iii) 将原文中的状语译为汉语的主语。

The newly-found building material is widely used home and abroad.

国内外广泛采用这种新型建筑材料。

(iv) 译成无主语的主动句。

如果英语原句中不需要或无法讲出动作的发出者，通常表示什么地方发生、存在或消失了什么，以及表达观点、态度、告诫、要求等的被动句，就可译为无主语句，动词前常加"把"、"将"、"使"、"对"等词。

The mechanical energy can be changed back into electrical energy by means of a generator.

利用发电机可以将机械能转化为电能。

(v) 加上不确定主语的主动句。

Salt is known to have a very strong corroding effect on metals.

众所周知，盐对金属有很强的腐蚀作用。

有些常用句型，也翻译成不确定主语的主动句。如：

It is well known that ... 众所周知    It is believed that ... 人们相信

It is taken that ... 人们认为    It is noted that ... 人们注意到

It should be pointed out that feed varies inversely with cutting speed for otherwise similar conditions.

必须指出，在其他条件相似的情况下，进给量与切削速度成反比。

（2）译成汉语被动句

如果英语句子是为了强调被动动作，则可以直接译为汉语被动句，通常加上"被"、"受"、"加以"、"得到"、"让"、"给"、"称"、"为……所"等词。

This kind of steel is not corroded by air and water.

这种钢不会被空气和水腐蚀。

Besides voltage, resistance and capacitance, an alternating current is also influenced by inductance.

除了电压、电阻和电容，交流电流还受电感的影响。

(3) 译成汉语判断句

如果英语句子所着重表示的是某种状态,如时间、地点、方式、方法等,可翻译为"是……的"或"……的是……"的句型。

Currently most solar cells are made from crystals of high-purity silicon.

目前,绝大多数太阳能电池是用高纯度的硅晶体制成的。

Produced by electrons are the X-rays, which allow the doctor to take aside a patient's body.

电子产生的是 X 射线,医生用它做透视。

## 5. 复杂长句的翻译

专业英语文章是书面语体,要求层次分明,严谨周密。复杂长句是专业英语语法的又一大特点,它能充分体现作者严密的逻辑推理思维。

长句之长,主要体现在修辞成分多,因此,要译好英语中的复杂长句,首先必须理清原文的句法结构,找到主句;分清主句的主语、谓语和宾语后,把句子的基本意思翻译出来;依次分析各个修饰短语或分句,弄清楚句子各层次之间的逻辑关系,分层次地将原文的意思翻译出来,不必拘泥于原文的形式。长难句的处理方法主要有下列几种:

(1) 顺译法

英语长句的结构顺序与汉语相同,可采用顺译法。

In order to obtain more accurate control, the controlled signal $c(t)$ must be fed back and compared with the reference input, and an actuating signal proportional to the difference of the output and the input must be sent through the system to correct the error.

为了获得更精确的控制,必须将被控信号 $c(t)$ 反馈回去与参考输入量相比较,且须将与输出和输入之差成比例的促动信号送给系统以校正偏差。

(2) 倒译法

英语习惯用长句表达复杂的概念,而且表达主要信息的主句前置,而汉语则习惯使用若干短句按主次顺序,层次分明地进行阐述,同时按由小到大的顺序安排语序,重点内容通常后置。这时可采用倒译法。从长句的中间或后面译起,最后翻译长句的开头。

Suffice it to say that a whole complex of properties in addition to structural strength is required of an alloy before it will be accepted into, and survive in, engineering practice.

在合金材料被采用和应用于工程实际之前,除需要掌握其结构强度外,还需知道它的综合性能。

(3) 分译法

将英语长句翻译成几个独立的句子,顺序基本保持不变,保持前后连贯的方法,为分译法。

The loads a structure is subjected to are divide into dead loads, which include the weights of all the parts of the structure, and live loads, which are due to the weights of people, movable equipment, etc.

一个结构受到的载荷可以分为静载荷和动载荷两类。静载荷包括该结构各部分的重量。动载荷则是由于人和可移动设备等的重量而引起的载荷。

# 参 考 文 献

[1] ROBERT L MOTT. Machine Elements in Mechanical Design [M]. 4th ed. Ohio: Pearson Education, Inc., 2004.

[2] SEROPE KALPAKJIAN, STEVEN SCHMID. Manufacturing Engineering and Technology [M]. 5th ed. 北京:清华大学出版社,2006.

[3] DAN NECSULESCU. MECHATRONICS[M]. New Jersey:Prentice-Hall, Inc., 2002.

[4] JULIAN W GARDNER, VIJAY K VARADAN, Osama O A WADELKARIM. Microsensors, MEMS, and Smart Devices[M]. 北京:清华大学出版社,2004.

[5] JAMES A REHG,HENNY W KRAEBBER. Computer-Integrated Manufacturing[M]. 英文版3版. 北京:机械工业出版社,2004.

[6] DAVID G ALCIATORE, MICHAEL B HISTAND. Introduction to Mechatronics and Measurement System[M].英文版2版.北京:清华大学出版社,2004.

[7] (美)约翰 J 克拉克. 机器人学导论[M]. 北京:机械工业出版社,2005.

[8] (美)罗伯特 N 贝特森. 控制系统技术概论[M]. 北京:机械工业出版社,2006.

[9] 章跃. 机械制造专业英语[M]. 北京:机械工业出版社,2003.

[10] 张维刚,钟志华. 现代设计方法[M]. 英文版. 北京:机械工业出版社,2005.

[11] 司徒忠,李璨. 机械工程专业英语[M]. 武汉:武汉理工大学出版社,2001.

[12] 唐一平. Advanced Manufacturing Technology [M]. 北京:科学技术出版社,2002.

[13] 刘小芹. 现代制造技术英语实用教程[M]. 武汉:华中科技大学出版社,2001.

[14] 李俊玲,罗永革. 汽车工程专业英语[M]. 北京:机械工业出版社,2006.

[15] 《汽车行业名词术语汇编》编委会. 汽车行业名词术语汇编[M]. 北京:人民交通出版社,1996.

[16] 沈希瑾,李京生,张文杰. 汽车工程图解英汉词典[M]. 北京:北京理工大学出版社,2001.

[17] 杨春生. 机电技术专业英语[M]. 北京:电子工业出版社,2001.

[18] 司爱侠. 电子商务专业英语[M]. 北京:清华大学出版社,2005.

[19] 黄渝祥,邢爱芳. 工程经济学[M]. 上海:同济大学出版社,2005.

[20] 王克强,王洪卫. 工程经济学[M]. 上海:财经大学出版社,2004.

[21] 赵国杰. 工程经济学[M].2版. 天津:天津大学出版社,2004.

[22] 朱超,尹小莹,汪治. 电子商务英语[M]. 北京:高等教育出版社,2002.

[23] 翟天利. 科技英语阅读与翻译实用教程[M]. 北京:新时代出版社,2004.

[24] 魏汝尧,董益坤. 科技英语教程[M]. 北京:北京大学出版社,2005.

[25] 姚国章. 电子商务英语[M]. 北京:北京大学出版社,2005.

[26] 李伏生. 专业英语的特点及其教学方法[J]. 高教论坛,2004,8(4):68-70.

[27] BENJAMIN C. KUO FARID GOLNARAGHI. Automatic Control Systems[M]. 8版. 北京:高等教育出版社,2003.

[28] HEISLER, HEINZ. Advanced Vehicle Technology [M]. London, Great Britain: London Melbourne Auckland,1989.

[29] Motorola. Automotive Local Interconnect Network(LIN) Application [EB/OL]. http://Motorola.com,2002.
[30] Motorola. Automotive Local Interconnect Network(CAN) Application [EB/OL]. http://Motorola.com,2003.
[31] 本书编写组. 英语应用文写作大全[M]. 北京:社会科学文献出版社,2003.
[32] 高成秀. 机械工程专业英语教程[M]. 北京:国防工业出版社,2005.
[33] 赵运才,何法江. 机电工程专业英语[M]. 北京:北京大学出版社,2006.
[34] 冯修文,赵琳红. 实用英语写作[M]. 上海:上海交通大学出版社,2007.